SINNING IN THE HEBREW BIBLE

How the Worst Stories Speak for Its Truth

ALAN F. SEGAL

Columbia University Press

New York

COLUMBIA UNIVERSITY PRESS

Publishers Since 1893

New York Chichester, West Sussex

Copyright © 2012 Columbia University Press

All rights reserved

Library of Congress Cataloging-in-Publication Data

Segal, Alan F., 1945–

Sinning in the Hebrew Bible: how the worst stories speak for its truth /

Alan F. Segal.

p. cm.

Includes bibliographical references and index.

ISBN 978-0-231-15926-5 (cloth : alk. paper)—ISBN 978-0-231-15927-2

(pbk.: alk. paper)

1. Sin—Biblical teaching.   2. Bible. O.T.—Criticism, interpretation, etc.

I. Title.

BS1199.S54S44 2012

√241′.3—dc23

2011046083

To all the dedicated people who work on the second floor
of the Luckow Pavilion and the weekend crew at the
Valley Hospital in Ridgewood, New Jersey

SINNING IN THE HEBREW BIBLE

CONTENTS

INTRODUCTION   *1*
The Bible and Myth

CHAPTER ONE   *22*
The Matriarch in Peril

CHAPTER TWO   *58*
The Golden Calf: A Lesson
in Chronology

CHAPTER THREE   *82*
A Historical Tragedy: The Short-
Lived Deuteronomic Reform

CHAPTER FOUR   *100*
The Concubine of the Levite:
A Complete Horror

CHAPTER FIVE   *123*
The Horror of Human Sacrifice: Sex,
Intermarriage, and Proper Descent

CHAPTER SIX   *152*
Ways of a Man with a Woman

CHAPTER SEVEN   *180*
No Peace in the Royal Family

CONCLUSION   *222*
Synoptic Sinning

NOTES   *259*
INDEX   *275*

SINNING IN THE HEBREW BIBLE

INTRODUCTION

The Bible and Myth

Terrible Stories in the Old Testament

We think of the Hebrew Bible as our moral fixed point. But the Bible is also a history book. Morality and history often conflict. The stories of days long gone by are unattractive, downright terrible, and even immoral, but they are even more evident in the Hebrew Bible than law codes and moral exhortations. Thus the Hebrew Bible presents us with many unexpected moral problems that are horrifying to contemplate. These difficult stories demand a greater explanation, which I will attempt to supply in this book. By asking why the Bible chooses to tell us such terrible stories, I hope to shed some light on the dating of various parts of biblical history. What I suggest is meant to supplement the many expert studies of the stories that have gone before.

The Hebrew Bible, the West's foundational book, tells us stories of Abraham, who tries to give his wife in marriage as his sister, twice. His son tries the same trick, making a total of three times in less than fifteen chapters of Genesis. The Bible also tells us that God commanded Abraham to sacrifice his child Isaac as a whole offering, slaughtering him as though he were a lamb. It tells us that Isaac was tricked into giving his blessing to his younger son Jacob when it belonged to the elder Esau by right. It tells us that Jacob was tricked into marrying and bedding Leah when he wanted to marry

Rachel, that he sired children from both of them, but also sired children from their handmaidens. He was only doing what his grandfather Abraham did. It also tells us that Reuben, his son, also slept with one of his father's concubines. No one could get to the idea that marriage institutes a loving couple of one man and one woman from actually reading Genesis.

Further on, during the period of the Judges, we hear about murder and mayhem, rapes, tribal wars, more human sacrifice, and general chaos. Moving a little bit later in time, we find that even King David was guilty of adultery with Bathsheba, murdering her husband Uriah, and subsequently attempting to cover up the crime. We know that David's son Amnon was attracted to his half sister and that he raped her. As a result he was killed by his half brother Absalom. And Absalom was in turn exiled and forgiven and then killed after rebelling against his father. Solomon eventually was appointed king, but, after inheriting the kingdom, he had his older brother Adonijah executed.

To be frank, they are terrible stories; their moral value is, at best, as negative examples. Parents are well warned to keep children away from reading these sections of the Bible until they are quite mature; pastors are cautioned against sermonizing on these stories too often; they are, with good reason, rarely read in church or synagogue. If the subject is morality, the safest thing to do is ignore them, to pass over them in discreet silence as momentary lapses in moral sense, and hope no one asks an embarrassing question.

But something else is at stake when we think about these terrible stories. They are stories whose reason for existence is not easy to fathom. In short they are not stories that you would make up to attest to your glory. In a way, the very terror that they instill may be important for discussing their historicity and authenticity. We shall see how in the coming pages.

The Argument of the Book

One way to understand these horrible stories is to view them within their historical contexts and try to understand what they meant at the time they appeared. A great many of these immoral stories merely testify to the ancient time period being discussed. But we are in a particularly frustrating moment in biblical scholarship because the consensus about the date of the traditions in the Bible is under strong attack from a variety of different perspectives. No new synthesis has appeared. It is hard to know for sure in which historical circumstances and in which contexts to put the stories of the Bible. Under such circumstances, one should look at the stories themselves and get a sense of relative chronology on how the stories develop. After we compare stories and see which is earlier, we will try in the last chapter to develop an absolute chronology that is sensitive to the archaeological data outside the Bible but coming from biblical lands.

The Beginning of Biblical History

The beginning of historical time for Israel, however, has remained the same for over a century, despite many attempts to dethrone it. The first time that the word *Israel* is mentioned in a historical source outside of the Bible is in the Stele of Merneptah.[1] In that Egyptian inscription from the New Kingdom, datable to 1206 BCE, the people Israel are described as a tribal people already living in the hill country of Canaan. In terms of biblical chronology that remains to be verified, that is the period of the Judges. This would put an entity called Israel in the hills of Canaan after the Exodus,[2] if the Exodus is historical, and before the rise of kingship.

By definition, that date is the current border between historical Israel and legendary Israel. That means that the stories of all the patriarchs—including Abraham and his trek from Mesopotamia and sojourn in Canaan, Isaac and Jacob's wandering, Joseph's adventures in Egypt, the Hebrews' descent into Egypt, the story of Israel's oppression in Egypt, the Exodus, the wandering of the people in the desert, the arrival of the people of Israel in the land of Israel and their victorious wars—are all within the realm of legend. If some other external archaeological datum were to show up, demonstrating the patriarchs' existence directly, we would be able to move the border between history and legend back in time.

That does not mean that everything in the Merneptah stele is automatically historical or that everything in the Bible after 1206 BCE is historical either. Although the Bible gives us an almost continuous narrative for the period of the settlement and the judges through the end of the Davidic dynasty as rulers of Judah (586 BCE), we lack external verification for a great deal of it, especially the early part. Arguments for the historicity of this early period—especially the reigns of Saul, David, and Solomon—must be very circumspect and convincing. We will evaluate their possible historicity at the end of the book. As for Israel itself, we have an intriguing thirteenth-century

BCE reference whose import is great but difficult to interpret. However they got there, we find a people called Israel by the Egyptians in the highlands of Canaan by approximately 1250 BCE.

Historical Study Is an Art

Of course, historical study is inherently uncertain. Writing history is not merely listing the facts and writing a narrative. The data are not continuous and are often contradictory. A historian must evaluate a variety of sources and make reasoned judgments about what to include and what not to include: 100 percent surety is never possible in historical study. There is no such thing as objective history. All history is written from one perspective or another. This is an inevitable part of human endeavor, as we each see the world through a particular set of experiences and outlooks.

But that does not mean that we cannot attempt to write history. It does mean that there is no single, universal history that everyone will agree upon. It does mean that we must take every precaution against our own prejudices and biases and then also accept the legitimate critique of our peers. And it does mean that we should not consciously attempt to write history from one ideological perspective or another but, instead, to do the best we can to explain the ancient data on its own terms.

Disinterest

Disinterest—in this case, studying the Bible without prejudice or favor—is a very difficult order, especially given the necessity of biases in every historian's perspective. In a very real sense, disinterest turns out to be impossible for any one person to achieve, since no one is completely free of bias. But the world of scholarship is a community of scholars who engage in a discourse of self-correction over generations, past, present, and future, imperfect and slow moving as correction may be. My rule of thumb is the following: If you think that you are 100 percent right about what the Bible says, then you are *not* working in the world of scholarship. You are in the world of religion or ideology, perhaps—stances that are renowned for their ability to command our assents absolutely. You are using the Bible to demonstrate some ideological or personal hypothesis. This is a wholly private test and depends on being as honest with yourself as you can possibly be. Rightness and wrongness in biblical scholarship is a matter of evaluating sources and judging between conflicting pieces of evidence. That is a corollary of knowing that, in history, surety must be a question of percentages, not absolutes.

I think we are correct to be suspicious of people who say that the Bible must mean that their own contemporary religion is right, that their own contemporary country is right, that their own contemporary people are right, or that their war is just. We all know many examples of this kind of use of the Bible, which is rightly called proof-texting because it just looks at the texts that support its own view of a matter and disqualifies opposition, rather than reading the evidence as impartially as possible and reasoning through what the evidence suggests. Disinterest, as an ideal, is the opposite of self-interest. A scholar should read all the perspectives with as much detailed knowledge as can be mustered—ancient languages, philology, archaeology, literary criticism—and make every attempt to be disinterested.

Nor is disinterest the same as lack of interest. One can be passionately disinterested. Rather, disinterest means achieving an attitude of neutrality that should be fostered about historical questions in universities. I do not mean that scholars should be objective; that is clearly an impossibility. Furthermore, disinterest does not imply agreement between scholars either. Disinterested scholars will continue to have differences, even large and vexing differences. Humans are always embedded in their own historical context and subject to personal perspectives. Neutrality toward contemporary social movements and politics, even if it is not entirely achievable by one person, is the reason that universities exist as centers of scholarship.

Philosophically, disinterest has been discussed in Western philosophy since Descartes. Its existence has been disputed by contemporary postmodern philosophers on many grounds, not only because impartiality is thought by postmodernist thought to be inadvisable, even immoral, but also because disinterest appears to define a sense of private mental space that may not exist. These grounds are also disputable. Disinterest is for me a social behavior that scholars can produce: disinterest actually is a group of socially defined professional ethics that characterizes a group of historians trained in the critical methods of a particular time period. Historians learn languages and how to read sources and how to evaluate data. Critical historians agree that the historical enterprise demands adherence to a group of rules that make historiography possible, not perfect. They disagree over details and theories. Postmodern writers claim that their philosophical acumen and close reading make them equal to any text and that their job is to point out bias among those historians who merely apply historicocritical standards. Actually, I believe that perceiving and pointing out bias in other historians is a fairly low-level skill that every historian learns at the beginning of professional education.[3] What postmodern writers have to augment historians' toolbox is their emphasis on postcolonial perspectives, a major and important addition but not a secret shortcut to omniscience. But their insistence on writing from an overtly decided assumption makes the kind of scholarship for which the university has been justly famous impossible.

In the case of the Bible, we need not privilege any text or perspective as basic, especially not the Bible. The postcolonial study of the Bible has helped us understand what the prophets are doing both in the First and Second Temple periods. And postcolonial studies may help us understand the very beginnings of Israelite culture, as we shall see. In the meantime, we must operate as independent judges of the material. Historians cannot be assumed to be theological or mythical in their analysis of the Bible, as postmodern critics sometimes do.[4] We must attempt to make decisions autonomously based on data, not personal sentiment. That seems to me to be a more important moral value.

But we may read other scholars—in fact, we must read other scholars, who have better understandings of the archaeology, the very difficult ancient languages, or even just a wiser point of view. But we must never accept another scholar just because the work fits a preconceived notion. Unfortunately, Bible interpretation has become extremely complex, with much philology and earlier historical material to read. But with the appropriate "hermeneutics of suspicion," we weigh each document and each scholar's opinion before we frame or accept any conclusions.

The Hermeneutics of Suspicion

The *hermeneutics of suspicion* is a complicated term meant to remind us as scholars to trust nothing when it comes to evaluating evidence, not even our own theories. *Hermeneutics* is a fancy word, derived from the name of the Greek god Hermes, who was the messenger of the gods but also the god of translation. The process of translating what is written into something that is meaningful to us is called hermeneutics. It currently means the study of reading and gaining meaning from any text. Hermeneutics certainly includes what a sermonizer does in religious services when explaining a text. The word was originally the name for a part of a divinity school curriculum, especially the part that helps preachers learn their skills. But today it also includes academics who, though trying to reconstruct the past, are also always adding unexplored hypotheses, details, and formulations to their explanation. It almost describes the whole process of reading and interpreting. Gaining meaning from any text is partly a function of what the text purports to be saying and equally much to what we think the words mean, including the assumptions that we ourselves bring to it. When we bring to bear the hermeneutics of suspicion, we must both interrogate the text for meanings that it might contain and also interrogate ourselves as well because we are predisposed to see the text in a particular context. So we must take stock of ourselves and the text as well, interrogate ourselves and the text as well. We have to ask the same hard questions of the Bible that we ask of other texts.

Two Types of Disinterested Analysis

Disinterest is neither confined to religious nor secular approaches to the Bible, but we can find it in both kinds of writing. For instance, in the historical study of the Bible, this means, practically, that we must face that the story of Adam and Eve, Noah's flood, and all the events of the primeval history (Genesis 1–11) are not literally true. They are interesting and important tales from the ancient Near East, a good deal of which appear to be adapted from the epic literature of Mesopotamia and Canaan. Believing them to be true is at odds with long established science and it is completely at odds with all good Bible scholarship of the last two centuries, which shows the relationship between Israel's cosmological stories and those of Canaan and Mesopotamia. They are all a special form of literature called *myth*. Scholars who adopt a fundamentalist point of view because of their own religious perspective are most often not displaying disinterest in their work.

That does not mean, however, that one must insist on these findings when studying fundamentalism. If we were studying the modern phenomenon of fundamentalism, recognizing that it has adopted a literalistic form of Bible interpretation is an important part of understanding the movement. One can appreciate its social organization, even the theology of a fundamentalist group, but when studying the Bible itself the mythical character of Genesis 1–11 must be recognized.

However, in studying the biblical text, there are many possible religious stances that can be called disinterested. But there are many varieties of faith that can survive with a more sophisticated reading of the Bible, which takes account of the historical development of biblical ideas. Furthermore, there are many varieties of secular thought that are helpful in understanding the Bible. What *disinterested* means in this context is that the scholar is using every tool available, taking every care not to allow his or her own personal perspective to bias the conclusion.

Likewise in nonreligious stances, we can see two extremes. A strong ideological stance—for example, that the Bible proves a modern state of Palestine should exist—is not trustworthy when applied to ancient scholarship because we know the person would not accept a conclusion determining the Bible says something different or perhaps has nothing to say about the issue at all. Or take a hypothesis that is related to the idea that a modern state of Palestine should exist: for example, that there was no First Temple period. If that hypothesis depends on the former, then it is not scholarship. However, it is possible to come to the same conclusion, that there was no First Temple period, disinterestedly. In that case, it is simply a case of mustering the evidence fairly and presenting it for other scholars to weigh and judge. Though in theory it can be very difficult to tell the difference between a consciously biased and a disinterested argument, in practice it is not very difficult because a disinterested argument deals quite fairly with evidence and produces an evidentially based argument. Biased cases often begin with theoretical discussions and arguments, obviating the need to consult opposing evidence.

Minimalists and Maximalists

It is customary to divide the camps of contemporary scholarship of the Hebrew Bible into minimalists and maximalists. The terms refer to the extent to which the information in the Hebrew text of the Bible itself is to be accepted for historiography. Maximalists, normally, believe a great deal of what the Bible tells us and minimalists believe a great deal less. Critical historians tend toward the middle of the scale to the end while postmodernists almost always tend to be minimalists. A few are so minimal in what they accept as historical, they should be called nihilists.[5]

Since minimalist and maximalist are relative terms, it is possible to be confused by their referents. Few scholars, as I said before, believe that Genesis 1–11 should be believed literally, though some fundamentalists do and should really be called extreme maximalists. So the arguments between minimalists and maximalists have nothing to do with the historicity of the biblical creation stories, Adam and Eve, or the flood. Virtually all modern scholars concede that these are myths that have been reused by the Hebrews to place themselves in a meaningful world.

Most of the current argument between minimalism and maximalism concerns the believability of the historical books in the First Temple period (approximately 950–586 BCE) and the believability of archaeology dated to that period. That is because the archaeological and scriptural evidence from that time period have been criticized as overinterpretations. An extreme minimalist might argue that there is no evidence for Israel in Merneptah's stele, that the reference has been misread or even that the inscription was an early-twentieth-century hoax. That is a far-fetched conclusion. Yet most contemporary scholars concede that the five books of Moses as we know them were finally and fully edited in the early Second Temple period (approximately 515 BCE–70 CE) out of a great many sources. Maximalists accept that a great number of traditions come from the First Temple period or reflect traditions that go back that far. Minimalists accept very few of the sources as actually describing the First Temple period.

Extreme minimalists often think that the Bible comes entirely from the Second Temple period, starting in the mid-sixth century BCE (550s BCE), and that it is in large part from the Greek period, a fictional reconstruction of a group of people who call themselves Jews and who have never been in the area before. Needless to say, this extreme minimalist position is largely the product of scholars who are Palestinian nationalists first, largely not Bible scholars per se, but who maintain that there is no such thing as accurate history, only the fictional master narrative of one socioeconomic group justifying rule over another. Their explanation, which ignores most of what moderate scholars call critical history, is, therefore, just as good as anyone else's. Just as fundamentalists tend to agree that their information comes not from reason but from faith, extreme minimalists tend to agree that their superior grasp of history is due to their superior ideology, which is fairer to both Arabs and Jews from an ethical perspective.

I believe that there are better and worse arguments. From my position, neither extremes are part of disinterested scholarship. Both extreme maximalists and extreme minimalists agree that they are giving a single narrative their primary credibility. Neither one, therefore, needs to be an expert in the field but prefers actually to be specialists in theory or theology itself. Disinterested scholars, whether they be maximalists or minimalists, tend to be scholars in the field and tend to argue from the data or archaeology and the Bible, each in relative importance, depending on the specific problem under scrutiny.

From my own point of view, only disinterested scholarship needs detailed analysis, and that disinterested scholarship will provide us with the best understanding of what actually happened, even if no one completely agrees on what did happen. In the end, I intend to show that biblical history will show us that the stories of the patriarchs can be understood as the mythical system supporting life in the First Temple period, and that study of myth and folklore will allow us to see some insights about how the Bible has come down to us. Moreover, my position will come out somewhere between the classic maximalist and classic minimalist position, but it will, I hope, be a disinterested opinion.

History Is Terrible, but So Is the Human Imagination

We know that history is cruel and that terrible events may yet help us understand which stories withstand the test of historicity in the Bible. But the human imagination is capable of constructing terrible stories too. The myths of the Greeks, for example, also relate rapes, murders, incest. What makes us sure that what the Bible tells us is history?

Actually, it will turn out, we shall see, that some of the most terrible stories in the Bible will serve as myths for the people living in the period of the First Temple (from roughly 950 BCE until 587 BCE). Other stories did happen, and we can demonstrate that they did because they were so disturbing that they caused the society of that time to question its assumptions—for example, to give up some tribal authority and priestly authority and opt for a king. And, indeed, very often mythical material helps the people of that time to come to terms with terrible events, as we shall see. Consequently, the stories will sometimes tell us a great deal about the distinction between history and myth and how they interacted in the Old Testament. They will help us resolve the quandary about which of these terrible stories is likely to be true and why and give us a reason for understanding what biblical truth means.

Since It Is Fiction We May Safely Believe It

The Bible, whether historically true or fiction, is a foundational book in our society. No book would have to be true in every detail to serve in this capacity. The works of Shakespeare are also foundational to our society, and almost everything in Shakespeare's plays is fictional or so heavily fictionalized as to amount to the same thing. I personally would allow that the Bible, even when fictional, functions to help understand ourselves better, just as Shakespeare's plays do. Indeed, we read fiction thinking that we will be not just amused but also edified by it. Because we know we are reading fiction in advance, we are relieved from having to believe it to be literally true.

For me, there is likewise quite a bit of fiction in the Bible; some of it, like Ruth, Job, and Jonah, was even intended to be fiction. Like other fiction, when the Bible is indulging explicitly in fiction, it is often truer than history, a narrative we can expect to be manipulated by one party or another. I want to affirm the ironic truth that "history will tell lies, as usual. But since it is fiction, we may safely believe it." By this I mean that it is easier to identify moral seriousness in fiction than it is in tendentious historical writing. We know how to identify truths in a fictional document. Normally, we do understand that fiction tells us something true and enduring about ourselves, even as it amuses or terrifies us. We accept the conventions of a fictional world because of the power that reading and watching drama has over our imagination. I will suggest that knowing this helps us whether we look at the world through reason alone or want to add faith. A great deal of all writing depends on our imaginative faculties, whether it be deemed history or fiction.

The Bible as an Anthology

The Bible's name in Greek—*ta biblia*—arguably means "anthology." Since *ho biblos* means "the book" in Greek, *to biblion*—a neuter diminutive form— would mean "the little book" and its plural, *ta biblia*, means "the little books." So though we think that the Bible means the paramount, zenith, or cynosure of books, it actually means something quite different: a collection of little books, an anthology. One can ask what kinds of literature are enclosed within any kind of anthology. I will maintain, and I am not the first to do so, that some of the early parts of the Bible are myth. I will also maintain, like the minimalists, that a great deal of the Bible is shaped by political myth. But I will try to show that the nature of the political myth in the Bible is quite different from what most scholars have described.

Myth

Within the anthology of the Bible, there are many different types of literature. Within those genres of literature is a great deal of myth. In fact, I will be arguing that there is more myth and legend than is commonly recognized. Myth is not a word that can be completely understood or always easily identified. My description of the book of Genesis would certainly start with the word *myth*. A lot of people find that word troublesome, but, when I use it, I do not mean to be negative, rather the opposite: myth is very high praise for the function of this ancient literature. *Myth* is an auto-antonym or contranym, a word like *oversight, sanction,* or *cleave*. All these words can mean two opposite things, one good and one less so.

From ancient times, myth could mean a respected story or foolish nonsense. For example, the word *myth* could be used to describe the "old wives' tale" that handling frogs will give you warts—a story that is patently false. But there is also a high view of myth that points out the sacredness and centrality of certain stories in a society, a positive and productive part of any society's beliefs. That is the way I intend to use it.

But use of the term *myth* to describe the religious assumptions of a society has grown controversial because academics like to have their terminology clear (if not uncomplicated). For a long time anthropologists and scholars of religion agreed to use it when they meant that it was a crucial story for giving meaning to a culture or society. The first 11 chapters of Genesis were certainly that kind of myth; in fact, they still function that way in a large section of American society. Myth represented whatever was viewed as obviously or self-evidently true in a society. But other scholars are troubled by the ambiguity of the word and do not use it at all.

The tenets of modern American democracy, especially as interpreted by the popular media, can be described as myths, since they are treated as self-evident truths. In this "high" view of myth, a "foolish myth" is a contradiction in terms, at best referring to a myth that has ceased functioning in a mythological way. But because myth continues in ordinary parlance to have the unwanted implication of a false or foolish story, some anthropologists and students of religion prefer to coin a term like *root metaphor* or *conceptual archetype* to suggest without prejudice that we are studying a very important and formative story for that culture. I have no objection to using either set of terms, as long as the intention is clearly explained.

A root metaphor or myth usually takes the form of a story about the cosmos or the ancient history of the group. Although the story may be amusing or enjoyable or scatological or even sexually explicit, it must also have four serious functions to qualify as a myth: 1. to explain the beginning of time (archetype) or history (prototype); 2. to inform people about themselves by revealing the continuity between key events in the history of the society and the life of the individual; 3. to illustrate a saving power in human life by demonstrating how to overcome a flaw in society or personal experience; and 4. to provide a moral pattern for individual and community action by both negative and positive example.

The most important rituals in a society are usually closely connected with myths. The ritual, whether a complete dramatization of the story or just a casual reference to it, is an expression and embodiment of the myth in the society. For me, therefore, the Bible's mythic stories, Genesis 1–11, for example, are extremely important, even though they are not literally true. They are connected with biblical notions of time, the seven-day week, the Sabbath, marriage, eating meat, wearing clothes, and many other things.

Some of the Bible Is Myth for People Living in Biblical Times

I am going to try to make the case that the stories of the patriarchs, no matter whether they be legendary, history, or fiction, served as myths for the people living in First Temple times, roughly 950 BCE–587 BCE). This means that I will try to demonstrate what some skeptics of the Bible find impossible to believe: there were Israelites living in the land of Israel during that time and that they have both a history and, what is miraculous, an imaginative life—the patriarchal stories—which is available to us if we study them carefully. In those myths, we find the record of their religious experience.

The Hebrews left us a continuous narrative from creation until the end of the Davidic monarchy in the sixth century BCE. With some patience we can divide up that narrative, assess its historicity, and actually reconstruct some of what they were thinking in the early parts of the first millennium

BCE. Myth will take up far more of the first five books of Moses than has been ordinarily considered. That we have their religious thinking, for me, represents a new kind of miracle about the Bible, not just because it has been insufficiently recognized. When we put the stories in their correct context, we see how the myth and the history functioned together to help the Israelites resolve issues in their own society.

Covenant: The Overriding Myth of the Hebrew Bible

Whenever we are dealing with an anthology, which the Bible is, the first question ought to be: "Why were all these little books put together?" What is the organizing principle of the anthology? The answer is that they all concern the relationship between God and the people Israel. That relationship is known as the *covenant*. In fact, the word *covenant*, when translated into Latin, is *testament*. So that is how we understand the names of the two biggest divisions in the Christian Bible: the Old Testament and the New Testament. They are talking about two different groups of books that deal with *the old covenant* and *the new covenant*. Since the covenant is between a historical people and a supernatural being, it is clear that covenant is itself *myth*. As such, it fits into a more complex structure of beliefs that is easiest to call a mythology.

The Hebrew word for *covenant* is *brith*. The concept was in use in First Temple times (ca. 950 BCE–587 BCE) as well as in Second Temple times (534 BCE through 70 CE). *Covenant* is actually a legal term that means much the same as *contract* does today. According to the ancient Israelites of the Hebrew Bible, the relationship between themselves and their God—a supernatural person called the LORD or, as his name is conventionally transliterated from Hebrew, Yahweh—was governed by the rules of a contract, which he initiated with the people of Israel. This contract not only specified a relationship with their divine partner YHWH, it also specified the rules by which Israelites should behave and treat each other.

The model for this root metaphor came from formal agreements in ordinary human relationships—such as treaties or even marital contracts. Both treaties and weddings, as well as several other agreements in the ancient world, had one thing in common. They were enforced by an oath. That oath taking became a central aspect of the myth and ritual of the Old Testament and continues today even in some of the language of modern Judaism,

Christianity, and Islam, all of which base themselves on the stories of the patriarchs and revere the Old Testament in one way or another. All those who were party to the covenant became known as the people of Israel, whether they lived in the southern kingdom of Judah or the northern kingdom, also called Israel.

The Hebrew claim of the divine origin of law was unique among nearby peoples. Although all the great ancient Near Eastern cultures at the time of the Israelites, and for centuries before them, thought of themselves as subject to laws that were guaranteed by their gods, only the Israelites actually said that all their laws came directly from the divinity. Moses is the law giver but not the law writer. He was merely a conduit. The Babylonian king Hammurabi, for example, was said to have presented his law code to Shamash, the god of wisdom. This very act is depicted on the most famous copy of the Code of Hammurabi. It is also quite clear from Hammurabi's edicts that the law code was created by him, in the sense that he ordered it created by his school of scribes and that he takes credit for it. The Israelites, however, for all that, declared that God was the direct author of their law code and that this divine law was the basis of all behavior between members of the society and also between God and the people.

The Hebrew concept of covenant was unique in some other crucial respects. It conceived of the entire universe as under the sway of one deity. The law was not simply revealed; it was based upon an actual agreement and guaranteed by an actual oath sworn between the people of Israel and that God. This was a myth with a ritual behind it. We find evidence of periodic covenant renewal ceremonies in the late First Temple period (ca. 950–587 BCE), at Josiah's Passover celebration (621 BCE) and Ezra's covenant renewal (515 BCE).

There is actually some room for thinking that the Israelites achieved monotheism after a struggle between Yahweh and the other gods of Canaan and after considering that Yahweh was their God, though there may have been other gods who governed other nations.[6] This is called *henotheism*. Eventually, they considered that the Hebrew God was not only reliable and just in his responses to his people but also single and unique and, lastly, that he was the one and only God. This suggests, in some fashion, a progression from henotheism to monotheism. Hence, his ordinances of law were for the common human good. Nowhere else in the ancient Near East was there so systematic an appropriation of the concept of a lawful, contractual obligation to express the relationship between a whole people and their god and consequently to define morality within society. These concepts, derived from the root metaphor of covenant and later expressed by terms like *monotheism* and *ethics*, evolved through many stages in Hebrew thought as the social institutions and historical situation of Israel changed.[7]

The most mature notion of covenant comes from the latest layers of the Bible. But covenant is present in some of the early levels as well. Whatever its date, it was not merely a theological idea but a pattern for ritual and lore and a model for social practice. The Hebrew legendary ancestors of the Israelites—Abraham, Isaac, Jacob, and Moses—were pictured as having made archetypal covenants with God. In these agreements, YHWH always promised them long life, many offspring, and the land of Israel (for example, Genesis 15, Genesis 28:10–20). But they were also of a piece with the agreements that the patriarchs also made with their neighbors: Abraham (Genesis 21: 22–32, with Abimelech), Isaac (Genesis 26:26–31, also with Abimelech), and Jacob (Genesis 31:43–54, with Laban), for example, are also depicted as having made rather similar covenants with neighboring kings.

In other words, a covenant was not an unknown literary convention before God revealed his covenant with Abraham. This was a legal aspect of their society, as it is of ours. It represents a grant or an agreement, enforced with an oath, with many different ritual requirements (in the ancient world) that change over the centuries. These legendary accounts of covenanting with the patriarchs are paralleled in the historical covenanting of Josiah (621 BCE) and Ezra (515 BCE) as well as some of the narrated behavior of David and Solomon. And so the ancient legends became part of the pattern for later rites and rituals.

The interspersing of covenantal, legal material with historical narrative, epic, and saga in the Bible is a unique aspect of Hebrew covenant literature. Depending on the time and place in which the account was written and the purposes for which it was written, the covenant would contain slightly different characteristics. Biblical stories of the covenant express the perspectives and politics of the narrator, which were supposed to have taken place in the most distant past.

The covenant can appear like a primitive ritual in which God and Abram encounter each other in Abram's trance or dream. They make an agreement and may even take part in a covenantal meal, as tribal chieftains might—as in Genesis 15. The result of that agreement is that Abram becomes a worshipper of Yahweh. It almost appears as if God himself allows a curse to be invoked upon himself if he is foresworn by ritually passing between the pieces of the cut-up animals in the form of a flaming torch. This may be considered the *durable* aspect of a myth, while any ritual reenactment of it, like Josiah's covenant renewal at Passover (2 Kings 23:23) or Ezra's reading of the law on Sukkoth ("Tabernacles," see Ezra 10, Nehemiah 10), which might have taken place in ancient Israel, would be considered the *punctual* aspect of the covenant. The *durative* was meant to depict the true and enduring aspect of God's providence. In this case, what God promised Abram, and through him all Israel, was the prophecy the LORD gave to Abram:

> ¹⁷ When the sun had gone down and it was dark, a smoking fire pot and a flaming torch passed between these pieces. ¹⁸ On that day the LORD made a covenant with Abram, saying, "To your descendants I give this land, from the river of Egypt to the great river, the river Euphrates, ¹⁹ the land of the Kenites, the Kenizzites, the Kadmonites, ²⁰ the Hittites, the Perizzites, the Rephaim, ²¹ the Amorites, the Canaanites, the Girgashites, and the Jebusites."
>
> (Genesis 15:17–21)

Offspring and homeland have paramount importance. And the text tells us that the people will have an Egyptian bondage but come out and inherit this land. The general boundaries of the land are mentioned. The "river of Egypt" is not the Nile but the Wadi Arish south of Gaza. The Euphrates is high in the North, not to the East in Mesopotamia. The only time the Bible records an empire of that size is during the united monarchy of David and Solomon, and we shall see that it is itself an idealization. Clearly, the passage was written long after the time of the Egyptian bondage or the Exodus or even the time of David and Solomon. But the text is extremely interested in establishing the rights of the Israelites to live long in this special land, to have many offspring, and to "go to your fathers in peace." The latter can have no possible meaning of resurrection or immortality but rather promises a peaceful death and proper burial, as the archaeology of Israelite grave sites show. The root metaphor of family descent set the Israelites apart from the Canaanites, earlier inhabitants of the land of Israel, whom the Israelites partially defeated but whose religion they were tempted to emulate.

According to the Bible, Yahweh, the Israelite God, was not neutral toward the Israelites' accommodation to Canaanite ways after their settlement in the promised land. He found the Canaanite religion abhorrent because of its practices of ritual prostitution and child sacrifice. He wanted the Israelites to separate from the Canaanites, forbade them to sacrifice their children, gave them substantial parts of Canaan as punishment for the Canaanites' sins, and promised the Israelites progeny, long life, and a good burial if they obeyed his covenant. The moral is apparent in these mythical stories.

In the archaeological record, however, we find many goddess figurines in Israelite settlements and other evidence that the Bible's ideals were too difficult for the Israelites. The covenant, then, if it existed in this time, was surely an ideal to live up to and not the norm of the society.

The greatest of the covenants in the Bible, however, is the giving of the Ten Commandments at Sinai (Exodus 20:2–17) where Moses received the commandments directly from YHWH. It is but the beginning of a law code that continues through Exodus 23:27 and goes into considerably more detail about the legal requirements of the law. The story is so important to the Israelites that we see many different voices at work in narrating it, voices we will explore. The Ten Commandments, or the Ten Utterances as they are literally called in Hebrew, serves as the civil code for the society that lives in the land and mediates legal problems by its example.

This mythical event (whatever may have happened in the desert) is represented throughout the society in big and little observances of the society:

> You shall take some of the first of all the fruit of the ground, which you harvest from the land that the LORD your God is giving you, and you shall put it in a basket and go to the place that the LORD your God will choose as a dwelling for his name. You shall go to the priest who is in office at that time, and say to him, "Today I declare to the LORD your God that I have come into the land that the LORD swore to our ancestors to give us. . . . A wandering Aramean was my ancestor; he went down into Egypt and lived there as an alien, few in number, and there he became a great nation, mighty and populous. . . . The LORD brought us out of Egypt with a mighty hand and an outstretched arm, with a terrifying display of power, and with signs and wonders; and he brought us into this place and gave us this land, a land flowing with milk and honey. So now I bring the first of the fruit of the ground that you, O LORD, have given me." You shall set it down before the LORD your God and bow down before the LORD your God.
>
> (Deuteronomy 26:2–10)

Here is a ritual occasion. The book of Deuteronomy specifies a particular liturgy for the action of paying a tithe of summer produce. The history of the people is rehearsed at the very moment that a farmer is paying his taxes to the priests. YHWH brought the people out of Egyptian bondage and brought them to the land where they could raise this produce. Out of the bounty that YHWH produced, the law says, you should remember the priest, the Levite, and the aliens, orphans, and widows, in accordance with the law code YHWH gave to Moses. The ritual enforces the story of national origins. The story provides a justification for the ritual. As a result, it is also true that the ritual, and the myth behind it, supports the taxes given to the priests. That is one of its functions. Myth quite frequently not only gives meaning to the past and present, it also supports and benefits a professional class whose job is to maintain and tell the story. This is one example.

Since the highest form of covenant, and the kind that would busy the most scribes, was treaty, many of the covenantal ceremonies of the Hebrew Bible take treaty forms. That would include the renowned story of the giving of the law at Sinai. Moreover, it would cover the punctual events in Israelite history, including the dedication of the Temple at the festival of Sukkoth, the dedication of the Second Temple, also at the festival of Sukkoth, and the Temple purification of Josiah, which famously took place at Passover, the spring festival holiday. Each of them, to the extent that they are historical, represent a punctual and ritual appropriation of the myth of the covenant.

It took a long time to see that the prophets were also aware of the covenant root metaphor, even though they rarely address it in treaty language. Amos, for example, reminds his hearers that Israel entered into a contract with Yahweh, sealed with an oath, on which the people have defaulted. Yahweh must therefore seek redress by lawful means, which includes sending his prophets to sue for nonperformance of contract. Amos concentrates on describing his divine lawsuit as God's lawyer, spokesperson, and prosecuting attorney. Even the words *love* and *lover, know* and *knower, master* and *servant* have covenantal and legal implications in the mouths of the prophets. They are technical terms referring to covenantal partnerships in ancient Near Eastern texts.

Even more famously, Hosea pictures the covenant relationship between Yahweh and Israel as a marriage, though a bad one that has to be repaired or ended. A marriage, too, is a contractual relationship that, unless the father or husband is king, cannot be fairly reduced to a treaty form. Like treaties, however, marriage contracts are covenants that were enforced with oaths, even in earliest times.[8]

Israelite history is mythical in the further sense that it sees the past as a paradigm for the present. Past events, we have already seen, are used consciously as liturgical models for the covenantal meaning of human destiny. For instance, the entire people, whether if actually came from Egypt or only knows of the story, take the event of the Exodus to be the foundation of its identity, a metaphor of going from slavery to freedom, to becoming a people with a destiny and a purpose. The Passover liturgy today contains the ancient lines "Every Jew should look upon himself as though he too came forth out of Egypt." That is a Second Temple statement, but one of the characteristics of myths is that they are often enacted ritually. The ritual provides the participant with an reenactment of the events that are narrated in the myth.

As the service continues, each Jew is instructed to hope for the future redemption of Israel and, indeed, all of humanity. Thus identification with the history of the covenantal community helps define an individual Jew's religious purpose. Fidelity to the covenant makes deliverance possible. Past historical events, remembered either directly or within a liturgical context, express evolving notions of the covenant and the salvation it offers.

Some of the covenant stories are quite ancient. But most of the stories and the use of the covenant as a central organizing principle of the anthology of the Bible come from Second Temple times. This chronology makes them later than the stories I want to discuss. But myth functions in the same way in both First Temple and Second Temple times, so this is exactly the same function of myth that we shall be looking for most assiduously in this study of the Hebrew Bible's oldest and most puzzling layers. For sure, in the literature of the Bible, the latest era of time when the anthology is being redacted and edited shows up a great deal in how the stories are being understood. The myths that we see being enacted by the patriarchs or the past heroes of Israel, I will try to show, are going to serve as clear prototypes and paradigms for Israelites living not just in Second Temple times but in First Temple times as well.

It is no surprise that Second Temple times show up often, because that is the time period during which the stories were redacted. More surprising and apparent among the most terrible and inexplicable stories in the Bible is the presence of the First Temple period's interests and desires. The result is that the terrible stories of the Pentateuch witness First Temple times occasionally and not just the layer of their redaction in Second Temple times.

First we shall see how patriarchal stories function in these relatively early times. That will help us find a relative chronology for how the traditions of the Hebrew Bible were laid down. Then we shall look at the external archae-ological evidence and, in some cases, actually discover an absolute chronol-ogy for when these stories began or reached final form.[9]

CHAPTER ONE

THE MATRIARCH IN PERIL

Stories Told Again and Again

The Old Testament is a great saga. The stories are told and retold throughout our society. But they are also told and retold within the text of the Bible as well. The stories always fascinate children, even as they puzzle adults. Furthermore, the stories have an uncanny way of repeating themselves, just at their most puzzling and mystifying moments, as if crying out for extra attention. The more the stories are repeated, the more important they become. We will take a closer look at the most puzzling and horrifying of these stories and try to understand them. We shall learn that repetitions and reformations of the story are an indicator of the importance of the story to the narrators. And one of the most difficult and puzzling things to investigate is the mysterious repetition in the text of the Hebrew Bible.

Tropes, Type-Scenes, Doublets, Allegories, Prototypes, and Hypertypes

Hebrew Bible scholars categorize repetitions in many different ways. It is not important to expose them systematically here because we need only talk about the ones that occur as we need them in context. Nevertheless, it is beneficial to have an overview of what repetitions might imply about the text. One of the first and most important repetitions to be isolated has been called a trope (a conventional scene) or "type-scene." Robert Alter, one of the greatest Old Testament literary critics, uses *type-scene*, a term derived from the study of the Greek epics, to describe a specific kind of scene that recurs repeatedly in the text.[1] For example, in the *Iliad* and in Near Eastern epic, there is often a scene of the mother or wife of a warrior watching him from the window or the walls of the city as the hero heads off for combat. The prototypical one is when Andromache watches Hector from the walls of Troy, *he teichoskopia* (the view from the city wall) in Greek. Or, in biblical tradition, it is quite conventional for the patriarch to meet his future wife first at a well, where some interesting event brings the couple closer together. That can be called a type-scene. There is also a famous trope or type-scene in the biblical birth of a hero. Usually the mother is barren, and the birth of the hero is a direct response to the mother's prayers to God to open her womb. The implication is that this is the much desired child for whom God has miraculously opened the mother's womb. It functions like the trope we know as a virgin birth in the Greek tradition.

Another kind of repetitious scene characteristic of the Bible is called a *doublet*. It is somewhat different from a type-scene since it is not a trope told at a specific moment so much as an exact, or almost exact, repetition of the biblical story in a different place. A doublet is quite often told about the exact same character in exactly the same way, even with almost exactly the same words. Sometimes the doublet can be retold about different characters, but using almost the exact same language. There is also a long history of interpreting doublets in modern biblical studies. The modern assumption about such doublets is that when they occur we are witnessing two different sources, both of which told the same story but were edited far later so as to preserve each version. So the most common explanation for a doublet in historicocritical Bible interpretations is that it indicates two different sources. By studying the differences between the two texts, historicocritical Bible scholars attempt to characterize the different sources or even the different editors.

A lot of the issues that characterize different sources and editors or narrators are far more complex and difficult to unravel. There will yet be other pairs of stories that can be understood as allegories—where one story stands in for another or represents another symbolically.[2] Allegory is explicitly a Greek rhetorical form. In Greek academic literature, allegories are normally added by a later interpreter who is embarrassed or bothered by something in the original text. For example, at a certain point in the academic tradition of teaching the works of Homer, the Greek teachers and interpreters became embarrassed by the depictions of the gods and their petty human motivations. Almost all the actions of the *Iliad* and the *Odyssey* were allegorized in the Greek academic tradition to refer to ethical values as a way of keeping the text relevant to an increasingly philosophically sophisticated audience. In Jewish academic traditions based on the Greek model—such as the work of Philo of Alexandria in the first century CE—the Bible is allegorized to represent relationships between virtues and vices, and the reasons for doing so were exactly the same. The stories seemed crude and needed to be allegorized to remain interesting to a philosophically sophisticated Jewish community in Alexandria.

Another pair of stories that speak symbolically one to another is a *typology*, where one story prefigures or serves as a prototype of the other. There are actually several kinds of typologies: prototypical story pairs as well as hypertypical stories. A hypertypical pair of stories occurs when one story is meant as a paradigm for another, and a prototypical story, a subcategory of the first, is when the story is understood to have happened long before and therefore serves as a pattern that is repeating in the second story. We shall spend most of our time looking at hypertypical and prototypical stories. Eventually we shall see that the prototypical story in the pair is often written later, serving as mythical justification or legend to help understand a more current event. All of this is excessively theoretical here. But it will be clear when we look at cases. What is most important to understand is that we must study these stories in pairs or larger groups as all these forms of typology develop between two or more stories analyzed together. Let us see how helpful this method of comparing similar stories can be in interpreting material in Genesis.

Abraham and Sarah

In this case, we begin by looking at Abraham. Abraham is an enormously important character in the Bible. He is explicitly the progenitor of most of the tribes living in or near the land of Israel in the first millennium BCE. The Bible promises to Abraham that kings shall stem from him and Sarah: "⁶ I will make you exceedingly fruitful; and I will make nations of you, and kings shall come from you" (Genesis 17:6, see Genesis 17:16).[3] Most importantly for the Israelites, since the Hebrew Bible is the story of the Israelites, he is the father of all Israelites—tribes from both north and south—as well as the nation that rises and falls from them. So he is explicitly the eponymous ancestor of all the tribes of Israel. We shall be studying some of the most difficult stories in Genesis and wondering why such an important figure as Abraham does some incomprehensible and terrible things.

We will begin by taking a *doublet,* or actually a *triplet* of stories about Abraham and Sarah, because virtually the same very puzzling story occurs three times in a very brief period in the book of Genesis. This story has sometimes been called a type-scene and dubbed "the wife-sister motif" or "the matriarch in distress." This categorization belies its horrifying intent by seeming to suggest that it is a convention that we understand. To the contrary it is only told these three times in the early part of Genesis and it is completely incomprehensible. In fact, some aspects of the story are so mysterious that we will not be able to understand them until the end of the book. But we start with the story to show the power of reading stories against each other in the Bible.

Genesis 12:10–20, 20:1–18, and 26:1–17 seem to tell a single story, even the same story, about a matriarch in peril, though it is told about different characters. If read separately, as we shall do at first to see the contrast, the three versions would offer the critical Bible scholar almost insoluble problems in narration. They concern the same main characters—Abram/Abraham and Sarai/Sarah. The two stories use slightly different names for the main characters. The third version concerns Isaac and Rebecca, but some of the other characters are the same and the events are essentially the same, so it is arguable that we have a *triplet* in this case.

The Wife-Sister Motif

Let us look at the stories in more detail. In the first story, Genesis 12, the patriarch, whose name in the story is Abram, takes his wife Sarai into Egypt because there was a famine in the land of Canaan (Genesis 12:10). Abram tells Sarai that the Egyptians might steal and rape her after killing him (Genesis 12:12). To prevent this tragedy, and it would be as much of a tragedy for him as for her, Abram suggests that he tell the Egyptians that Sarai is his sister so that he will be saved because of her: "That it will go well with me because of you" (Genesis 12:13). He is suggesting that Sarai is in some way more dispensible than he is. Presumably, this means that if Sarai becomes a wife of Pharaoh, they will also protect Abram as her guardian. Nevertheless, whatever Abram's statement means exactly, it is quite a difficult story to understand morally. In fact, it is a horrifying story, which threatens to subject the matriarch to the worst kind of sexual abuse. The story threatens to negate completely the promises made to Abram and Sarai about their manifold offspring.

How could Abram, the father of the Hebrews, the Israelites, the Jews, and the Arabs have done such a cowardly and immoral deed? How could he have treated his wife as an object to be bought or sold? The mind of a modern Bible reader recoils from such behavior, even in the planning stages. But it is his fatherhood of the multitude of nations that is at stake.

What makes reading this passage even more frustrating and difficult is how little the text actually does tell us about Abram's reasoning process, either his inner thinking or his emotional state. We learn what we can from what Abram does, not from his thought processes, which are not described. Abram never reflects on his actions, never tells us why this is the only available course of action, never tells us whether he is proud or ashamed of taking any of the strange courses of action that he performs. The story is, from our point of view, full of "gaps," missing bits of information that we would expect to be present to understand the narration.[4]

Thus, we have few clues as to what the narrator of the passage wants us to take away from the story. Are we to blame Abram for his callousness toward his wife or (what seems to be the point of the story, though it is almost impossible for us to believe) admire him for his cleverness? God rewards him after the incident, which seems as if it is telling us that we are to admire him. But neither interpretation is ruled out by the text. There is no sure way to understand the narrative by our moral standards. The ambiguity appears deliberate. We shall see that it puzzled commentators, scholars, and probably some ancient minds as well.

What Abram fears about Sarai's beauty is the very thing that happens.[5] Pharaoh sees the couple, admires Sarai, and takes her into his house. Abram receives a great fortune in flocks and servants, presumably as a bride price, as Sarai's guardian (Genesis 12:16). Pharaoh immediately has difficulties: he has to endure unspecified plagues (Genesis 12:16). Pharaoh calls Abram into his presence and readily learns the truth. Pharaoh's behavior has been guiltless; only Abram's has been culpable, from our point of view. In fact, Pharaoh may seem to us to be the moral center of the story, which is surprising when one considers Egypt's future role in the Exodus narrative. But here Pharaoh asks the very question we would ask: "Why would Abram do such a thing?" Then Pharaoh orders his soldiers to escort the patriarchal family out of Egypt (Genesis 12:17–20), which is about the lightest "punishment" one could imagine for his lack of judgment. Abram leaves with his wife, who is miraculously saved intact, and they take with them the property of Egypt.

With its sojourn in Egypt, miraculous salvation, and exit with the goods of the Egyptians, this version of the story contains many key motifs in the Exodus story. It appears to be the Exodus story writ small.[6] The repetitions of the wife-sister confusion suggest that this is central issue of this version of the story. Strangely enough, though, that is left unnoticed by the narrator, who instead concentrates on the escape from Egypt and Abram's gain in worldly goods. But it is a key point that we are to understand Abram and not Pharaoh as the moral center of the story.

The narrator is deliberately giving the story a *typological* meaning. In this case, this story is meant to be a *prototype* of the Exodus story, which it prefigures and of which the narrator seems quite aware. It seems unlikely that an Exodus story would be very important to a group of people returning to Israel from Babylon. Neither would a story of taking the possessions of the Egyptians be very congruent with a time period in which Israel was part of the Persian Empire. But the story might well have meaning to a people who think that they were later rescued from Egypt by God after being enslaved there. Logically, however, it would have to be posterior to the Exodus story. In a way, typological studies point out the harmonies that exist in the text while type-scenes are more like looking at the melodies. Without it, we would have missed the seemingly impossible fact that Abraham and not Pharaoh is the hero of the story.

The Matriarch in Distress Again

But the mysterious story repeats almost exactly in about eight chapters in Genesis. In Genesis 20:1–18 a very similar story is told about Abraham and his wife Sarah, the same couple with slightly different names,[7] though now the foreign king is not Pharaoh of Egypt but Abimelech of Gerar, a Philistine king. The story is a doublet with the first, although several important details and narrator evaluations are different. In this story Abraham journeys to the south again, but not as far south as Egypt, dwelling in Gerar between

Kadesh and Shur (Genesis 20:1). Abraham again presents his wife as his sister, whereupon she is taken into the household of Abimelech, king of Gerar (Genesis 20:2). But God intervenes in a dream and tells Abimelech Sarah's true identity, threatening Abimelech's life (Genesis 20:2–3). In this case the story is not meant to be a prototype of the Exodus. Again it is not at all clear why anyone should tell such a story. But God's direct communication to Abimelech warning of the lethal danger of bringing Sarah into his household, a slightly different way to reveal the plot knowledge, is key to the successful conclusion of the story. This is a God who will intervene even in the lives of nonbelievers, especially where the progeny of Sarah is concerned.

If we were reading the narrative of Genesis straight through, thinking we have one continuous narrative from Genesis 12 through Genesis 20, we might think that this story merely shows Abraham repeating a successful gambit at the expense of his wife and God, a story that would distress us immediately, so we tend to disallow it without even analyzing it.

Abimelech is rudely warned of the consequences of his seemingly innocent action. Abimelech asks the divinity much the same question that we associate with Abraham himself, pleading for the righteous of Sodom (Genesis 18). In this case Abimelech pleads for his own nation as righteous (Genesis 20:4). He even says that both Abraham and Sarah maintained that they were brother and sister (Genesis 20:5). This time we learn that Abraham is a prophet and his prayers will benefit Abimelech (Genesis 20:8). Abimelech accuses Abraham of the very senseless sin, with no rationale to the reader (Genesis 20:9), but, as with Pharaoh, it is hard not to grant Abimelech's perspective some validity. Abraham then says that he was sure the fear of God was not in this place and that he feared for his life (Genesis 20:11). He is wrong, in terms of the story; he should not have feared, for God is looking after him. (Again, this is a key point in the story and perhaps this is how best to explain it—as a way to expose the idea that God follows Abraham even on foreign territory.) But, if this were a true continuous narrative, we might guess that he expected divine intervention, like the last time, and another "happy ending" brought about by God's having chosen him for greater deeds.

Then the narrator adds something quite unexpected: Not only is Sarah Abraham's willing accomplice, she is actually Abraham's sister: "And yet indeed she is my sister; she is the daughter of my father, but not the daughter of my mother; and she became my wife" (Genesis 20:12). That makes Sarah Abraham's half sister, which would violate Hebrew incest laws, as explained in Leviticus and Deuteronomy (Leviticus 18:9, Leviticus 18:11, Leviticus 20:17, and Deuteronomy 27:22).

The explicit statement that Abraham and Sarah are half siblings is also a very interesting piece of information for us because it gives us a possible relative chronology. The meaning of the story may adhere to its precedence to the major, later law codes. And that may help us establish a relative date for the stories, if we press these seeming contradictions to their logical conclusion.

But comparing Abraham and Sarah's relationship to the law in Deuteronomy and Leviticus only increases the moral issue. Abimelech then does the same as Pharaoh. He rewards Abraham with servants and kine and restores his wife (Genesis 20:14), thus successfully ending a second story in which Abraham gains financially by promoting his wife as his sister, though this time he is telling a partial truth. Furthermore, Abimelech invites Abraham to dwell in his land, a considerable gain for Abraham (Genesis 20:16). Abraham reciprocates by praying to God, who heals Abimelech and his wife. The women and the flocks bear again, because, we are now told, God had previously stopped up all their wombs (Genesis 20:17).

Yet Another Matriarch in Peril

The third story takes us forward another six chapters in Genesis and in a new direction, as it is Isaac who serves as patriarch and Abimelech who again serves as foreign king. If we were considering this as three separate stories, we might think that trapping and outsmarting foreign kings using Sarah as bait has become the family business. But this incident really counts as the last of a triplet of stories telling more or less the same event. In other words, this story makes little sense if we are to restrict ourselves to understanding these stories as three different events. It must, in fact, be three versions of the same story, with different people serving in the roles. We think of this as a *structural* similarity, which ensures that we are dealing with a very close parallel or, in short, an elaborate triplet.

Though it is conceivable that another Abimelech is meant, no notation is made in the text, which only increases the mystery. If this is the same Abimelech who met Abraham, should not Abimelech have been more careful this time? Even if the son or grandson of Abimelech is meant, would he not have told his offspring to be careful of those wily Hebrews?

The narrator tells us that it was a second famine, as in the days of Abram, showing that the narrator is aware of the story in Genesis 12 and wants us to believe that it is a second occurence for him. Perhaps the narrator is merely removing a loose end: that the patriarchs could have avoided all this trouble with Pharaoh by going somewhere else. But no, even Abimelech would have given them the same hard time in the famine.

In any event, this time Isaac is forced to go to the lands of Abimelech, the king of the Philistines in Gerar (Genesis 26:1). A dream makes clear that God intends to give this land to Isaac and his descendants (Genesis 26:2). Isaac already knows that he may have to pretend that Rebecca is his sister (Genesis 26:7). After they had lived there a long time, Abimelech, who lives in a house, not a tent, looks out his window and sees the beauty of Rebecca, as they are playing (Genesis 26:8). The confrontation happens rather obliquely in verse 9. Abimelech accuses Isaac of having endangered the people. He charges all his subjects not to touch Isaac under penalty of death (Genesis 26:11). So Isaac and his people continue to grow and succeed in the land: "Then Isaac sowed in that land, and received in the same year an hundred-fold: and the LORD blessed him" (verse 17).

The moral of this story is that the patriarchs belong here because God means them to flourish here, both as pastoralists and eventually even as farmers. That only increases the mystery. What could be seen as God's favor that they give their wives as sisters and that accounts for their success? But all the stories end before anything untoward could be done to the matriarch, who is expected to continue the line of this special family. The stories all end with the promise of fertility and affluence, the patriarch becoming more wealthy, because he has rights in the land. But the only moral value to the story is a very parochial one: God will help the patriarch get rich and gain land and will protect the matriarch in distress from ruin at the hands of foreign kings, even if the plan risks the matriarch's offspring and, indeed, her well-being.

To conclude from our reading: they are indeed three unusual and distasteful stories, unusual and horrifying enough to make incomplete sense to us when read in narrative order. There are too many unanswered questions about how Abimelech could have made the same mistake twice or why Abraham seems actually to hire out his wife, to say it bluntly. The text seems to take inordinate trouble with a few details that seem unimportant to us, leaving out details that we would consider crucial for understanding the motivation of the characters.

Three Different Stories or One?

Why do the stories report such immoral behavior by the patriarchs and yet show the patriarchs gaining materially from the incidents? And if there is continuity in character, as we normally assume, why do these characters never seem to learn from their previous experiences? Because the same puzzling attempt to pawn off a wife as a sister repeats three times, even though it brings everyone in the story into peril, it is almost as if the patriarch is daring God to intervene and resolve the story to his advantage, which is exactly what happens in all three stories.

But, as we noticed very early, a greater number of questions are resolved if the stories are considered to be three versions of the same core story, though they were adumbrated in different ways, were told for different purposes even by different narrators, and were related about different patriarchs.[8] The threefold retelling suggests that the story had already become troublesome enough that several different narrators tried to approach the story in different ways to get to the nub of what the story means. Although each narrator resolves a great many narrative problems, the threefold retelling raises some other problems immediately. For one thing, it might mean, to our normal way of thinking, that the editing process in the biblical text is imperfect, for we would certainly have eliminated two of the three stories as repetitious.

But luckily they did not leave two stories out. The narrators left all three intact, giving us three different possibilities for significance and a sense that they had as much difficulty as we do in understanding this story. In a way, the repetition of three different stories with different but similar morals means they accepted them as myth, too horrifying, too puzzling, and perhaps even too ambiguous to be easily understood, but so important that they could not be forgotten.

We can, as Bible scholars have done, explain them as coming from different voices. This is what we shall explore, as a first approach. We can tentatively assign names to the narrators. Bible scholars usually identify the narrator in Genesis 12 as "J." They identify the narrator of Genesis 20 as "E." The third narrator, of Genesis 26, who is aware of the previous story about the famine and the plague, has been identified as "J" again. That does little to help us in terms of the sense of the story. But the separation of sources is a handy way to deal with the repetition.

The worst aspect of these three parallel stories is that they assume a world of violence and usurpation, where men and women must defend themselves against being murdered and having a spouse kidnapped and stolen. None of us has, I hope, experienced such a brutal and lawless world, though, sadly, places still exist in our own times where these dangers can be encountered. We must not think we have wiped out these kinds of crimes. Yes, the choice taken by the patriarch is also horrifying morally and incredibly puzzling from any moral perspective. We must think hard about whether the narrator's perspective could be better than our first impression. There is some chance we can clarify the mysteries as we study these cases.

The patriarchs seem willing to pretend that their wives are their sisters and marry them off to a king who might threaten them. This pretense certainly counts as a terrible story. Obviously, it reflects very badly upon the biblical view of women as a class, though much worse on these two men. But we want to understand the phenomenon, not just condemn it.[9] Obviously, we have seen that the Bible characteristically leaves out details of the discussion between the couple that we would like to know. It is a horrifying mystery.

By mysterious, I do not mean the story is somehow primitive and must be seen as the result of a backward culture. Quite the contrary is true—though it may have been written by people in the Iron Age, the text is generally understandable and the result of a sophisticated literary imagination. That is what makes these sudden difficulties so mysterious.[10]

Before the Bible was formed into a single book, this episode appears to have been seen as quite strange, mysterious, and difficult morally. Even by then, I think, not everyone could understand the story, as each of the narrators tries to give the story meaning by building a context for it, and none of the three actually agrees with each other, either in terms of the characters or the setting. Just as there is a certain mystery about the stories that eluded the Bible's ancient readers, some of their deepest meanings will elude us as well. Modern theories of myth and literature may help us to an extent, but since the ancients told the story three times in three ways it must have hit a nerve with them too.

One Story with Oral as Well as Written Phases

The stories themselves look like they have a common stem and yet also some independent life, because each time one of them is narrated, the narrator

sets the story in slightly different circumstances and derives a slightly different conclusion.[11] The base tradition concerns the wife-sister motif, the patriarch's willingness to conceal his identity as husband to his wife, and their
eventual deliverance because of God's intervention, even though it seems to
be beneath the moral dignity of anyone who is called a patriarch. But anyone
who allows that the Bible may be a compiled document (and that not every
story must have a moral ending that we understand) can see that the ribs
of the composition are similar. It will pay us to look at the so-called documentary hypothesis about the composition of the Pentateuch on the basis
of these observations alone. But let us take a quick look at the differences
between the three stories as well as their similarities before we do.

Although the motivations of the narrators are sometimes unclear, they
are not totally hidden, despite the strange emphases and repetitious details.
We can tell already that three somewhat different morals and explanations
have been extracted by the narrator(s). The first story, we have already seen,
is a kind of mini-Exodus, a prototype for the coming story of the Exodus
when God will save the whole people; the second stresses God's promise to
live in the Canaanite land in which the patriarchs wander; the third shows
that Hebrews were also invited to live on land controlled by the Philistines,
both with their flocks and to raise crops. Together all three recapitulate
the sojourn in Egypt and the settlement of Palestine. So all three treat the
story as being proof that the Israelites are different, but that they belong in
the land and have the right to flourish there, both in terms of offspring and
herds, though the connection between the action and the conclusion may
seem obscure to us. They are three explanations that never quite manage to
clarify the central, common problem of the wife-sister motif.

All of them contain morals that would make more sense to a people who
had known the other stories of the life of Israel: a sojourn in Egypt with an
exodus, carrying the wealth of Egypt, a land-taking in which the Canaanites
and the Philistines have to make way for the Israelites. These are three morals, but they are all related because they prefigure and build to the other stories of the patriarchal period. All of this suggests that they have been shaped
into a mythology—a group of myths or stories that ground people in their
times and space—in this case what we call the Israelites' remembered history and geography.

Since there are three different morals, the morals themselves must be
later than the basic story. They each seek to explain the central problem of
the story, the wife-sister motif, by adding something that an editor thinks

may help clarify it. Who provided these adumbrated meanings and when they were written down is obscure, but they must be later than the core story and so they represent an editorial attempt to make the story understandable. Even though the story is repeated three times, we do not actually find anything in the text that explains the wife-sister motif for us. But we do get three different interpretations about what the behavior meant in terms of the larger story of Israel's arrival in the land, three slightly different perspectives about the problematic moral predicament of passing one's wife as one's sister.

So, besides the basic story, there must have been an ongoing editing process as well, because we have three slightly different morals and yet one underlying story. In other words, one possible conclusion is that the narrator(s) who kept the stories intact did not quite understand the root story completely and were ready to accept all three related morals as helpful. The editor, on the other hand, knew exactly what he wanted the stories to mean, even though the central connections between the story and moral might have remained a bit obscure to him as well.

The editing was not complete to our standards either because we would have preferred one story to cover all three cases. We assume that a final editor must have taken all versions seriously, perhaps as holy writ, very early. Luckily, through this complicated and repetitious editing process, we see that there are different morals, perhaps growing up in different places, with different heroes, but all related. In short, the whole editing process must have been very complex and probably not accomplished just once. Maybe it is a case of one story bumping up against another in the course of its history, picking up some similarity, and eventually all three were written down, freezing them in the form we have.

Oral and Written Layers

One of the most obvious and perhaps the best hypothesis to explain the similarities and differences is that the stories were for a time oral stories, during which time they maintained a more fluid form, and that they eventually crystalized into three written stories and that the written form happened after the oral stories had achieved a core as well as possible individual form. In this way, they could be understood as three slightly different versions of the same base story, each of which received an individual moral from the narrator, who also tried to frame a meaning for the difficult to understand wife-sister-matriarch motif in the oral tradition.

This hypothesis of an oral/written text claims more than a change from oral to written: it claims that there was an oral phase at the beginning, when story-telling kept the stories fairly fluid, and that the stories then continued in a written phase, even in the very ancient period.[12] If we assume that we have one motif being reiterated in different places by different writers, we see that each writer did reach individual and quite different but related conclusions about the meaning of the story. Though connected, the stories are truly individual as well.

Stories from Many Sources

We have seen how important the notion of composite authorship can be in explaining the biblical text. Indeed, with regard to the passages under consideration, logic virtually compels us to admit that we have three versions of the same or similar story, and that an editor or editors put the stories together, though they were each puzzled by the meaning of this unusual story. An oral followed by a written phase of the development seems like a very easy way to explain the development of the present biblical tradition. Perhaps another editor put them all together, but possibly the same editor or one of the narrators serving as editor. It will be hard to clarify these issues exactly. But we have a story that grew up in three different forms, and that one or two or even three editors combined them into a similar form. It is, further, likely, when one thinks about it, that the oral and written forms overlapped because the repetition of three related forms is probably due to an oral period, while the exact editing suggests a later written form as well. We shall see that this complex process of oral and written traditioning is actually a good way to understand the scribal school in ancient Israel.

The Documentary Hypothesis

To ordinary readers of the Bible everything we just concluded about the three stories will be puzzling. Wasn't the whole Hebrew Bible given at Sinai? That is a traditional idea which is, nevertheless, never exactly found in the Bible itself. The realization that we have contradictions and repetitions, again and again in the Bible, virtually forced nineteenth- and early twentieth-century scholars like Julius Wellhausen (1844–1918) to a larger theory of composite authorship, today known as the documentary hypothesis of the composition of the Pentateuch (the five books of Moses). The documentary hypothesis is one of the true intellectual accomplishments of the nineteenth century, as important in its own way as Darwin's theory of evolution. It is, in fact, a theory of the evolution of the Bible out of many different sources and the combination of those two theories coming at the same time changed the Western world forever, in large part because it changed our understanding of what the Bible is.

According to consensus view of the documentary hypothesis, the Pentateuch is composed of approximately four large documents or sources—named by the letters J, E, D, P—in the fashion of the wife-sister story we have just studied, only far more complicated. Wellhausen actually pictured them as written documents right from the beginning, but subsequent scholars have shown that they were originally oral "voices" that were eventually written down after some development, just like the three stories of the matriarch in peril. Sometimes the voices go over the same material and, just as we could see in the wife-sister stories, the differences and seeming contradictions become important tools in distinguishing sources. Other times the sources simply narrate different incidents. For example, both J and P narrate the flood story, while only E tells the story of Joseph's journey to Egypt.

The hypothesis of sources has become a revolutionary difference in how to understand the Bible. Until the nineteenth century (with a few perspicacious rare exceptions),[13] when discrepancies or repetitions were noted (as they surely were, because people read the Bible assiduously), they were explained away by means of an exegetical distinction between the two occurrences or by special pleading: for example, God meant us to understand slightly different morals from the slightly different outcomes of the stories. But after the nineteenth century, Bible scholars could also utilize these repetitions and seeming contradictions to define different documents and different "voices" in the text, concluding something historical about their location in the society. According to the theory, a person or school of persons became the redactor of the JE epic and can be seen at work in combining the three versions of the matriarchal stories that we have seen. This redactor is often designated by the siglum Rje—the redactor of the JE epic.

Unlike the wife-sister stories, the JE epic is a very large body of tradition with a discoverable history at least in part: it is the result of the combination of a source that uses a word beginning with Y = J (the first letter of the name YHWH, as spelled in German) as a name for LORD and E, the source that uses ELOHIM for GOD. Bible translations today almost always reflect these differences by translating YHWH by the English word LORD, in small capital letters and the E word for God by the English word GOD, again in small capitals.

D, the third source, is primarily found in the book of Deuteronomy and also in a few places in the other four books, where material that sounds like Deuteronomy interrupts the narrative. In future chapters we shall have the opportunity to analyze D and also another, later writer deeply influenced by D, who is conventionally called the Deuteronomistic Historian (DH).

That leaves P. The material we discuss in this book is largely non-P, so we do not have to analyze P at length. But I include it to explain the full import of Wellhausen's hypothesis. P is, in Wellhausen's estimation, the last chronologically of the four sources, which Wellhausen took from the word *Pentateuch*, because P edited the Pentateuch as we know it. Nevertheless, most scholars call the P source "the priestly source" because the material in this strain of tradition takes a priestly perspective and also recounts a great many priestly understandings of the law and history. Indeed some of P is too early to have been the redactor of the Pentateuch. Very often the priestly version of the material has suggestively different interpretations of Israelite lore and history from the other versions.

A number of people have criticized Wellhausen's evaluation of D and especially P. He was relatively unfriendly to D and P for theological reasons, considering both of them to be later sources, more centered on a text devised by bureaucrats and priests and consequently, in his estimation, less a product of direct revelation from God. J was the most direct and so the most spiritual of all the strands of tradition. One way to evaluate Wellhausen on this matter is to admit that Wellhausen, being Protestant, was simply less able to appreciate scribal and priestly interpretations of religious experience, which he associated with Catholicism. Conversely, Wellhausen romanticized the epic traditions J and E and especially the prophetic ones in the literary prophets as the real beginning of monotheism.

Though he has been accused of antisemitism, no doubt his judgments come from a time when Catholic and Protestant stereotypes were foremost in the minds of Bible scholars. For roughly the same reasons, a number of Jewish scholars refused to accept Wellhausen's theory because they considered P to be the earliest of all the sources. The truth seems to depend on the particular passage and the moment at which the piece of tradition was edited into the whole. Since we will be dealing with smaller units of tradition, we can ignore a great deal of the larger discussion about the extent of J or E and settle for smaller and relative judgments about what seems earlier or later, original or derivative, narrative or editing.

The Social Basis for the Sources

According to the classical form of the theory, associated with Julius Wellhausen, the Hebrew epic was created when the northern kingdom and the southern kingdom's traditions were brought together into a single story by a power important enough to have recorded and redacted them. Originally, he thought the J source and the E source to be written documents, but soon it became clear that a great part of the tradition must be oral or, as we have seen, some combination of oral and written sources. Wellhausen and his school of successors thought that the initial two documents—J and E source—were carved from earlier traditions coming from the south (who characteristically used the name YHWH or LORD for God in everyday speech) and north (who used the word Elohim for God in their dialect), but they were originally a set of traditions of the south and north, respectively, which were combined into a single national epic of Israel sometime during or soon after the united monarchy, the kingdoms of David and Solomon (the incredibly early period of 1000 BCE to 922 BCE). They also thought they were two completely written documents combined in various ways by an explicit editor, working with written sources, who just fastened the two epics into one by taking a few verses from one, then the other, and building a single narrative out of two.

Theoretically, this was the first layer of the Pentateuch, but exactly when it achieved the status of prose epic has been hard to define. Wellhausen thought the combination was during the united monarchy itself, the reigns of David and Solomon (ca. 1000 BCE–922 BCE), or very soon thereafter under the auspices of the south, because the editorial perspective is always from the southern kingdom of Judah. It is reasonable to suppose that some strands of tradition were in existence during the tenth century BCE even today, if oral tradition is counted, but there is far less agreement and outright skepticism about what could have existed in written form at that early period, when Hebrew itself was forming as a language.[14] Very few pieces of writing seem to fit this earliest style, whereas quite a bit more fit a developed and robust royal style of a later period.

Some scholars believe that the P source is much earlier than Wellhausen thought, as I mentioned. This is not just because they honor and respect it more than Wellhausen did but because the P source contains priestly material that seems older in formulation than we find repeated in the laws in Deuteronomy (which can be fixed to 621 BCE or earlier). Thus, some form of P, perhaps quite a lot of it, seems earlier than D, which can be dated exactly to 621 BCE, as we shall see.

P, in addition, also includes a more universalistic perspective than any of the other strands. That perspective fits well with Persian imperial times, when the Israelites were aware of a greater world than their own little kingdom. Since the Bible's narrative does not extend far beyond the exile, it makes sense to think that P is its latest manifestation. The Persians, who ended the Israelite exile in Babylon, preferred to rule through priestly groups (they found kings to be too nationalistic and rebellious) and so it is to the priests that the final word was given in the building of the Pentateuch, though their traditions went back far earlier than that period. After the exile, it is also possible to begin using the word *Jew*—*yehudi* in Hebrew—to refer to the people of Israel, as it originally meant an inhabitant of Judah.

Before the exile, it is more historically and linguistically correct to use the word *Hebrew* for the earliest periods of Israelite history and *Israelite* or *Judean* for the inhabitants of the monarchies in north and south. So the postexilic Jews were deliberately appropriating as their history the stories that the Hebrews and Israelites produced because they were, in large part, biological, cultural, and ethnic descendants of those who were taken away into exile.

More recently, J (and hence JE) has come to be dated later and later.[15] Since we have looked at J and E in "the matriarch in peril" stories, we know that there is little explicit moralizing in them, though great moral principles certainly are being discussed in them. Moralizing, however, is quite characteristic of Deuteronomy and the Deuteronomistic Historian. Whether to date the Pentateuchal stories before or after Deuteronomy is always a problem, but stories with strange moral outcomes are always candidates for being historically early. We have already seen that the Abraham stories do not assume the rules of incest we find in P and D. These are hints that tell us relative chronologies. We shall see in future chapters that there are many reasons to think that JE was evolving into our current form during the Judean monarchy and not after it.

Recently some scholars have suggested that there never was a J at all, just a collection of patriarchal stories—particularly Abraham stories. That same perception had already been quite successful in understanding the E source, which is now regularly understood as supplementary material from the north, mostly about Jacob, added to the J material. Again, we do not have to resolve these issues because we will be dealing with small episodes of text and not large chunks of text. Some scholars argue that the historical traditions in the Bible may be earlier still, including the matriarch in distress, as its purposes are scarcely comprehensible to us.

At the other end of the spectrum, some extreme biblical minimalists have even suggested that the JE epic was written in the Persian or Greek times (the Persian period begins in 534 BCE and the Greek period in 332 BCE) and that everything earlier than that was just made up either out of the imagination or based on the skimpiest of previous stories. Luckily, we shall find that stories that come entirely out of the imagination are usually easy to spot. But, given the recent lack of consensus about the date, we should be aware of different ways to date the material. At first we shall only be able to make relative judgments about our materials: this tradition must have preceded this one and superseded another. By the end of our study, we shall occasionally be able to find a few absolute dates.

The documentary hypothesis in its classical form says that a great deal of the material in the first five books of Moses were composed by the people of Israel living in their homeland—who knew that it belonged to others before them and who believed that their well-being depended on YHWH, in a way that explained their past and outlined their purpose and future. They were a people who knew that they had come from other places and displaced the original inhabitants. All three of the wife-sister stories share this moral, as we have seen, though they articulate it in recognizably different ways. Though the patriarchs may misbehave in these lands, they are flourishing there and are good stewards of them. The stories argue strongly that it was God's will that the patriarchs and their descendants take over the rule of the land because the Canaanites were sinful (Exodus 23:20, Deuteronomy 18:9–14, and frequently elsewhere).

The Bible also tells us that the Israelites gave in to idolatrous practices of the Canaanites. After sending them prophets to warn them of catastrophe,

God eventually punished them by sending first the northern kingdom, then the southern kingdom, into exile. Since the Bible was viewed as an impeccable source, this story was thought to be the literal history for generation after generation of Western scholars.

But archaeology has shown us that Canaanites and Philistines continued to live in the land with Israelites long after the Israelites concentrated their power and took over the rule of the country from their original center of power in the Judean highlands. Archaeology also shows us, for example, that female devotional deities can be found all over the land and that at Kuntillet Ajrud, for example, YHWH was viewed as having a goddess named Asherah or another goddess named Anath as a consort. So while the story that the Israelites told is sometimes supported by archaeology, it still offers us many surprises, especially in the extent of alternative voices to the Bible in First Temple society. We now know that the Bible is a prescriptive document, with a distinct point of view on history, and not so much a neutral, descriptive history. For me, that is not shocking. All historical sources need to be read critically and suspiciously.

The History of the Documentary Hypothesis

As with the Bible itself, so with the documentary hypothesis: At first, the hypothesis was believed to be the literal history of the text. But a theory of such explanatory value must evolve as it is used, due to the very astute critique of scholars who work with it. And the documentary hypothesis is no exception. A great deal of the original system has been shown to be helpful, but some has proven to be inaccurate in details or even false. Enough of it has been proven again and again to have interpretive power to consider that scholars still use it as a shorthand for the various, much more complicated, voices in the Bible. The result of the century and a half of discussion and research has not exactly disproven the theory; rather it has just as often strengthened and innovated the documentary hypothesis to make the multiple source theory more sophisticated and more important as a tool for interpreting the Bible.

What was clear from our quick analysis of Genesis 12, 20, and 26 seems beyond dispute: we have one story, as told in three quite specific places in the Pentateuch, which shows us three different attempts to understand its very problematic elements. The Bible can no longer simply be considered a document revealed by God at one time, pure and simple, perfect with no contradictions. The seams in the document are too easy to see, and sometimes the narrators are providing meaning to traditions that puzzle them, as we have seen in the case of the matriarch in peril stories.

Theologically, that does not, however, rule out the idea that revelation is progressive, that the various persons who contributed to the books of Moses each brought their own revelation, so that the whole is a sum of revelations edited into a single story. But it does say that the Bible was written by human beings in specific human contexts and was not one book written with a single meaning that was eternally correct. It suggests that God's will in any situation emerges as various persons puzzle over the same ambiguous and difficult stories, and, indeed, that the meaning will change over time.

Revelation Must Be Progressive

Anyone who sees the point of the documentary hypothesis and wants to use the Bible as a basis for theology needs to adopt some kind of theory of progressive revelation, where God spoke to Moses but also to a variety of other writers in the society, each adding a dimension of truth appropriate to the period of origin of the writing and sometimes contradicting another voice in the society. That seems implicit in acknowledging that Abrahamic religions are historical religions. History, we now see, is always the medium of revelation and also partly a human endeavor because people have the responsibility of telling the story.

So in our case of the matriarch in peril. Those who do not wish to speculate theologically have to come to terms with the document that started as an oral tradition, evidenced several times, which became part of the Israelite national epic, full of ambiguities, polemics, and special pleadings, and not necessarily coming to a single or unambiguous notion of historical or moral truth. That is a great deal to comprehend. The continuing difficulty of many Americans in seeing the Bible for what it is—both its remarkable value as history and its brilliantly ambiguous characteristics as ancient literature—still shapes our national conversation in the contemporary United States.

Those who read in the field know that the conversation has been spirited and interesting. It has gone through a source criticism phase, which isolated J, E, D, and P, associated with the Protestant interpreters of K. H. Graf and Wellhausen. Underlying all these critiques is textual criticism, which compares the different readings, different versions, of the Bible's literal text. The discovery of the Dead Sea Scrolls, for example, gives us evidence that part of the biblical text itself was fluid in the first century BCE and did not remain fixed until the end of Second Temple times, a century later. So anyone who wants to interpret the Bible has to take the textual differences into account.

There are a series of other phases in the development of the documentary theory, each of which adds a new dimension: a pan-Babylonian phase in which ancient literature of Babylonia was compared to and subsumed into our understanding of the Bible; a genre criticism phase in which scholars realized that traditions come down to us in specific *genres*, or *Gattungen*, and that these forms suggest their original purpose in the society; a social scientific phase in which the Bible was subjected to the analysis of anthropology, sociology, and economics; a Canaanite phase in which the more fragmentary documents from neighboring Canaanite cities were read and compared to the Bible, various literary phases; and, lastly, a concerted attempt to dissect the documents into a series of fragments instead of a complete narrative. All these methods continue to be practiced by scholars of the Bible throughout the world. They continuously give us interesting new information about the early history of the biblical text and new theories with which to come to terms. In truth, they have not solved as many problems as we would like, but they have, in some cases, dramatically altered our understanding of the biblical text.

Albright's Synthesis

There is one moment in the debate that deserves special recognition because it brought a rare synthesis between the Bible scholars and the faithful. The person who accomplished this seemingly impossible task was W. F. Albright (1891–1971), an American Bible scholar, resolute believer, and archaeologist, who saw in the archaeological record a partial justification for believing in the Bible as it was written. It was not, of course, a full synthesis down to a literal reading of every line of the Bible. Albright did not go back to the absurd stance that the prehistory of Israel—Adam and Eve and Noah's flood for example—could be proven archaeologically. He affirmed that everything in Genesis 1–11 was myth, based on other myths that had by then been discovered in the sands of the Middle East, mostly in Egypt, Canaan, and Mesopotamia. But he left open that some of the events narrated about the patriarchs might have happened. He thought the Hebrews brought these traditions with them when they left Ur of the Chaldees, when they exited Egypt, or learned them from their forefathers in Canaan.

And he might have been right about some of them, though it is likely that the Israelites were influenced by these documents far later in their history than Albright thought. For example, we now know that the great epics of Mesopotamia, like the Gilgamesh epic, had been found in Megiddo, a Canaanite city that became an Israelite city. But Albright did hold out that the patriarchal period (Genesis 12 right through to the conquest of Canaan in Joshua and Judges) was historical. Some archaeological material could substantiate those chapters of the Bible.[16] Other prominent scholars, especially Ephraim A. Speiser, expanded the point of view with their own research, which culminated in the inaugural volume of the Anchor Bible Commentary, a volume universally known as Speiser's *Genesis*.[17]

Speiser's argument about the composition of Genesis was very powerful, based as it was on a combination of the literary evidence of the Bible and the presence or absence of evidence from the known archaeological record. Certain details in the biblical patriarchal stories correspond to known features of second millennium culture in Mesopotamia, Syria, and Canaan. The same details, however, seemed not to be present in the Israelite monarchy, when the Pentateuchal stories were written down. So while we could not prove that there were actual people like Abraham, Isaac, and Jacob, some details preserved in the Pentateuch included authentic legal and ritual elements of the patriarchal period, the early second millennium BCE, which the monarchy, a first millennium culture, could not have known because they were no longer practiced in the first millennium. For example, the names Abraham and Abram (or its close cognate Abiram) and even Jacob were very common in the second millennium BCE in West Amorite culture, but they were thought to have disappeared in the first millennium.[18]

Within this argument neatly fell the stories of the wife-sister motif or the matriarch in peril. Speiser and others maintained that newly deciphered evidence unique to the second millennium BCE, found in the remains of Mari and Nuzi, two recently excavated ancient cities, illuminated the core of this biblical tradition. For example, the ancient city of Mari in Western Mesopotamia, found in the first half of the twentieth century, was a flourishing city that in the eighteenth century BCE was inhabited by West Amorites. They are quite close culturally to Israelites, and their culture resembled the patriarch's culture. Names in Mari are close to biblical names. The rulers of the second millennium in Canaan also report many Amorite migrants who are bothering them. Their word for these people was *Apiru* or *Hab/piru*, which looks like it could have evolved into *Hebrew* when Hebrew became a language in and for itself.

Similarly excavated in the first half of the twentieth century, the Nuzi tablets reflect the practices and customs of the Hurrians, a people who flourished in the eastern Tigris region in the middle of the second millennium, with a significant group of tablets from the fifteenth century BCE. Although no one has attempted to associate the patriarchs directly with the Hurrian kingdom of Mitanni (which is more ancient still), Hurrian influence was widespread in Syria and Canaan in this period. The Hurrians inhabited the city of Nuzi, a provincial center, in the ancient kingdom of Arrapha whose capital lies today underneath the city of Kirkuk in northern Iraq. These texts give us examples of many customs found in the Bible.

Most important for our story is that they appear to tell us something quite relevant to the puzzling wife-sister motif. In Hurrian society, according to Speiser, a wife could enjoy a special status if the law recognized her simultaneously as her husband's sister.[19] This means, more or less, that the title "sister" indicated a special wife, perhaps a principal wife, perhaps even the wife of one's youth, to whom primacy was given.

The Bible, as well as these cultures, certainly recognized that a man could marry more than one wife at a time. The wife-sister stories, according to Speiser, are fundamentally attempts in the first millennium BCE to understand customs that must have come down from an actual patriarchal period but that were no longer understood in their entirety when the JE epic was put together. Although this theory does not actually tell us why the stories should feature the wife-sister status in this scurrilous way, it allows us to interpret the motif as an incompletely understood datum from the second millennium which shows up in a text from the first millennium BCE. That is, according to Albright and Speiser, we have a custom of the second millennium BCE that is being recounted in writing by a first millennium author who no longer understands it completely, which means it existed in oral form for most of a millennium.

As G. Ernest Wright, another student of Albright, said: "We shall probably never be able to prove that Abram really existed, that he did this or that, said thus and so, but what we can prove is that his life and times, as reflected in the stories about him, fit perfectly within the early second millennium, but imperfectly within any later period."[20]

This explanation struck like a thunderbolt; it seemed to be everything that a scholar could possibly want or need. Some averred there was nothing left to discover conceptually about the structure and dating of the Pentateuch: the patriarchs show us second millennium culture while the kingdoms of Judah and Israel show us first millennium culture. The Albright synthesis held on for decades because of its powerful explanatory value. Even so, some scholars immediately noted that the explanation—and many others as well—is strangely unsatisfactory because it does not give us a full accounting of the story itself, with all its moral ambiguities, only the recognition that the full explanation was lost even to the compilers of the story. To understand it, we have to posit a relatively long period of oral retelling of the story widely and then a later period in which we get several narrators trying to write it up in a way that is intelligible to them. The oral stories may have existed at the same time and been known to the others, but each writer or editor found unique material in the story, which bore on the promises of God to the patriarchs: that the Israelites would be saved from Pharaoh in Egypt, that they would inherit the land, and that they could live at peace among the Philistines but would come to dominate them. What we have then is three different first-millennium BCE attempts to understand how the second-millennium BCE patriarchs could have called their wives their sisters, editorialized as being perhaps a necessary evil, which was destined to play a role in revealing that the Israelites would obtain dominance in the area. It is not morally edifying to us, but it does give the stories an overriding and iron-clad historical significance.

Although this appears to solve the issue, it ignores the central problematic in the text of what each narrator thought was moral about the patriarch's behavior in pretending that his wife was his sister. It tells us instead that editors in the first millennium BCE no longer understood that the word *sister* meant a principal wife. The problems include issues of redaction and moral—that the first story appears to prefigure the Exodus, the second reiterates the promises to Abraham in Genesis 15, and the last tells us that the Israelites have the right to live in Philistine lands.

But it was not very long before other scholars of Mesopotamian languages objected to this neat synthesis. It appears as though the translations or, in truth, the understanding of the actual legal situation of the wife-sister in Hurrian society, was a bit skewed by Speiser. The Hurrian custom was apparently far more complicated than originally thought. First, the legal situation seems to be a product of an individual circumstance rather than a widespread custom. It is created when one reads the same names as the exact same characters into several different tablets. Second, the brother in Hurrian society might take upon himself the responsibility of marrying off his sister to another man, if there were no father to conclude the marriage agreement. And there are provisions by which the marriage may be annulled and the sister returned to her brother. In yet another law, the wife is given the guarantee that if she bears a son the husband cannot take another wife. And, finally, it appears as if the women who entered into these arrangements were not aristocratic but usually poor. It is apparently not the case in the Nuzi texts that most husbands were seeking sister *(ahatutu)* status for their principal wives; it appears rather that this is an unusual case, something like one man trying to marry his "ward."[21]

But what was worse for the synthesis was the discovery of more textual and archaeological material in which calling a wife a sister, and many other customs from the life of Abraham, Isaac, and Jacob, was known in the first millennium BCE. It turns out, as more archaeological material became known and revalued, that many customs and laws supposedly unique to the second millennium were also well known in the first millennium, which is fatal to the logic that there must have been a patriarchal period in the second millennium when customs were entirely different from the first millennium, the time of the kingdoms of Israel and Judah.

Wife-Sister Elsewhere in the Bible

Take a very simple example. The Song of Songs (Song of Solomon) actually calls the lover, "my sister, my bride" no less than four times: 4:9, 4:10, 4:12, and 5:1. These extremely well-known verses and other first-millennium evidence cast serious doubt on the theory that the customs were only known to the second millennium. If they could be traced to the first millennium, there was not just reason to believe that we have any real evidence that dates to the period of the patriarchs. On the other hand, we know that the Israelites did in fact use the word *sister* to refer to their beloved brides, at least in this one beautiful song. In other words, it may be true that the Israelites, like other people in the first millennium, called their wife, or the wife of their youth, their sister. It is not so clear that this custom has anything to do with the Hurrian custom in the second millennium BCE.

In point of fact, we became aware that a number of the details of the patriarchal period in the Bible were actually anachronisms. For example, the patriarchs are pictured as riding camels before camels were domesticated. Abraham is said to have originated in Ur of the Chaldees, but we have no record that Mesopotamia was called by that name until the first millennium. Or again, Abraham has dealings with the Philistines before the Philistines appear to settle the land. That suggests that however old the stories may be, later periods have put their individual stamp on the traditions by updating them with more contemporary names or customs.

Further study of the customs of the Amorites and Hurrians did not in every case negate the work of Albright. For example, we know that childless couples could appoint an agent to work for them and take care of them in their old age. As a result, they would inherit some of their fortune. This explains the relationship between Abraham and Sarah and Eliezer of Damascus. Unfortunately, we know that this custom continues into the first millennium too. So we can no longer prove that the material from the age of the patriarchs is accurate to the second millennium BCE.

Tamar and Amnon: Sisters and Wives

There is another place where wives and sisters become tragically confused. This is in the Court History (1 Samuel–2 Kings) where Amnon, son of David, develops an unhealthy attraction for his half sister Tamar and tries to rape her (2 Samuel 12).[22] Amnon grabs hold of her, but she rebukes him: "[12] She answered him, 'No, my brother, do not force me; for such a thing is not done in Israel; do not do anything so vile! [13] As for me, where could I carry my shame? And as for you, you would be as one of the scoundrels in Israel. Now therefore, I beg you, speak to the king; for he will not withhold me from you'" (2 Samuel 13:12–13).

Marriage between half siblings is forbidden (Leviticus 18:9, Leviticus 18:11, Leviticus 20:17, and Deuteronomy 27:22). But Tamar is trying to convince Amnon not to rape her because David, their father the king, would allow their union. It could have been a desperate and untrue statement. But it makes more sense if this narrative is correct, inadvertently disclosing a time before the Levitical and Deuteronomic law codes, when half siblings might still marry. In that case, Abraham and Sarah could have been married and the wife-sister motif could have been a real possibility in the second millennium BCE and have remained known in the first millennium BCE. The ancient custom in fact did change, albeit not at the borderline of the first millennium, in the ostensible time period of the united monarchy in the tenth century BCE, but some centuries thereafter.[23] If that is the case here, then the narration of the Tamar-Amnon story would have had to originate before both Deuteronomy and the Pentateuchal (priestly) source were edited or popularized.

1 Samuel, then, might be thought of as consisting of many sources, of which one is likely to be a kind of inside, gossipy voice retelling the goings-on in the court. In any event, it raises a difficult contradiction in this society of late First Temple times. The writing seems both to condemn and allow marriages between half siblings and that seems unlikely on first consideration.

Perhaps the story of Abraham and his wife Sarah's relationship is meant somehow to bridge this gap in the earlier period. If so, the story would have been written or even edited perhaps to this specific kind of situation. In this interpretation, the version which includes the fact that Abraham and Sarah were actually half siblings (Genesis 20:12) would be crucial. It especially might be written directly to the Amnon and Tamar story or to a story like it. This is speculation, but it is not far-fetched. We will explore the intimate connection between the Court History and the patriarchal stories in several of the following chapters.

The Folklore and Literature of the Wife-Sister Motif

The Albright synthesis slowly gave ground and finally disappeared, but the puzzling wife-sister motif remains unexplained and unjustified. It is still possible that the status signifies a special kind of marriage, but it is no longer provable and, more importantly, it is not an exclusively second-millennium custom. Instead, it looks like we are dealing with traditions that are rather closer to the time of the Davidic monarchy but likely before the promulgation of D in 621 BCE and later. This is a chronology that will repeat and repeat as we look at these stories.

So it no longer can be used as evidence for the historicity of stories from the period of the patriarchs. But it might still very well speak to the time period of the monarchy, as the story of Amnon and Tamar has shown.

Scholarship then attempted to understand the tale in terms of other stories in the Bible. The reader sat down with the text and only concluded what could be gleaned from the text itself. One might even frame as a hypothesis that these wife-sister stories have something to do with the fact that there was no clear ruling yet on whether one could marry one's half sister. The culture was conflicted and needed guidance. Myth can bridge contradictions like this. If Abraham and Sarah or Isaac and Rebecca could have done so, then it is acceptable sometimes.

Literary Studies

With all the doubt cast upon the source theories, it is no wonder that literary approaches took over from the earlier documentary study of the texts. Starting from the perception that reading the text was more reliable than traditional Bible criticism, Bible scholars did not have to import a huge theory into their appreciation of the stories themselves. In fact, the literary approach has not been particularly good at cracking the nut of these strange stories.

We know, for example, that in the ancient environment, as well as traditional modern ones, a man's masculinity can be brought into doubt by shame if he cannot protect his wife's honor. That is particularly true in cultures that depend on honor and shame, as did biblical culture. One is very tempted to treat this incident as a deliberate reversal of the conventional honor/shame story. Abram/Abraham/Isaac is being tested by being asked to put his wife in danger and rewarded by God for passing the test of having put everything in the hands of God. In this interpretation, the incident is very like the incident of the binding of Isaac, in which Abraham is explicitly being tested by God (Genesis 22:1). The rabbis come close to this interpretation in their manifold turning and turning of the story.

The problem is that not only Abraham is tested but so are his wives and the entire promise of progeny. If Sarah/Sarai is not rescued, there would be no Isaac or succession of the patriarch. And the second problem is that Genesis 22, the story of the binding of Isaac, explicitly says that God is *testing* Abraham, while none of the versions of the wife-sister story in the Bible explicitly make that point.

Close to this is the interpretation that the entire story is being narrated from an ironic point of view. This is an interpretation of Carolyn Sharp in her recent book.[24] Much as I admire any literary critic who is willing to investigate the Bible's use of rhetorical devices like jokes, deliberate ambiguities, and ironies, even Professor Sharp's analysis may not explain all the difficulties, though she has an acute sensitivity to the text. If the story meant to tell us that Abraham had given up his prior sense of masculinity to obey God, you would think that there would be a "tell" in the text, something in the text to tell us it is defensible to look at it ironically. But none has occurred to me. Perhaps this story is so old that we will never entirely understand its meaning.

The Folkloric Approach

The folkloric approach offers another path. Folkloric study too is a kind of literary approach, looking at the structure of the stories, which was pioneered by many of the most famous German Bible scholars as an ancillary tool for their research. It was inevitable because the Germans had pioneered the study of a genre of story in their own heritage—*die Maerchen*, or roughly what we call "fairy tales" studied by the brothers Grimm—so the famous Bible scholars Hermann Gunkel, Albrecht Alt, and Martin Noth all took considerable interest in the folkloric content of Genesis especially. Eventually, that became part of American Bible scholarship as well.

One could easily outline many different phases of the folkloric approach. But the most interesting of the more recent scholars to approach the Bible in this way is Susan Niditch, whose *A Prelude to Biblical Folklore: Underdogs and Tricksters* contains a whole chapter of very carefully defined analysis on the wife-sister stories.[25] Characteristic of her approach is to employ the trickster motif to show how Abram/Abraham/Isaac outwits the foreign kings by means of his wife, Sarah/Sarai/Rebecca. She also is careful not to decide which of the stories is prior, which derived from the others. They are all equal stories, with none to be taken as prior or more important. But they still are three forms of the same story. Her understanding of *trickster* is as follows:

> The term *trickster* is used by anthropologists and folklorists to describe a particular character who appears in the lore of various cultures, including those of West Africans and Americans. Robert Pelton, commenting on the work of Daniel Brinton, describes the North American

Indian trickster as "gross deceiver, crude prankster, creator of the earth, a shaper of culture, a fool caught in his own lies."[26] Mac Linscott Ricketts suggests that "the trickster is man . . . struggling by himself to become what he feels he must become—master of his universe."[27]

He is "noble and foolish, heroic and cowardly, daring and deceitful, often beaten but never defeated."[28] Paul Radin emphasizes the trickster's liminality, his "undifferentiated" quality (he is often pictured as a man/woman or human/animal), and his status as wanderer[29] and suggests that this traditional character is a creation of the common man rather than of priests and shamans, an interesting suggestion recently challenged by Pelton's seminal study.[30] Deceiver, creator, acculturator, unmasked liar, survivor—these qualities of the trickster do apply to the deceiving, ethically ambiguous survivor Abram of Genesis 12:10–20. [Nor does she mean to eliminate the next two examples of the biblical story, either.]

Nonetheless, Niditch seeks to resolve the core issue, rather than the morals extracted by the narrator of each particular instance of the wife-sister motif. Further, Niditch resolves the moral dilemma at the center of the story by showing that our moral reaction to the patriarchs' behavior is not the point of the story. Instead, the patriarch's wily image as a trickster is the deepest point that we can recover. And, of course, invoking the worldwide image of the trickster does, in fact, further relieve the reader of having to make moral sense of the patriarchs' puzzling behavior. By bracketing our sense of morality in the text, we get back to a level assumed to be something like a group of people telling tales about their clever ancestors who outwitted their enemies, gained land and riches, and, in the process, fathered many children.

Given the second story, the Tamar-Amnon reprise of the same issues, chances are it would need to be early enough so that the story of David's descendants was a live issue, which would mean, whatever its original oral context, that the written form of the story is likely to be after the succession to Solomon, since it speaks to that issue but not necessarily by much: the relevant time must be after Solomon's reign (930 BCE) but before Deuteronomy (621 BCE). This is well short of an exact date, but it is a time frame that will keep popping up. So is Abraham a trickster or the ironic servant of God who must give up even his sense of masculinity to appease his master, who is trying to test him? It is not entirely clear that any of us can capture the sensibility of stories of such antiquity.

Instead, perhaps we should posit that this particular level of antiquity in the stories is characterized by our incomprehension. We realize that we are talking about the period of the story's oral composition, sometime in the period of the First Temple (950 BCE to 587 BCE), but likely before Deuteronomy with its explicit moral loading (621 BCE). It is for the written level to take the trickster motif and reimagine it in the editorial work of each of the three writers—each of whom, in some way, deemphasizes the trickster in favor of an editorial interest, whether it be to emphasize the Exodus, to stress God's promises to Abraham, or to posit that Isaac's dependents have the longtime right to settle in Philistine lands.

But, as I intend to argue in this book, it strains credulity to think that any such explanation would have been going on exclusively at the end of the First Temple period, or even in the Second Temple period at all, because stories in those periods are a good deal easier to understand. In the Second Temple period there was no need or desire to depict Abram/Abraham/Isaac as a trickster. Also the literary conventions of Hebrew of the Second Temple period are well known, and they do not appear in this material. We shall need to settle the dating problem at some point, but not now. What is important to note is that this story seems so old as to defy interpretation.

Scribal Schools: Oral and Written Traditions at the Same Time

We have already seen that the triple wife-sister tradition virtually demands that there was both an oral and written phase of the story and that they needed to overlap to both account for the similarities and differences between the two stories. Several books lately have stressed the fluidity of the written and oral texts, not just in biblical transmission but in all the scribal traditions of the ancient Near East.[31] All the scribal traditions of the area stressed memorization of oral traditions, even as it taught the young scribes how to write. The fact is that none of the writing systems of antiquity completely expressed all the sounds of the language; few separated between words; and almost none contained anything that could be called punctuation. So enormous oral skills were needed just to write a simple sentence. The early Mesopotamian language, Sumerian, contained a fair number of ideographs, and even the later Semitic language, Akkadian, depended on an extended set of characters for each syllable rather than a true alphabet. They were truly difficult to write and required long years of schooling for literacy. Indeed, even the later languages—such as Hebrew, which is a great deal easier to write than syllabic cuneiform or hieroglyphic Egyptian—did not develop a true alphabet but allowed the short vowels to remain unexpressed. However, by comparison to the earlier writing systems, Hebrew, and Northwest Semitic dialects generally, could be mastered by ordinary people, not just an educated class of scribes.

Given the relative ease of writing Hebrew, it is possible that many people in Israelite society could read and write—or at least read—in some functional way. But scribal schools were still necessary for the elegant writing of treaties, documents, and national literature. Under such conditions, it is not surprising that we find young scribes bragging of their skills—and especially of their memorization skills. We may imagine that scribal arts were taught rather like *madrassahs* and other traditional schools today teach them. A limited number of texts were used as the curriculum, and the method of instruction progressed from memorization of characters to memorization of fixed texts.[32]

The training of scribes was onerous, though it must have been a rare opportunity for a young man, starting with a scribe's own sons. So we may even picture collections of good advice, like Proverbs, from fathers to their sons as they enter the scribal and bureaucratic services of the state, whether it be in Temple or Palace. What we need to posit, however, is only that the scribal school itself was one social location and situation in life (*Sitz im Leben*) for the interplay of oral and written traditions. Indeed, we can count on there being a fair amount of interplay between local traditions among the varied students in the scribal schools, as there must have been in the institutions to which young scribes graduated: royal, prophetic, and/or priestly bureaucracies.

We can no longer be sure that we have separate and distinct written documents, as Wellhausen thought. In fact, we can be rather sure, from the material we have already looked at, that the sources are not fixed documents so much as oral stories that get written down in stages and thus can influence each other in rather complex ways. There is obviously evidence in the wife-sister motif stories that they influenced each other without changing the moral and intent of the particular author or editor or redactor—so much so that they continue to puzzle us even today. They each clearly went through periods of oral development, though they eventually congealed into relatively different written texts, sometimes even doublets of the same story. So perhaps they are three stories from one source that no longer have a single underlying point because they have undergone enough evolution as to have disguised it.

The Patriarchal Stories Serve as Myths to the Israelites: Study Patriarchal Stories Parallel to the Stories in the History

To me, the right of the Israelites to live in lands that once belonged to others seems the most basic and the most striking of the themes that cut across these stories. Even in the stories about the succession of the kingship, these stories are about ordinary family issues. Of course, the monarchy is a family writ large, to a certain extent. But the stories of the patriarchs are like monarch stories for every person, about how families endure many crises and still manage to continue. So they may come from very ancient times.

But they also seem to show the issues of the later transmitters of the tradition. One theme that seems to have been forgotten is that every time the patriarchs put their wives in danger they are also risking an intermarriage between themselves and outsiders. That others desire Israelite women as brides also seems fundamental. It appears that the text is basically opposed to this mixing but chooses a strange way of expressing it: by showing the patriarchs being forced into the position of sharing their wives, and, in this situation, it is right that they connive, with the help of God, to avoid it. So the trickster motif is the other side of this issue. Peter Machinist has described these kind of stories as the making of a "counteridentity."[33] The stories have the function of reifying Israelite identity over against that of the Canaanites and Philistines, and this is, we shall see, a theme that includes legitimate offspring, endogamy, and fertility.

But this is not the kind of argument or polemic that we would expect in historical discourse from the second millennium BCE. It is very much an issue starting when the Israelites get to the land, as the book of Judges tells us. When we have a historical figure from long ago talking about issues in the historical present of the first millennium BCE, we have a great deal of editorial reordering. I would suggest that these difficulties and format are actually the stock and trade of mythic structures. The stories may in fact have long prehistories in oral form. But they are prescriptive, not descriptive, for the first millennium BCE. The stories tell us something otherwise not understandable about these early Israelites. They are being told by their literature not to mix with their outsider neighbors. Looked at in a positive light, the literature is saying that it is God who gives the patriarchs what they need, very nearly at the cost of everything dear—fertility, increase in wealth, and increase of their flocks.

The mythic structure of the story is the very thing that makes the thoughts of each character less important. In myths it is the narrative, the plot, that is important. The psychological disposition of the main characters is not nearly so important as it is in our novelistic literature, for example. The writers did not care in the way we do what the main characters were thinking. Then how do we reconstruct experience in the Hebrew Bible when they do not use the description of our internal states in the way we expect?

One way is by paying attention to the narrative structure of these stories and how the narrators evaluate the stories they recount. To do this, I plan to compare the mythical models in the Pentateuch with the legendary stories of the former and later prophets. There are a surprising number of explicit comparisons between the two time periods, and they relate to each other in a revealing number of ways. I will investigate these comparisons and contrasts. I am planning to explore the comparison between Genesis 22 (the sacrifice of Isaac) with Judges 11 (the sacrifice of Jephthah's daughter), Genesis 19 (Lot in Sodom) with Judges 19 (the concubine of the Levite), and Exodus 32 (the golden calf of Aaron) with 1 Kings 12:28–30 (the golden calves of Jeroboam). What I propose to do in the rest of this book, then, is to compare terrible stories, difficult stories, from what appear to be different time periods, to see how the difficulties in each story were handled by tradition, and assuming that they may have been able to influence each other during the history of their transmission. From their similar motif, I hope to extract a mythic pattern of what these writings meant for the society and then talk a bit about what the different editors were trying to do with them. It is a pattern that will be highlighted in each chapter in this book, where we will see an issue in the patriarchal period turns out to be the basis of a crisis in later historical books, particularly in the Court History, which traces how the north and more particularly the south's royal families continue from generation to generation.

Though he did not use the word *myth*, this style of presentment was noticed by Erich Auerbach in his famous work *Mimesis*.[34] He noted that all the stories in the Pentateuch were written against a black backgroud. They were stories stripped down to their most general form. Another way of expressing this form is to say that the mythic form of the story has been emphasized in these early stories. But the recognition of a mythic generality in the stories has rarely been followed up in a systematic way. As I have noted, there has been episodic interest in the "gaps" in the texts but the majority of scholars think that they can automatically understand the story by adding our own values to complete the text. It is something that the Hebrew Bible's style virtually demands, and it is one of the things most responsible for the rich tradition of interpretation of text in the Bible.

In contrast to the characters in the Pentateuch, the prophets do tell us what is on their minds in a particularly personal way. We can often tell which prophet is talking to us without looking to see where we are in the Bible. They each have a personal voice, even as they all ironically describe their words as coming directly from God. It is the very act of receiving the revelation from YHWH that brings out their personal voices while the narrators of Pentateuchal stories and the stories of the former prophets—Joshua, Judges, 1 and 2 Samuel, 1 and 2 Kings—are impersonal. We will for now keep our mutual study confined to the difficult stories of the Bible and hope that we can find reasons why the narrators felt the need to tell us these terrible, often morally outrageous stories. From it, I hope we can gain a sense of what is likely to be historical in the text, what is not, what functions as myth, and what the biblical text seeks to have us know about the ancient world from which it came.

CHAPTER TWO

THE GOLDEN CALF

A Lesson in Chronology

The Golden Calf

Twice in the recent past, calf figurines have emerged from the soil of Palestine. Sometime in the early 1980s an on-duty Israeli soldier, Ofer Broschi, looked down at his feet while standing on a hilltop in Northern Samaria. Close enough to the surface to be partly visible, Broschi glimpsed an object and then dug out an intact seven-inch cast bronze calf. He brought it back to his home kibbutz Shamir, where it was displayed for a time in its small archaeological museum. The importance of the find, however, demanded a greater audience with easier access, especially for scholars. It was traded for study and display to the Israel Museum, for which the kibbutz was compensated by the gift of several antiquities found in their specific area. Despite the calf's removal from the original location, Amihai Mazar easily identified the original collection site for further detailed study and tentatively dated the find to about 1200 BCE, when the Israelites were beginning to settle the northern area of the country.[1] It is quite difficult to decide who may have constructed it and what use he may have made of it.

A second calf find luckily had a strictly archaeological provenance from the beginning. In 1990, archaeologists working at the southern coastal site of Ashkelon discovered the small cast silver and bronze figure of a calf (approximately four inches high and four and a half inches long) inside the shattered fragments of a ceramic shrine (approximately a foot high). The calf and its model shrine had apparently been deposited in a Canaanite sanctuary located below the slope of the Middle Bronze Age city of Ashkelon and dated to 1600–1550 BCE,[2] a date between the patriarchal period and the period of the Judges, if we can graft the Bible's chronology correctly into the archaeological record. So one calf appears to come from the north on the eve of Israelite occupation; the second is from a Philistine settlement some time before the Israelites arrived.

These two tiny finds had a huge effect on our understanding of biblical history. First, while they are small finds, they give us actual religious cult objects—young bull calves in the prime of life, vibrant and energetic. The bull is also a symbol for the god Baal (lit. "husband," "master"), the son of El, the object of a great many polemics by the prophets, and the Canaanite fertility god who brings the autumn and winter rains and, at the same time, stud to the herd. As such, he is given a variety of names, including Hadad and 'Add.

These small calf replicas are not toys, then, but personifications of the great forces of the weather and its life-giving effects in the eastern Mediterranean, a small meditative symbol for a god who was worshipped all over the Canaanite world. They seemed to confirm that molten-cast calves (one of bronze; the other of silver), if not golden calves, were being worshipped in the area during the First Temple period and before.

We also know that "a golden calf" was the object of Israelite worship from the Bible itself. Aaron and the children of Israel offered sacrifice to a golden calf while Moses climbed up Mount Sinai to receive the Ten Commandments. This quintessential scene of sinning has been prominently displayed throughout the history of Western painting. And in Cecil B. DeMille's famous classic, *The Ten Commandments*, it actually received more time on-screen than the giving of the Ten Commandments itself. In fact, in spite of the high moral and historical purposes the director took upon himself in his unprecedented direct address to the audience, his camera spent more time lovingly depicting the affluence of ancient Egypt and the sinning of the Israelites in the desert than most of the other parts of the Exodus story. When it comes to the Bible, just as in a screenplay, the snake has all the lines. But, in terms of the Bible, the golden calf is in the category of the greatest sinning the children of Israel ever did. What was especially galling is that it took place almost in earshot of the giving of the Ten Commandments. The calf then is as much an Israelite symbol as a foreign one. In fact, we shall see that the calves are also a major interpretation of Israelite religion, not really a foreign import.

The Bible, and specifically the E source, which specializes in the Exodus account, recounts the terrible sinning of the golden calf in Exodus 32: "When the people saw that Moses delayed to come down from the mountain, the people gathered around Aaron, and said to him, 'Come, make gods for us, who shall go before us; as for this Moses, the man who brought us up out of the land of Egypt, we do not know what has become of him'" (Exodus 32:1).

The people are obedient to Aaron, who tells them to donate their wealth. He even tells them to take their wives' jewelry away (32:2). With these he smelts and casts a "golden calf." When Aaron is done, he presents the calf to the people as the god of the Israelites: "He took the gold from them, formed it in a mold,[3] and cast an image of a calf; and they said, 'These are your gods, O Israel, who brought you up out of the land of Egypt'" (Exodus 32:4). The exclamation directly quotes the first statement of the Ten Commandments and only points up the terrible sinning inherent in this verse. Then Aaron builds an altar and proclaims a festival for the next day (32:5). The horror of the actions is mirrored in the Bible's use of eating, drinking, and reveling: "and the people sat down to eat and drink, and rose up to play" (32:7). There are very obvious sexual implications in the last "rose up to play" (32:7), which are immediately taken up.

Meanwhile, high on the mountain, the LORD warns Moses of the perversity of the people, telling him to go down there at once, and adding sarcastically that Moses himself brought them out of Egypt merely to act perversely (32:7). The LORD complains angrily of their behavior and threatens to wipe them out entirely (32:8). Moses, however, implores the LORD, pointing out that they are indeed his people (32:11) and that he has promised to make them a multitude with many descendants to inherit the land forever (32:13). In the end, Moses changes the LORD's mind about the disaster (32:14).

Then Moses turns and goes down from the mountain. Joined by Joshua, Moses returns to the camp and finds it raucously celebrating a festival in honor of the calf. Moses throws the tablets down, breaking them (32:19). He then breaks the calf, burns it, and even grinds it to powder, which may parallel the ritual stages of grain preparation that was characteristic of the worship of Canaanites goddesses, and then makes the Israelites drink the powder (32:19–20). Aaron then intercedes for the people as well: "And Aaron said, 'Do not let the anger of my lord burn hot; you know the people, that they are bent on evil.' They said to me, 'Make us gods, who shall go before us; as for this Moses, the man who brought us up out of the land of Egypt, we do not know what has become of him'" (32:23).

Moses imposes a test on the people, asking: "'Who is on the LORD's side? Come to me!' And all the sons of Levi gathered around him" (32:26). Moses then commands the Levites to kill the inveterate sinners (32:28). The fallen comrades form a kind of human sacrifice as much as an act of retribution: "Moses said, 'Today you have ordained yourselves for the service of the LORD,[4] each one at the cost of a son or a brother, and so have brought a blessing on yourselves this day'" (32:29).

The text wants us to be astonished at the heresy of the Hebrews: not free from Egypt more than a few days, having personally witnessed the miracle of the crossing of the Red Sea, they still fall into worshipping another god, who is no god but a golden statue of a calf. But, in spite of the position of the narrative, one must be equally horrified at the extent of the slaughter. It is so terrible that one hopes it to be a fantasy of bloodshed, rather than an actual event.

The next day Moses makes atonement for the sins of the remaining Israelites. Here is the first reference to a "book of life," obviously a scroll here but also a roll book that Jews still believe God consults at every High Holiday season to decide who shall live and who shall die: "But now, if you will only forgive their sin—but if not, blot me out of the book that you have written." Moses again offers his life for those of the people. But the LORD said to Moses, "Whoever has sinned against me I will blot out of my book" (32:32–33). Finally, the LORD appoints an angel to lead the people and promises that he will not hold back punishment on the day of judgment: "But now go, lead the people to the place about which I have spoken to you; see, my angel shall go in front of you. Nevertheless, when the day comes for punishment, I will punish them for their sin" (32:34). That punishment appears to be a plague, which attacks the people the next day (32:35), causing yet further damage. But the statement is available later to support a notion of a day of judgment at the end of time. Clearly, this is a passage with many mythic reverberations down through the centuries for Jews and, later, for apocalypticists everywhere.

The story is meant to put fear in the heart of anyone who thinks of worshipping a calf or any other idolatrous object. We may suspect that the audience is living in a later time, however. And perhaps it is also trying to explain the significance of any more contemporary sickness and plague. But, in any event, it is a very terrible tale of vengeance, perpetrated by the LORD. It seems almost impossible to justify this kind of terror. But events in the future of Israel will at least help us to understand what is happening in these verses and why the plague and the slaughter are so terrible. The passage is a terrible *prototype* to scare "sinners" living at a far later moment in Israel's history.

The Golden Calves of Jeroboam I

Almost as famous as the golden calf of Aaron are the golden calves that were set up by King Jeroboam (922–901 BCE) as the centerpiece of his rebellion against the house of David:

> ²⁸ So the king [i.e., Jeroboam] took counsel, and made two calves of gold. He said to the people, "You have gone up to Jerusalem long enough. Here are your gods, O Israel, who brought you up out of the land of Egypt." ²⁹ He set one in Bethel, and the other he put in Dan. ³⁰ And this thing became a sin, for the people went to worship before the one at Bethel and before the other as far as Dan. ³¹ He also made houses on high places, and appointed priests from among all the people, who were not Levites. ³² Jeroboam appointed a festival on the fifteenth day of the eighth month like the festival that was in Judah, and he offered sacrifices on the altar; so he did in Bethel, sacrificing to the calves that he had made. And he placed in Bethel the priests of the high places that he had made. ³³ He went up to the altar that he had made in Bethel on the fifteenth day in the eighth month, in the month that he alone had devised; he appointed a festival for the people of Israel, and he went up to the altar to offer incense.
>
> (1 Kings 12:28–33)

This biblical passage from the former prophets, the historical book of Kings, tells the story of the most terrible rebellion against the Davidic dynasty and hence against the wishes of God. The story, we note, especially singles out the use of nonlevitical priesthoods. The story demands a preface for those who are not familiar with the biblical story.

When Solomon died, his son Rehoboam (c. 922–915 BCE) succeeded him as king of Judah (1 Kings 11:43). Rehoboam then traveled north to Shechem to secure his claim to the throne of Israel as well. The account of the ensuing negotiations preserved in 1 Kings 12 suggests that the leaders of the northern tribes were only prepared to accept Rehoboam's rule if he released them or at least diminished the tax of his father (the tax was payable in labor, since there was no currency as yet). The tax supported Solomon's building projects (1 Kings 4:7–28), but the only grievances expressed in the Bible's account of the Shechem parley are "the hard service of your father and the heavy yoke that he placed on us" (1 Kings 12:4). According to 1 Kings 9:15–23, Solomon had imposed a corvée, a tax of manual labor, on the foreign, non-Israelite population, while the Israelites involved in his work projects served as overseers and officers (1 Kings 12:22–23). Nevertheless, the language of the northern leaders' complaint indicates that it was probably more onerous than the book of Kings admits and that the northerners felt oppressed by the corvée. The secession of the north from the rule of the dynasty of David became inevitable at this point.

Thenceforth, Israel was ruled not by the descendants of David. Instead, the ten tribes in the north followed a new leader, Jeroboam, who was succeeded by other dynasties. Scholars call the southern kingdom the Kingdom of Judah, and the northern kingdom the Kingdom of Israel. The southern kingdom is known in ancient extrabiblical sources quite often as "the house of David," where *house* signifies *dynasty*. The northern kingdom of Israel could be known as Israel, but was, just as often, known by the name of Jeroboam's own tribe, Ephraim. It was also called "the house of Omri," after a later, eighth-century BCE dynasty. But the north was never again to return willingly to the rule of the south.

Thereby, Jeroboam became the traitor and heretic par excellence, the Judas, Quisling, and Benedict Arnold in the eyes of the southern kingdom. Of course, none of those figures yet existed; so how will the narrative pick a prototype important enough to put in the tradition of Jeroboam? The answer is the golden calf.

The Perspective of the South

The book of Kings gives us only the perspective of the southern kingdom on this matter, so Jeroboam thereby becomes not only a rebel but the archheretic of the Old Testament. In the north, we will see that there was a divided opinion about Jeroboam's actions. Some no doubt thought of him as a political and religious reformer; others thought of him as a religious rebel, as we shall see.

This rebellion/reform occasioned a great deal of frustration and general discontent in the south, which thought of the whole area as rightfully belonging to the Davidic dynasty, not just because of David's conquests but also by divine right. Nathan had said: "Your house and your kingdom shall be made sure forever before me;[5] your throne shall be established forever" (2 Samuel 7:16). This would preclude a king in the north. But after the death of Solomon there certainly was one, the same Jeroboam who had earlier been a rebel in Solomon's court (1 Kings 11:26–39).

Although a descendant or scion of David continued to sit on the Judahite throne in Jerusalem for more than four hundred years, until the Babylonian conquest in 586 BCE, the northern kingdom was forever lost to it. This was a crisis of huge proportions, and when the northern kingdom is destroyed the southern editors of the books of Kings know just what sins to blame for its destruction: Jeroboam's golden calves. Jeroboam, for his part, set up a more loosely associated form of government, probably closer to the tribal confederacy that had been the ideal form of government before the rise of the Davidic kingship. In spite of Jeroboam's religious reform, this form of government was inherently weaker, even unstable. Even the necessity of making two cultic centers, one on the southern border and the other on the northern border, suggests a looser form of organization than the south.

In fact, the northern kingdom witnessed a succession of unrelated rulers and periodic putsches, revolutions, and rebellions, yielding many different dynasties, each worse than the previous from the point of view of the biblical book of Kings, a book whose narrative reflects the perspective of Judah and the "house of David." It is easy to see that the dynastic principle that took hold in the south around the scions of David never did hold in the north, which kept closer to the original charismatic form of leadership where God himself would appoint a leader by pointing out his (or occasionally her, i.e., Deborah) inherent powers to rule.

As a young man from Zeredah (a town west of Shiloh in the Ephraimite highlands), Jeroboam son of Nebat had started as a bright young man in Solomon's employ. He had come to Solomon's attention because of his administrative skills and energy. Solomon placed him in charge of the corvée labor of the house of Joseph—that is, the conscript labor battalions of the territories of the half-tribes of Ephraim and Manasseh (1 Kings 11:26–28). But the good feeling did not last long, as Solomon soon understood the threat that Jeroboam might present if he acted against the kingdom (1 Kings 11:40). With Solomon's agents seeking his life, Jeroboam fled to Egypt and found refuge with Pharaoh Shishak (c. 945–924 BCE), the Egyptian pharaoh Sheshonq, in whose safekeeping he remained until Solomon's death.

The occurrence of Shishak in the Kings narrative, both here and in 1 Kings 14:25, is very important. It is crucial in arguing against a Second Temple date for these traditions and makes impossible the position of the extreme minimalists, who claim that there was no First Temple period. This is why: the second occurrence in 1 Kings 14:25 records the campaign of Shishak against the kingdoms of Judah and Israel, removing a great deal of the wealth accumulated by Solomon. This punishing campaign during Rehoboam's reign is also commemorated on a stela in Egypt, which makes it the first explicit event mentioned in both Bible and an outside source. It is hard to imagine that a late editor could have situated this event so exactly. It must have come from some earlier, unimpeachable Israelite source, since the Egyptians used a completely different calendar. Furthermore, the damage inflicted by Shishak on the southern kingdom could easily have been an important reason why the country was not united for several centuries. We shall take up the issue of historicity again in the last chapter.

According to the account in 1 Kings 12, Jeroboam exercised a leadership role in the parley at Shechem. Rehoboam, the Davidic monarch, might have been able to win over the northern tribal leaders if he had dealt with them respectfully and assured them of less oppressive treatment. Indeed, his senior advisers recommended this course of action (1 Kings 12:7). But Rehoboam followed the advice of more junior advisers, his contemporaries, and replied to the petition of Jeroboam and his companions with hostility and even a sexual insult: "My little finger is thicker than my father's loins" (1 Kings 12:10).

Having been threatened by Rehoboam with policies even harsher than Solomon's, the northern leaders took up the slogan of a previous revolt, known as Sheba's Revolt: "What share do we have in David?" (compare 2 Samuel 20:1 with 1 Kings 12:16), and withdrew from Shechem. When Rehoboam sent Adoram (or Adoniram; compare 1 Kings 4:6), his chief corvée officer, to raise a work levy, the Israelites stoned him to death (1 Kings 12:18), and the division of the kingdoms became an accomplished fact. Rehoboam was obliged to flee back to Jerusalem for his own safety (1 Kings 12:18).

Even a quick look at a map will show that all that remained under the sway of the Davidic king in Jerusalem was a small and pitiful remnant of the whole, only the semiarid and marginally arable land in the south, mostly given over to grazing. The north, by comparison, was far more affluent, with gorgeous and relatively well-watered valleys and farm lands, which had made it a very rich and powerful agricultural area. No wonder there was constant pressure to revolt. The north is more likely to feel gratitude to a more explicitly agricultural deity. But Elohim and El could be easily given responsibility for the affluence since they resembled Baal in having the characteristics of a sky god who also brings stud to the herd.

The south was much more uniformly pastoralist, though its capital was Jerusalem, a city favored with many natural defenses. David, the military hero, succeeded in conquering the north for a time and, almost miraculously, had conquered Jerusalem. But the north is easy to conquer because the capital city of Samaria was weakly defended by contrast to Jerusalem's impressive fortifications. Though the Bible is written from the point of view of the south, it was the north that dominated during much of biblical history. And that would mean its religion was more common than the south would like to admit.

Jeroboam I is only described by the books of Kings, which are sources very biased toward the south. According to them, Jeroboam feared that his people would still want to offer sacrifices at the Jerusalem Temple and might revert to the rule of the Davidic dynasty (1 Kings 12:26, 27). According to Kings, to keep his people's allegiances, Jeroboam established two shrines at opposite ends of his kingdom—one at Bethel, in the southern part of his new kingdom, and the other at Dan, in the northern sector, where he set up two golden calves. "These are your Gods, O Israel," he declared (1 Kings 12:28). That is another direct parallel with the Exodus golden calf account. It surely points up that the Bible intends to propose these two incidents as related. It is a very significant detail; but the significance of the parallel does not come into focus at first.

One problem that the doublet addresses is surely that the calf worship itself is not so much foreign worship and not Egyptian worship, as the Exodus account seems to imply, but an alternative way of worshipping El or Elohim, as God was called in the north. Proof positive of the Israelite nature of the golden calf comes from Jehu, a king of Israel, who killed the worshippers of Baal and abolished the worship of Baal in his kingdom. Yet the north continues to worship the golden calf that Jeroboam instituted: "But Jehu did not turn aside from the sins of Jeroboam son of Nebat, which he caused Israel to commit—the golden calves that were in Bethel and in Dan" (2 Kings 10:29). It is a sin in the mind of the Kings narrator, but it is a quite different piety than worshipping Baal or the Egyptian Hathor, no matter what the Exodus account wants to imply.

Hosea also tells us that the calves were a matter of contention in the north.

Hosea's Witness

The prophet Hosea also opposes the worship in the north. He reports that there is worship of an angel at Bethel, which certainly invokes the angel whom Jacob struggles with at the cult place of Penuel (Genesis 32:24–32).[6] The story of Jacob at Bethel is a very "orthodox" Israelite story of divine conflict ending with Jacob's name change to Israel—exegeted in context as "one who strives with God." So this is a very important angel indeed. In Hosea's opinion, this is Israelite worship and not Canaanite worship. Even so, in Hosea's opinion, it is all improper:

> He strove with the angel and prevailed,
>> he wept and sought his favor;
> he met him at Bethel,
>> and there he spoke with him.[7]
> The LORD the God of hosts,
>> the LORD is his name!
>
> (Hosea 12:4–5)

Hosea's description shows that this worship was Israelite. The calf was a symbol of the Israelite God. Hosea contradicts the claim that the angel was Jacob's savior: "the angel who has redeemed me from all harm, bless the boys; and in them let my name be perpetuated, and the name of my ancestors Abraham and Isaac; and let them grow into a multitude on the earth" (Genesis 48:16). This suggests that YHWH was the name of the angel and thus held a secondary spot in the north's pantheon. It is significant in this regard that after the sin of the golden calf in Exodus, God says that his angel will go before them and be part of the punishment. The correct angel, whose name contains or personifies the name of YHWH, is revealed with Moses at Sinai, just as Hosea has it:

I am going to send an angel in front of you, to guard you on the way and to bring you to the place that I have prepared. Be attentive to him and listen to his voice; do not rebel against him, for he will not pardon your transgression; for my name is in him. But if you listen attentively to his voice and do all that I say, then I will be an enemy to your enemies and a foe to your foes. When my angel goes in front of you, and brings you to the Amorites, the Hittites, the Perizzites, the Canaanites, the Hivites, and the Jebusites, and I blot them out, you shall not bow down to their gods, or worship them, or follow their practices, but you shall utterly demolish them and break their pillars in pieces. You shall worship the LORD your God, and I[8] will bless your bread and your water; and I will take sickness away from among you.

(Exodus 23:20–26)

It seems clear then that the two incidents are speaking about the same northern worship, which is viewed by the south as being the equivalent of foreign worship but is a variant of Israelite religion in which YHWH is the principal angel and God can be worshipped by means of the symbol of the calf. That means that the golden calf in Exodus is really the normal form of worship in the north, which is just viewed as a "heresy" after the reform of Jeroboam.

Unfortunately, the events related in 1 Kings, Jeroboam's religious reform and rebellion, cannot be historically verified in every archaeological detail. But we have plenty of archaeological evidence suggesting that the northern kingdom practiced religion a little differently from the south. We have probably found the remains of the royal shrine where one calf once stood, at Dan, built in the late tenth century BCE. These remains include a large platform, about sixty feet wide, made of large blocks of stones. This structure, we believe, is an example of an open-air shrine known in the Bible as a *bamah*, often translated as "high place" (in Leviticus 26:30 and in dozens of other passages).

Besides this southern polemic against the north, containing an extremely negative view of Jeroboam, there is occasionally another, even more explicitly negative view of Jeroboam from one of the editors of the books of Kings, a person whom we can call the Deuteronomistic Historian (as we shall see in the next chapter). Here is an example of what could be summoned against Jeroboam by someone who had plenty of time to reflect on his sins:

While Jeroboam was standing by the altar to offer incense, a man of God came out of Judah by the word of the LORD to Bethel ² and proclaimed against the altar by the word of the LORD, and said, "O altar, altar, thus says the LORD: "A son shall be born to the house of David, Josiah by name; and he shall sacrifice on you the priests of the high places who offer incense on you, and human bones shall be burned on you." ³ He gave a sign the same day, saying, "This is the sign that the LORD has spoken: 'The altar shall be torn down, and the ashes that are on it shall be poured out.'" ⁴ When the king heard what the man of God cried out against the altar at Bethel, Jeroboam stretched out his hand from the altar, saying, "Seize him!" But the hand that he stretched out against him withered so that he could not draw it back to himself. ⁵ The altar also was torn down, and the ashes poured out from the altar, according to the sign that the man of God had given by the word of the LORD. ⁶ The king said to the man of God, "Entreat now the favor of the LORD your God, and pray for me, so that my hand may be restored to me." So the man of God entreated the LORD; and the king's hand was restored to him, and became as it was before.

(1 Kings 13:1–6)

This voice is obviously a later voice than the main narration of the religious and political secession with which we have been detailing. In the first place it knows explicitly about the birth of Josiah, the great king of the south who ascended the throne around 640 BCE, almost three centuries after the events of the days of Jeroboam and Rehoboam. But the voice that speaks the attitudes of Deuteronomy may be later than Josiah, even much later than that. We normally associate this voice with the Deuteronomistic Historian, who writes under the influence of Josiah's reform in 621 BCE, but who could be writing even in the early postexilic period under Persian rule, putting together a series of moral meanings in the biblical text. Apparently, the Deuteronomistic Historian here is a bit frustrated with the lack of moral tone in the narrative and wants to emphasize even further the sinning of Jeroboam and its eventual results.

It is certainly true that two centuries after Jeroboam I, the Assyrians conquered and eventually destroyed the northern kingdom. Then some eighty years after that Josiah was able to claim the land back for the Davidic monarchy. But during the two centuries before this Deuteronomistic Historian's narrative, no such moral and punishment for Jeroboam's rebellion would have been evident to anyone. Indeed, it looks a great deal like Jeroboam got away with the better part of the kingdom—that is, unless one makes clear the connection between the sinning of the northern tribes and the sinning of the Israelites at Sinai. Before the Deuteronomistic Historian, the story of the golden calf at Sinai served as the mythical prototype to demonstrate that the LORD was angry at the north. After the Assyrians, the narrator merely had to recite the facts. God had destroyed the northern kingdom through the might of the Assyrian army. So the golden calf incident only makes full sense before the destruction of the northern kingdom.

Amos and Hosea

The first two literary prophets—that is, prophets who left us biblical books titled with their name—were Amos and Hosea. They preceded the great prophets of Isaiah, Jeremiah, and Ezekiel, but the actual chronology is disguised because the longer, more famous prophets' books are found before theirs in the order in the Bible. Amos and Hosea were active in the north in the eighth century BCE. Hosea, as we have already seen, particularly prophesied against the calf worship in the north. Unlike Amos, who came from Tekoa, a town in the south, quite close to Jerusalem, Hosea was a native, northern prophet. Though he lived a century and a half after Jeroboam I, he does not accept or agree with Jeroboam's religious reform and he criticizes the religion in the north from within the northern tradition. He gives us quite a bit of information about the "heresy" of the northern "calf cult." From Hosea's point of view, it is folly and will end in failed crops and foreign conquest:

> Your calf is rejected, O Samaria.
>> My anger burns against them.
> How long will they be incapable of innocence?
>> For it is from Israel,
> an artisan made it;
>> it is not God.
> The calf of Samaria
>> shall be broken to pieces.[9]
> For they sow the wind,
>> and they shall reap the whirlwind.

The standing grain has no heads,
　　it shall yield no meal;
if it were to yield,
　　foreigners would devour it.
Israel is swallowed up;
　　now they are among the nations
　　as a useless vessel.

(Hosea 8:5–8)

The last verse particularly seems to be a gloss written into the text after the destruction of Samaria by the Assyrians (721 BCE). Hosea explicitly mentions the calf of Samaria, which is the capital city of the north as well as the name of the area. He must be talking about the area of Samaria, rather than the city, because Bethel is in Samaria, while Dan is in the Galilee. Both appear to be national shrines of the northern kingdom.

Amos and Amaziah

We know this not only because of the way Bethel and Dan are singled out by the narrator of 1 Kings and the way Hosea describes Bethel but because the prophet Amos is involved in an altercation at Bethel in one of his earliest prophecies (7:12–15):

> And Amaziah said to Amos, "O seer, go, flee away to the land of Judah, earn your bread there, and prophesy there; but never again prophesy at Bethel, for it is the king's sanctuary, and it is a temple of the kingdom." Then Amos answered Amaziah, "I am no prophet, nor a prophet's son; but I am a herdsman, and a dresser of sycamore trees, and the LORD took me from following the flock, and the LORD said to me, 'Go, prophesy to my people Israel.'"

The priest Amaziah tells Amos to go back where he came from—namely, to the south. He is protesting that Amos has no right to be speaking at a royal cult center like Bethel. He assumes that successful prophets can be hired by the king and supported in their prophetic duties. Prophets who eat at the expense of the king are not likely to anger him with negative prophecies but rather to support the policies of the king.

But Amos is different. Amos answers with a puzzling turn of phrase, a phrase that makes perfect sense in his particular context but demands explanation: "I am no prophet or a son of a prophet." It looks as though he denies his very profession. But, given that he is at Bethel, probably he is only denying that he is a "professional" northern prophet, eating at the king's table, as Amaziah describes it. At the same time, he is explicitly denying that he is tuning his prophecies to the whim of the northern king and implicitly critiquing the prophets employed there who did.

In context, this appears to mean that Amos is not a trained prophet, in the northern style. He does not accept the northern term, *nabi*, for his profession. The term in the south might still be *hozze*, "seer," anyway. So Amos may be saying all these things—that he is not a member of the professional prophets in the north and that he is not in the king's pay—in denying he is a prophet.

Nor is he a son of a prophet: apparently, this means that Amos is denying that he is a member of a prophet guild, educated at a prophetic scribal school. So Amos is apparently telling us that he distinguishes what he is doing from what the northern prophets do. They are trained in scribal guilds and are retained by the king. Amos, by contrast, has been called by God, and he speaks only the word of God. So in a way we are looking at the birth of literary prophecy in the Bible. It begins in the north with a southern prophet criticizing the northern religion.

In place of these more professional ways to become a prophet, Amos relies on his amazingly effective language. He is a prophet because God chose him for this occupation. Again, we see that literary prophecy is quite similar to judgeship and kingship. YHWH chooses the most unlikely people to make clear that all of history's effects are due to God's intervention. Amos claims only to be a southern farmer, a herdsman and a dresser of sycamore trees, two quintessentially rural activities. All of this makes Amos's great oratorical skills more obvious.

Since we are aware of Amos's great oratorical talents, we perhaps should not conclude that Amos was a poor farmer. The word he uses for herdsman, *boqer*, may in fact refer to either a small herdsman or to a giant supplier. Mesha King of Moab is also called a *boqer*, a supplier of meat for the king's table, though he can hardly be running a small business. Perhaps Amos is another larger agrarian producer. In any event, Amos speaks Hebrew extremely well, well enough that his language itself gives him the authority to be heard.

Amos seems to be describing himself in terms reminiscent of David's call to be king of the south, a man who followed after the sheep until YHWH chose him to become a leader in Israel. During David's time, we may imagine that there was not a lot of distance between the roles of shepherd and king. By the middle eighth century social class appears to be better developed.

More Prophetic Testimony

Both Amos and Hosea are writing during the time of Jeroboam II (786–746 BCE), some century and a half after Jeroboam I and a time of unusual affluence in the north. But it was also a dangerous time, a mere two decades to the fateful date 721 BCE, when the northern kingdom is destroyed by the armies of Assyria. Though Hosea is from the north and reflects a northern perspective, he rejects the calf and tells us that worship of the calf continues, even some two centuries after Jeroboam I set up the shrines. Hosea warns that God will cause the wheat crop to fail and that others will eat it. There were always crop diseases and an ongoing war with Syria to worry about, so we cannot use these events to date the prophecy exactly. Destruction is promised, but it is rather vaguely described. So one may well believe that these are authentic prophecies written before the destruction of the north by Assyria.

From the prophet's point of view, Jeroboam's gold statues are not gods, merely two statues of calves. This is something of a misunderstanding of "idolatry." Normally people who venerate images are aware of the difference between the image and the god itself. Perhaps they ask the god to take up residence in or on the image. But they do not confuse the image with the god. They are aware that the image of the god is a representative of the god.

We also know that worship there, at least in this crisis time, involved kissing the image of the god:

> When Ephraim spoke, there was trembling;
> he was exalted in Israel;
> but he incurred guilt through Baal and died.
> And now they keep on sinning
> and make a cast image for themselves,

idols of silver made according to their understanding,
all of them the work of artisans.
"Sacrifice to these," they say.[10]
People are kissing calves!

(Hosea 13:1–2)

Not only does the northern worship involve an image, it involves a cast or molten image of a calf, evidently. The polemic of the prophet ends with the comical taunt that worshippers are kissing calves. Though the silver calf that was found in Ashkelon was Canaanite and the Galilee calf of ambiguous background, here we have some literary evidence that the Israelites worshipped their own silver and golden calves as part of the worship of their God, which involved kissing calves. In a later prophecy that appears to know about the final fate of the northern kingdom, we have Hosea claiming:

> The inhabitants of Samaria tremble
>   for the calf[11] of Beth-aven.
> Its people shall mourn for it,
>   and its idolatrous priests shall wail[12] over it,
>   over its glory that has departed from it.
> The thing itself shall be carried to Assyria
>   as tribute to the great king.[13]
> Ephraim shall be put to shame,
>   and Israel shall be ashamed of his idol.

(Hosea 10:5–6)[14]

The prophet even calls Beth-El, Beth-Aven, not a house of God but a house of iniquity. Obviously, this is to be dated to the time after the destruction, because the prophet seems to know what happens to the calves after Assyria conquers the north. Perhaps some of the rites involved ritual mourning. In the end, the people will come to mourn and be ashamed of the image. Here Assyria is specifically mentioned as the agent of destruction, so the oracle is undoubtedly written later, by someone after Hosea with certain knowledge of the outcome. This also tends to confirm that besides kissing the image itself, as a ritual of worship and ritual mourning, the worshippers were indulging at other times in various celebrations and festivals and, as a result, would be brought to grief by Assyria's entrance on the scene.

The Parallels Between Aaron at Sinai and Jeroboam I at Dan and Bethel

In 1967 and 1969, Leivy Smolar and Moses Aberbach published a spectacular pair of articles in the *Journal of Biblical Literature*.[15] They changed the study of the story of the golden calf forever, but, as is more likely than not in scholarly journals, it was not at first noticed or heeded. One reason must have been contemporary events: Israel was involved in the Six Day War, what seemed at the time to be war for its survival; the Vietnamese War was gearing up; and ghettoes across the United States were burning; 1967 was a very hot summer. Furthermore, the articles did not argue the most dramatic implications of their study; rather they left them for the reader to conclude independently.

Here is what they demonstrated. They compared the story of the golden calf episode in the wilderness (Exodus 32) with Jeroboam's erection of the two golden calves at Bethel and Dan (starting at 1 Kings 12:2). They explicitly compare the actions of Jeroboam with those of Aaron throughout the narrative. The results are so striking that they cannot be due to chance. They outline thirteen points of contact or identity between the principal characters of the two stories:

1. Both Aaron and Jeroboam construct "golden calves." Although the motivation of the two sinners may differ, the language used to describe the act is quite similar. And the use of repeated words or what the German scholars have called *Stichwörter*, "stitch words," or repeated vocabulary "stitches together" the two stories. Stitch words can be used to unify a single story. But it is even more important when the same words are used to stitch together two parallel biblical texts.

2. Jeroboam announces exactly the same statement as Aaron: "Behold your Gods, O Israel, which brought you up out of the land of Egypt" (Exodus 32:4 with 1 Kings 12:28).

3. Both build an altar for calf worship (Exodus 32:5, 1 Kings 12:32, and 2 Kings 23:15). After the construction, they both ordain a feast, using similar vocabulary (Exodus 32:5, 1 Kings 12:32f).

4. In both narratives the sacrifices are offered to the golden calf (Exodus 32:6 versus 1 Kings 12:32). Both Aaron and Jeroboam function in a priestly capacity.

5. Jeroboam appoints priests not from the tribe of Levi (1 Kings 12:31, 13:32), while in Exodus the Levites are steadfast opponents to the calf worship and take a militant stand against calf worshippers.

6. In both accounts, the sin is described as sin par excellence. Aaron and Jeroboam are both described not only as sinners but as leaders who caused others to sin (e.g., Exodus 32:21, 1 Kings 12:30, but continuously in the narrative as well).

7. Both Aaron and Jeroboam come under severe divine displeasure and both are threatened with annihilation.

8. In both accounts sinners benefit from intercession. Moses beseeches God to spare both Israel and Aaron (Exodus 32:11, Deuteronomy 9:20), while the unknown prophet from Judah entreats the LORD to restore Jeroboam's paralyzed hand (1 Kings 13:6).

9. The desecration of Jeroboam's altar at Bethel by Josiah, king of Judah, was accomplished by the act of slaying the priests of the "high places" on it and also by burning human bones on it. At Sinai the Levites are told to "slay every man his brother" (32:27). If this is so, we can see an exact parallel with Josiah's slaughter of the priests of the calf cult, introduced by Jeroboam, just as 1 Kings 13 predicts. And perhaps we can also posit that refugees from the destruction of the northern kingdom in 721 BCE came south and began new lives in the south. The sudden growth of the southern cities after the Assyrian invasion may tell us even more than the text does.

10. The destruction of the golden calf made by Aaron (Exodus 32:20, Deuteronomy 9:21) and of Jeroboam's altars at Bethel by Josiah (2 Kings 23:15) is carried out in a similar manner, and even the wording of the two accounts is similar: Aaron's golden calf and Jeroboam's *bamah* altar dedicated for the calf are both burnt and ground into fine dust (Exodus 32:20, Deuteronomy 9:21, 2 Kings 23).

11. Both the Levites suffer additional retribution at the hands of God, who "smote the people because they made the calf." The chronicler, a still younger source with access to older material, uses the same expression in describing Jeroboam's death: "And the LORD smote him and he died" (Exodus 32:35, 2 Chronicles 13:20).

12. The two eldest sons of Aaron, Nadab and Abihu, and the two recorded sons of Jeroboam, Nadab and Abijah, bear almost identical names. They all die in the prime of life. The sons of Aaron die because they burn incense and offer "a strange fire," two presumably

idolatrous acts, while exactly the same is reported of Jeroboam (1 Kings 14:3).

13. After their deaths, the sons of Aaron are extolled as having been close to the LORD. All Israel bewailed their death (Leviticus 10:6). Similarly, Abijah, son of Jeroboam, is praised because of his good deeds toward the Lord. He was privileged to die in peace, and all Israel made lamentation for him (1 Kings 14:3).

This long list of similarities could imply one or more of four causes. One is, of course, the simplest explanation: all the parallels are pure coincidences brought on by similar subject matter. This seems to me to very unlikely, given the depth and importance of the similarities. The Bible sets these two events against each other, clearly trying to tell us something about both of them by describing them in such comparable language. As we have already seen, the second possibility is that the rebellion of Jeroboam is being deliberately framed in terms of the previously available story of the Exodus. After all, the Exodus happened many centuries before the Jeroboam revolt, and perhaps the writers are deliberately using an event from the past to apply to a present event. We have several examples of this kind of use of the past. More recent misfortunes of the Jews, for example, are often described in terms appropriate to the holiday of Purim, where the Jews were saved from extinction by the righteousness and intelligence of Esther and Mordechai. Or we can observe that many things that fall short of genocide (thank God!) are often discussed as if they were a repetition of Hitler's actions. These always have rhetorical as much as real effects. But it is possible that the revolt of Jeroboam is deliberately being reframed to look like the already well-known golden calf revolt in the desert.

Third, the exact converse is certainly possible. It is possible that the story of the golden calf near Sinai is being invented and inserted into the story of the desert wanderings to make clear how terrible is the sin of Jeroboam, especially since the punishment for such sinning would not have been visible to anyone for at least three centuries after the events. This would be a deliberate use of the mythical past for political propaganda and, if the term can be used, an example of polemical mythologization. In a real way, the story of the golden calf in the Bible could be redesigned as a polemic against the northern kingdom, with its different kingship and opposing notions of religious truth.

Last, if either two or three is true, it seems likely that both traditions grew up together and in coordination with each other. This seems likely in all cases where there is any relationship between them at all. In short, we already know that these two events form a kind of extended doublet, and the most likely explanation is that there was an oral/written connection between the two stories that continued for some time. We are already familiar with this process in previous chapters, even though we can only speculate how the connection took place.

Is there any information that might resolve the ambiguity? Aberbach and Smolar opt for the last of the options. They say the list of correlations is striking and bespeaks a relationship. They do not make clear if they believe that one preceded the other and would further account for the development of the tradition. They do entertain quite thoroughly that the Aaron story was inserted in the Exodus narrative on account of the south's annoyance with the rebellion of Jeroboam. In other words, it is Jeroboam's rebellion that caused the earlier story to be written rather than the other way around. They do not affirm it either.

I tend to agree with that assessment, but I find reason to believe that one is definitely prior to the other. The two stories did in fact develop in that peculiarly oral/written environment that we have seen is the background of Israelite traditions. I would point out one more thing, which Aberbach and Smolar note as well but do not argue. I am struck with the implication of saying the performative utterance "These are your Gods, O Israel" (compare Exodus 32:4 with 1 Kings 12:28). The number of Gods specified makes me suspicious. The plural occurs in the noun, with the appended also plural personal pronoun "your" in Hebrew. This form can be grammatically ambiguous in Hebrew because *Elohim* in Hebrew can be treated as a plural term, though normally it is not. But in both cases it is accompanied by a plural pronoun, suggesting that the term is very definitely an intended plural: "*These* are your *Gods*, O Israel." The plural form is not absolutely certain, so it cannot be taken as undeniable proof, but it does raise the likelihood that Jeroboam I precedes the story in Exodus.

There is only one place in the two Bible passages where there actually are two calves—that is, in the rebellion of Jeroboam. Jeroboam puts up two golden calves. Aaron only forges one golden calf. The controlling passage among these two is actually the place where the plural of *Gods* occurs, in the story of Jeroboam (1 Kings 12), not in the story of Aaron (Exodus 32). So I suggest that the controlling narrative event is the rebellion of Jeroboam and that the story of the single calf in Exodus is an echo of that narrative event, pushed back into the patriarchal era. The reason for the story will emerge shortly.

Even if this is not accepted, it is obvious that the two stories are connected. It seems clear that the description of the golden calf in Exodus is a kind of satire on the actual worship of a calf in the north and that this worship involves the calf or bull as a symbol for God or perhaps even the beast on which the God of the north rides, just as the cherubim are the place where YHWH of the south chooses to dwell and ride. From the point of view of tradition history, the story of golden calf at Sinai is from the E source. But the polemical perspective against worship of the calf is even more likely to be from the south. For me the best way to explain this agreement in polemic is that the E source is being included into the Exodus narrative under the watchful eyes of the editor of the JE epic, the southern redactor known as Rje because he redacts J and E together to form a single narrative. This suggests that the redaction of the story has to be close to or after the destruction of the northern kingdom in 722 BCE.

This is not exactly like saying that the 1 Kings story is historical while the Exodus story is purely fiction. Neither is guaranteed to be history, and certainly Jeroboam's rebellion is being told tendentiously from the point of view of the south. Since Hosea tells us that Jacob's struggle with the angel is an aspect of the Bethel worship, it seems clear that Jeroboam was not praying to a foreign god by setting up calves at Dan and Bethel. He is praying to the God of Israel, the same God to which the south prayed, only through different names and different symbols. Jeroboam's God could just as easily be symbolized by the calf or riding on a calf in the way that YHWH could be envisioned as riding between the cherubim, which are fantastical griffon-like animals in the ancient Near East. We have lots of depictions of ancient Near Eastern gods standing on the backs of their signature animal forms. Other rebellions are recounted in the wanderings of the children of Israel. 1 Kings has also had a chance to be reformulated in oral and written form and rewritten to correspond to the text in Exodus 32.

Jeroboam's Calf Is Historical: The Calf at Sinai—Not So Much

The events in 1 Kings happened in some fashion. The entirely independent reports of Hosea and Amos, completely different sources within the Bible, when taken together with the archaeological evidence, seem to guarantee the historicity of the religious reform of the northern kings and their policies. But there is no archaeological evidence anywhere guaranteeing the historicity of the stories in the Exodus tradition. Perhaps there is a context in which some of the events of the Exodus tradition make sense. That is all that can be said for sure. Given our current state of knowledge, there is a historical kernel to the 1 Kings 32 passage, while the Exodus story so far can only be verified as a story stuck into the Sinai narrative reflecting a southern polemic warning of the consequences of Jeroboam I's successful rebellion.

We have, however, a ready reason why the stories grew together in this way in the south. The largest group of tribes, the northern tribes, have withdrawn from the southern confederacy. They have spurned God's anointed ruler, the messiah of Israel sitting on the throne of Judah. The difficulties that this piece of cognitive dissonance would have caused in the south cannot be underestimated. One can actually feel the polemic in the description of the golden calf rebellion in Exodus. According to the Exodus account, Aaron gives the people what they want. They want other gods. It is easy to read this as the desire of the populace in the north and Aaron's cooperation as the partial cooperation of the Aaronides but the staunch defense of the Levites.

Then Moses imposes a test on the people: "Who is on the LORD's side? Come to me" The Levites serve as the agents of punishment and kill the sinners (32:26). This can be read as projected vengeance against the north and a plea for northerners to immigrate south and reaffirm their fealty to the Davidic king. It says, in short, that the northerners need to come south to avoid the vengeance. This is, in fact, what happened after Assyria attacked and conquered the north. We know that the population of Jerusalem increased greatly after the Assyrian conquest. The south is proposing in the story of the Exodus golden calf that the deaths of the rebels is a kind of sacrifice. And there is no escape because everyone's name is written down. Vengeance is complete. The Exodus story of the rebellion of Aaron is a polemic meant to help understand what great sinning the rebellion of Jeroboam was. And to my mind there is no need to make that polemic if it were already known in advance that Josiah would break down the *bamoth* of the northern kingdom and Assyria would destroy the northern kingdom.

The Deuteronomistic Historian Has a Better Explanation

No matter how much history is actually encoded in the Jeroboam story, the golden calf story in the Exodus story is a myth, and it is a myth that makes the most sense of the situation before the northern kingdom is destroyed.

After that, the Deuteronomistic Historian's explicit polemic of the destruction of the north as a result of their sinning and rebellion from the south makes far more sense as moral literature. Noting that the northern kingdom was destroyed is the final, and unassailable, historical argument, whereas the story of the golden calf is a mythological polemic. The historical facts beat the mythical polemic. But, before that moment, the argument against the north has to be a bit more oblique because no one knew in advance that Assyria was going to destroy the northern kingdom entirely and carry all its inhabitants away into servitude. That could not have been evident until after the destruction of the north.

The story of the golden calf in Exodus is therefore more than fiction; it is a myth—a polemical myth at that—the purpose of which is to make the rebellion of Jeroboam understandable as the horrifying sin that the southern kingship thought it was, even before the punishment of the Assyrian destruction and reconquest of Josiah made that crystal clear to the Deuteronomistic Historian. It was, as it were, the previous, less effective explanation for Jeroboam's rebellion. So it must have evolved long before the Assyrian destruction and the reconquest by Josiah to make clear what a sin Jeroboam had committed before the punishment was obvious to everyone, but then be brought up into the larger aims of the redactor afterward. It is therefore a demonstration that historical events we find in Kings generated moral ambiguities and cognitive dissonances. Mythological stories projected back on the Exodus tradition or the patriarchal period helped clarify moral lessons of the superiority of the south. For Israel, the patriarchal period and the Exodus serve as *illud tempus*, "that time," the name scholars of religion give to the period in which the myths take place. During those periods God appeared directly to intervene in actions and made clear moral lessons possible. To use the correct Latin in the oblique tense, everything before the settlement in the land, whether some of it happened or not, takes place *in illo tempore*, "in that (mythic) time," for the Judeans. And that is why we are justified in calling the material in the patriarchal period and the Exodus a myth. The rebellion of Jeroboam I is the real cause of the story of the rebellion of the golden calf at Sinai. And the story clarifies that the people of the north are terrible sinners, before the destruction of the north, when that was to become obvious.

CHAPTER THREE

A Historical Tragedy

The Short-Lived Deuteronomic Reform

Four Books of Moses and a New Explanation of History

By the time we get to the end of the First Temple period (950–587 BCE), we grow more certain of the historicity of the biblical narrative.[1] We saw this clearly in the last chapter. Traditionally, we say that the Bible begins with the five books of Moses. From a literary point of view, the Bible is probably best divided up into a tetrateuch, four books comprising Genesis through Numbers, leaving Deuteronomy and Joshua through 2 Kings as a great history of the Davidic kingdom and the dynasty of David or, as it was known by its neighbors, "the house of David." When we compare the root stories in Genesis through Numbers to each other and to the stories in the former prophets, study of myth and folklore seem like the most important tools for understanding them. This does not mean that the events in them did not happen in some form, but it does mean that they were greatly affected by oral transmission and the events in the great history, transforming into myth for the people living in the First Temple times. And we can see that the latest periods of transmission are usually the most clearly identifiable in the narrative.

Deuteronomy: From Mythology to Piety

But when we look to the book of Deuteronomy and the editorial work in the former prophets, we see a very different kind of historiography. Someone deeply imbued with the moral conclusions of Deuteronomy has edited the historical events in the books of Joshua, Judges, the Samuels, and Kings to represent not mythical but moral meanings. So Deuteronomy represents a watershed in the source theory and an enormous change in the narrator's perspective thereafter.

In fact, identifying the voice of the book of Deuteronomy is the keystone of the entire documentary hypothesis in biblical scholarship. It is the only source of the Pentateuch that can be associated with an entire book and the only source that can be dated with any certainty.

Finding the Book

The core of Deuteronomy appears to be the book that Josiah found in the Temple when he was having it cleansed and purified:

> The high priest Hilkiah said to Shaphan the secretary, "I have found the book of the law in the house of the LORD." When Hilkiah gave the book to Shaphan, he read it. ⁹ Then Shaphan the secretary came to the king, and reported to the king, "Your servants have emptied out the money that was found in the house, and have delivered it into the hand of the workers who have oversight of the house of the LORD." ¹⁰ Shaphan the secretary informed the king, "The priest Hilkiah has given me a book." Shaphan then read it aloud to the king. ¹¹ When the king heard the words of the book of the law, he tore his clothes. ¹² Then the king commanded the priest Hilkiah, Ahikam son of Shaphan, Achbor son of Micaiah, Shaphan the secretary, and the king's servant Asaiah, saying, ¹³ "Go, inquire of the LORD for me, for the people, and for all Judah, concerning the words of this book that has been found; for great is the wrath of the LORD that is kindled against us, because our ancestors did not obey the words of this book, to do according to all that is written concerning us."
>
> (2 Kings 22:8–13)

The book is authenticated and serves as the basis for Josiah's reform, which cleanses the Temple, reconquers the territory of the former northern kingdom (then an Assyrian possession), and centralizes worship in the south at the Temple in Jerusalem that Solomon built. No longer is the Temple to be just a royal chapel for the kings of Judah or the Temple of the Judean people but it will now be the Temple for a newly reconstituted kingdom of Israel, more or less on the Davidic model. In fact, the beginning of the rule of Josiah is greeted with a surprising formula in 2 Kings. Instead of the standard greeting, we see that Josiah's reign is met with a very positive judgment in a formula that, not surprisingly, is written in the style of the Deuteronomistic Historian: "Josiah was eight years old when he began to reign; he reigned thirty-one years in Jerusalem. His mother's name was Jedidah daughter of Adaiah of Bozkath.[2] He did what was right in the sight of the LORD, and walked in all the ways of his father David; he did not turn aside to the right or to the left" (2 Kings 22:1–2).

This is a stunningly promising summary statement, even for a king of Judah. And it introduces us to a voice we have heard before, the Deuteronomistic Historian (whom we shall call DH). Very few kings receive a favorable judgment. David, who though he sinned greatly also repented sincerely, receives nominally the highest positive notice. Then we find that Asa, Azariah, Hezekiah, Jehoshaphat, Jotham, Uzziah, and Josiah also receive positive evaluations. Since there were no kings deserving any praise in the north, the greatest kings are, in the eyes of the books of Kings, principally Hezekiah, Jehoshaphat, and Josiah in the south. But, really, only Josiah receives a wholly positive report; in many ways, his evaluation is far better than David's or Solomon's. It will turn out, of course, that these judgments are entirely made by the standards of the book of Deuteronomy, and so we think of these historical books—Joshua, Judges, 1 and 2 Samuel, 1 and 2 Kings—as the editorial product of the DH. That does not gainsay the importance of the historical sources DH must have used. But they cannot be traced as easily as the editor's voice, which we find both in Deuteronomy and in the historical books.

For example, in the book of Deuteronomy we find this advice, in very similar language to that which is applied to Josiah, directed to the ideal king: "You must therefore be careful to do as the LORD your God has commanded you; you shall not turn to the right or to the left" (Deuteronomy 5:32, see also Deuteronomy 17:11, 17:20 with regard to the king, and Deuteronomy 28:14). Even more obvious is the summary statement of Josiah's reign in 2 Kings 23:25: "Before him there was no king like him who turned to the LORD with all his heart and all his soul and all his might according to the law of Moses; nor did any like him arise after him." This too is repeated in Deuteronomy 6:5: "You shall love the LORD your God with all your heart, and with all your soul, and with all your might." Obviously, this is high praise. His success was due to his piety for the Lord. And the language again is specifically Deuteronomic. Moses is described in Deuteronomy with similar superlatives: "And there has not arisen a prophet since in Israel like Moses, whom the LORD knew face to face, none like him for all the signs and wonders which the LORD sent him to do in the land of Egypt" (Deuteronomy 34:10–12).

There was good reason to be enthusiastic over Josiah's reign. According to 2 Kings 22–23, he cleansed the south of its idolatry and then reestablished Judahite hegemony over the north, the former northern state of Israel. It was the first time that a Judahite leader had reigned in the north since the split of the kingdom in the tenth century BCE. That was three hundred years earlier.

Clearly, an enormous amount of excitement was generated by Josiah's reign. But since it began in his early youth, we should not expect the credit to be his alone. He was the spokesperson and king of a reform movement that had been growing underground all during the reigns of the previous two kings, Amon and Manasseh. They had both been vassals of Assyria. But Amon was killed by his servants in a palace insurrection, and a group of people called "the people of the land" (probably, in this period, the rural aristocracy) put the young Josiah on the throne: "The servants of Amon conspired against him, and killed the king in his house. The people of the land killed all those who had conspired against King Amon, and the people of the land made his son Josiah king in place of him" (2 Kings 21:23–24).

The Josiah of Deuteronomy

In fact, Josiah should receive Deuteronomy's praise for many reasons. He seems to obey Deuteronomy in virtually everything that he does, especially in his reform. If one compares the laws in Deuteronomy with the campaign of Josiah to centralize and purify the lands of Israel and Judah, one finds an almost complete agreement, down to the exact language:

abolition of the asherim:	Deuteronomy 7:15	2 Kings 23:4, 6–7
end the cult of stars:	Deuteronomy 17:3	2 Kings 23:4–5

end sun/moon worship:	Deuteronomy 17:3	2 Kings 23:5,11
destroy cult prostitution:	Deuteronomy 23:18	2 Kings 23:7
defile Moloch cult place:	Deuteronomy 12:31	2 Kings 12:10
destroy high places:	Deuteronomy 7:15	2 Kings 23:13
remove foreign idols:	Deuteronomy 12:1–32	2 Kings 23:13
break the pillar idols:	Deuteronomy 12:3	2 Kings 23:14
renew the feast of Passover:	Deuteronomy 16:1–8	2 Kings 23:21–22
forbid the cult of the dead:	Deuteronomy 18:11	2 Kings 23:24

There are other impressive agreements in vocabulary between Deuteronomy and the reform of Josiah. Deuteronomy calls itself "the book of the Torah" (*sefer ha-torah*) in Deuteronomy 33:4 and Deuteronomy 28:61. As opposed to most of the other traditions we have been following, which have an oral substratum, Deuteronomy is written down as a scroll (*sefer*). In Deuteronomy 17:18 we learn that the book has a purpose. The king should consult a "copy of the law" (*mishneh ha-torah*), which should be at his side when he rules. Deuteronomy 4:44 says this is the Torah that Moses put before the people of Israel through the mouth of YHWH by the hand of Moses. It seems, then, that Josiah's law book was some form of the book of Deuteronomy, whatever could be read publicly in one day, probably at the middle sections that run from chapters 4–28 and the curses at the end. They would have to be there to explain the dire reaction the book has on the king and those who hear it declaimed publicly.

The Stages of Josiah's Reform

If it all took place in the eighteenth year of King Josiah's reign, that would make the Josianic reform and the celebratory covenant renewal ceremony that takes place at Passover to be 622/621 BCE. And that is the most exact date we have for a literary source in the Pentateuch. It means JE comes before 621 BCE, that the Deuteronomistic history must be somewhat later. The final editing of P must come yet afterward, probably edited on earlier material starting in the Second Commonwealth, after the Babylonian exile (587 BCE–532 BCE), though some versions of the laws in P appear to be earlier than the book of Deuteronomy, so P, as a voice within the culture, probably is earlier than the identifiable voice of Deuteronomy. Of course, P continues into the Persian period (532 BCE–ca. 333 BCE) that succeeds the Babylonian exile, when the Judeans return from Babylonian captivity and begin a Second Commonwealth.

In the book of 2 Kings, Josiah appears to enact the entire reform in one single operation. But Josiah's reform is also described in 2 Chronicles 33–34, where it happens in stages—the eighth, the twelfth, and the eighteenth year of Josiah's reign. Though, in general, 1 and 2 Kings are to be preferred as more historical and closer to the events than the parallel accounts in 1 and 2 Chronicles, this later description of Josiah's reform in 2 Chronicles 33–34 has much to recommend it, especially when we look at the international politics of Josiah's day. We know that after the death of Assyrian emperor Ashurbanipal, the Assyrian empire collapsed rather quickly. Ashurbanipal died in 627 BCE but must have been unable to police his territories in the Galilee and Samaria because Josiah made two bold moves before the death of the emperor, the first in 632 BCE (Josiah's eighth year) and the second in 628 BCE (Josiah's twelfth year), just before the Assyrian emperor's death. From 627 to 612 BCE, Assyria had three or four weak leaders who engaged in costly internecine fighting and who therefore could not control the territory of their empire. In fact, Nineveh had already fallen, and the remains of the royal family had attempted to reestablish rule in Harran. Josiah and his party must have been watching international events very carefully, only extending his territory northward to the boundaries of the old Israelite state as Assyrian power waned.

The Tragedy of Josiah

Sadly, the political aspect, the national resurgence of the Josianic reform, was short-lived, as Josiah himself was tragically killed in battle against the Egyptians in 609 BCE. On the other hand, the religious and cultural aspects of the reform were much more long lasting, as the Deuteronomistic Historian, imbued with Deuteronomic theology, compiled the history that goes from Deuteronomy to the end of 2 Kings. As a result, however, we see an interesting phenomenon in the mixture of good auguries and dire prophecies that were offered at the beginning of Josiah's reign.

> Thus says the LORD, the God of Israel: Tell the man who sent you to me, 16 Thus says the LORD, I will indeed bring disaster on this place and on its inhabitants—all the words of the book that the king of Judah has read. 17 Because they have abandoned me and have made offerings to

other gods, so that they have provoked me to anger with all the work of their hands, therefore my wrath will be kindled against this place, and it will not be quenched. [18] But as to the king of Judah, who sent you to inquire of the LORD, thus shall you say to him, Thus says the LORD, the God of Israel: Regarding the words that you have heard, [19] because your heart was penitent, and you humbled yourself before the LORD, when you heard how I spoke against this place, and against its inhabitants, that they should become a desolation and a curse, and because you have torn your clothes and wept before me, I also have heard you, says the LORD. [20] Therefore, I will gather you to your ancestors, and you shall be gathered to your grave in peace; your eyes shall not see all the disaster that I will bring on this place." They took the message back to the king.

(2 Kings 22:15–20)

Part of the time, the voice of the prophetess Huldah must be supplied by a later writer, a voice that knows that the kingdom of Judah will be destroyed in 587 BCE. It will turn out to be the Deuteronomistic Historian again. But starting in verse 20 there is an earlier voice. This may be the authentic prophecy from Huldah because it promises a long, good life for Josiah, followed by a peaceful death. I say this because a peaceful death was not Josiah's end: he died in battle against Pharaoh Neccho. There is only one explanation for a prophecy that does not come true; it is the actual prophecy offered at the occasion, which somehow survived the incredible pressure to doctor it up to what actually happened.

The events of Josiah's demise could hardly have been anticipated and must have been heartbreaking to the Deuteronomic party, as we see in the later material forecasting doom in the prophecy but actually merely recounting events that had already happened. After fighting against Assyria for so many years, Egypt turned to become its ally only briefly at the very end of the Assyrian period, to prevent the Neo-Babylonian Empire from becoming the dominant power of the Middle East. Josiah was acting as an ally of the Babylonians and had gone out to meet the Egyptians to prevent them from joining the battle to rescue the Assyrian army. And it was in this strange last gasp of Assyrian influence that Josiah, unexpectedly, lost his life, making the original prophecy of his peaceful reign look false. On the other hand, the Judean army was able to claim the body and bring it back to be buried with Josiah's Davidic ancestors. That may have been enough to have convinced Josiah's contemporaries to preserve Huldah's original words in the longer prophecy, which should properly be called a *vaticinium ex eventu*, a prophecy written after the fact. In this case, the composer is again the Deuteronomistic Historian.

Covenant Renewal

Once the connection between Josiah's reform and the precipitous decline of Assyrian power is clarified, then another aspect of the book comes into focus—its interest in the covenant renewal ceremony that Josiah celebrates in 621 BCE, as related in 2 Kings 23: "The king commanded all the people, 'Keep the Passover to the LORD your God as prescribed in this book of the covenant.' ²² No such Passover had been kept since the days of the judges who judged Israel, even during all the days of the kings of Israel and of the kings of Judah; ²³ but in the eighteenth year of King Josiah this Passover was kept to the LORD in Jerusalem" (2 Kings 23:21–23). This public ceremony, no doubt, served as the ritual occasion for a renewal of independent government after so many years of Assyrian rule. The covenant renewal ceremony served as a national independence day and was accompanied by a religious reform. The covenant or contract with God had been part of Israelite lore throughout the JE epic. It is in fact one of the greatest mythic motifs underlying the Bible. But we see in the Deuteronomic form of the story a much more rationalized understanding of the covenant.

During the period of Josiah's reform the covenant becomes a major aspect of Israel's story as Josiah's advisers, his royal bureaucracy and the priests of the Temple mainly, understood the reform to be a national resurgence as well as a religious holiday. Their pattern for the covenant turns out to be something with which the royal and priestly bureaucracy was very familiar: an Assyrian vassal treaty. They had been subject to an Assyrian vassal treaty throughout the reigns of the previous two kings, Manasseh and Amon, who were judged to be evil in the eyes of the Deuteronomistic Historians. Together, the kings ruled some fifty-seven years by assuaging the Assyrian overlord. The political aspects of Josiah's reform were, unfortunately, much shorter, confined to thirty-one years, but the effects lasted much longer.

In fact the entire cultic book of Deuteronomy resembles nothing so much as an enormous Assyrian vassal treaty:

1. Preamble 1:1
2. Historical prologue 1:2–4:40

3. Ordinances 4:44–26:19
4. Provisions for reading 27:8
5. Curses and blessings 27–28

This is the outline of a general international treaty. It uses the legal language characteristic of treaties in the ancient world, but with a special emphasis on terminology from Mesopotamia. It has provisions for public reading of the treaty, which was a common rite of fealty in vassal treaties. It was enforced by oaths taken in front of the gods and the people. But what makes it most identifiable as an Assyrian treaty is the attention and emphasis on the curses. Just as a New York lease looks like leases from other places, except that it has a very healthy section of forfeits and penalties, so too an Assyrian vassal treaty looked like other ancient Near Eastern treaties, but characteristically contained a great many more curses than the standard ancient international treaty. The book of Deuteronomy follows suit, promising curses and more curses to those who disobey the Lord's covenant (e.g., chapters 27–28). And that, no doubt, was responsible for the reactions of grief from the king and his servants:

> [11] When the king heard the words of the book of the law, he tore his clothes. [12] Then the king commanded the priest Hilkiah, Ahikam son of Shaphan, Achbor son of Micaiah, Shaphan the secretary, and the king's servant Asaiah, saying, [13] "Go, inquire of the LORD for me, for the people, and for all Judah, concerning the words of this book that has been found; for great is the wrath of the LORD that is kindled against us, because our ancestors did not obey the words of this book, to do according to all that is written concerning us."
>
> (2 Kings 22:11–13)

The Deuteronomistic Historian

The hand of the Deuteronomistic Historian is most obvious in the stories of the conquest and settlement. The book of Joshua 1–12 presents us with one particular view of the period. According to the book of Joshua, the children of Israel cross the Jordan on dry land (Joshua 3:15–17). This reprise of the miracle at the Red Sea, when the children of Israel were fleeing the Egyptians, is a worthy start to a miraculous, short, conquest of Canaan. The victorious crossing of the Jordan sets up the first campaign, in which the children of Israel conquer Jericho, the walls falling to the sound of trumpets (Joshua 6). They then capture Ai by a ruse. This campaign takes the Israelites as far as Shechem with very little resistance. There Joshua builds an altar on a mountain overlooking the city (Joshua 8:30–35).

A second campaign takes the children of Israel southward. They wisely avoid Jerusalem, astutely making a treaty with Gibeon and other Canaanites (Joshua 9). This gives them time to regroup, but fails when the Gibeonites were threatened by a large coalition of Canaanite kings, including Adonizedek, king of Jerusalem. But Joshua defeats them in a large battle at Gibeon, in which both the sun and moon stand still (Joshua 10:12–13).

The text quotes a lost book, called the book of Jashar (see also 2 Samuel 1:18), to demonstrate the miracle. But it looks like the text is quoting the book of Jashar's hypothetical poetic exaggeration as if it literally happened.

In a third campaign the Israelites turn northward and win significant victories in the north, culminating in the destruction of the large fortified city of Hazor. The complete conquest of Canaan takes less than four years and ends with the whole land in their territory. "So Joshua took the whole land, according to all that the LORD had spoken to Moses; and Joshua gave it for an inheritance to Israel according to their tribal allotments. And the land had rest from war" (Joshua 11:23). This whole account is infused with the voice of the Deuteronomistic Historian, who clearly glorifies the account. The account is, in some way, just as miraculous as the conquests of Josiah some six centuries later, a conquest with which the Deuteronomistic Historian had more familiarity.

Judges

The situation in the book of Judges, also heavily redacted by the Deuteronomistic Historian, is very different. The children of Israel backslide again and again. To discipline them and reawaken their fear of God, YHWH must allow them to be repeatedly conquered by one of the surrounding peoples, who are still very powerful and whose culture is still very attractive. When they pray for deliverance from the Lord, God raises a judge to defend them. He throws off Canaanite domination and the land has peace again. But soon the cycle starts all over.

Of all the voices that make up the Bible, the Deuteronomistic Historian is the easiest to identify. The narrator is a moralist. Misfortune comes to the people and rulers when they sin and good comes when they cry out to the LORD. The cycle can be seen most clearly in Judges where editorial comments always underline that God wants his people to follow and acknowledge him:

¹¹ Then the Israelites did what was evil in the sight of the LORD and worshiped the Baals; ¹² and they abandoned the LORD, the God of their ancestors, who had brought them out of the land of Egypt; they followed other gods, from among the gods of the peoples who were all around them, and bowed down to them; and they provoked the LORD to anger. ¹³ They abandoned the LORD, and worshiped Baal and the Astartes. ¹⁴ So the anger of the LORD was kindled against Israel, and he gave them over to plunderers who plundered them, and he sold them into the power of their enemies all around, so that they could no longer withstand their enemies. ¹⁵ Whenever they marched out, the hand of the LORD was against them to bring misfortune, as the LORD had warned them and sworn to them; and they were in great distress.

¹⁶ Then the LORD raised up judges, who delivered them out of the power of those who plundered them. ¹⁷ Yet they did not listen even to their judges; for they lusted after other gods and bowed down to them. They soon turned aside from the way in which their ancestors had walked, who had obeyed the commandments of the LORD; they did not follow their example. ¹⁸ Whenever the LORD raised up judges for them, the LORD was with the judge, and he delivered them from the hand of their enemies all the days of the judge; for the LORD would be moved to pity by their groaning because of those who persecuted and oppressed them. ¹⁹ But whenever the judge died, they would relapse and behave worse than their ancestors, following other gods, worshiping them and bowing down to them. They would not drop any of their practices or their stubborn ways. ²⁰ So the anger of the LORD was kindled against Israel; and he said, "Because this people have transgressed my covenant that I commanded their ancestors, and have not obeyed my voice, ²¹ I will no longer drive out before them any of the nations that Joshua left when he died." ²² In order to test Israel, whether or not they would take care to walk in the way of the LORD as their ancestors did, ²³ the LORD had left those nations, not driving them out at once, and had not handed them over to Joshua.

(Judges 2:11–23)

A HISTORICAL TRAGEDY

This long passage is the summary paradigm for the mission of each individual judge. As a frame narrative for each of the judges, it is the Deuteronomistic Historian who creates the pattern of sin and atonement out of the raw material of tradition he had somehow gathered. Since the language is often uniform, it is clear he rephrases and retells much of the material that comes to him. But other pieces, like the Song of Deborah, were already fixed poetry. In this case he creates a prose preface (Judges 4) and then includes the Song of Deborah (Judges 5).

Other Editing Characteristics

One interesting aspect of the Deuteronomistic Historian's editing of the succession narrative and the Court History that follows in 1 and 2 Samuel and 1 and 2 Kings is how intimate it is. We do not get many background details. Since it is played against a black field, it would be almost as suitable for a rich surrounding. We moderns have tended to assume that the narrative takes place in opulent palaces, but we shall see that the archaeology shows the earliest stories, especially anything in the early history of the kingship, to have taken place in rather modest circumstances.

It is hard to know where the original stories come from. Some probably derive from official documents of state, as the formula for each king shows, listing the regnal years, the name of the mother, and other summaries details. It is quite possible that the original JE epic continued into this period. We add to that the summary judgment about the significance of the reign, which is supplied by the moralistic thinker, the Deuteronomistic Historian. Perhaps the intimate material was less formal—some oral, some coming from stories that grew up around the court but outside of the official court narrative. One wonders whether this is no accident and is instead a result of the multiple sources. As we have seen, the reader is treated to a number of puzzling gaps in the writing and a minimum of often telling details, so narrative skill is being used throughout. The editor is, in most cases, identifiable as the Deuteronomistic Historian, a redactor greatly influenced by the perspective of Deuteronomy. Wherever Deuteronomy originally came from, it quickly became a document passed on by the bureaucracies of the king and of the Temple. It recognizes what an Assyrian vassal treaty looked like and it espouses an ideology that reliably accords rewards to those who act well and punishment to those who do not. This *eudaimonism* in ethics is not a prophetic insight but the kind of ideology that adheres to bureaucracies and wisdom writers.

In fact, though many scholars have seen prophetic and northern influence throughout the book, which I do not gainsay, the book of Deuteronomy is the most critical of prophetic contributions and suggests that a true prophet can be identified by simply watching if his prophecies come true (Deuteronomy 18:22). The prophets themselves would never describe their prophecy in such simple terms. They speak out so that the people will listen to the word of the LORD, repent, and spare themselves the great punishments that are to come, which is, indeed what the Deuteronomistic Historian thinks as well. But the book of Deuteronomy is much more practical about it. The voice of Deuteronomy itself is the voice of the royal, scribal bureaucracy that is charged with training the king. The Deuteronomistic Historians, at least in their final redactions, have reason to agree more wholeheartedly with the prophets because they know what the outcome of the story is.

Myth and Moralism

The original stories in the Pentateuch and the former prophets were related to each other by chronological order. In effect the Pentateuch was the mythic life of the community, generated out of the difficulties that were worried about and remembered in the early period. As Lévi-Strauss has said, myth is a story that mediates contradictions. Myth can do a lot of other things, but we will see that mediating a contradiction is especially obvious in the story of the succession of Solomon. In spite of Solomon's youth and lack of position in the court, he succeeded to the throne. In spite of the fact that he was not a child of one of David's senior wives but instead a child of what had been an adulterous relationship, he inherits the kingdom.

None of this could have been accepted easily. The Deuteronomistic Historian helps the JE epic by adding comments of its own. But, basically, the Deuteronomistic Historian gives us the connected story of Joshua through 2 Kings by ranking the actions and the personages based on how closely they come to the superior moral promulgated by the book of Deuteronomy under King Josiah.

Later on we shall see that some of the ancient tradition appears to be made up—as in the exciting saga of how David slew Goliath with a sling. It turns David into a great military hero, even as a boy. This is understandable in folklore around the world. It was not necessarily made up by the Deuteronomistic Historian, only retold by him, and the indiscretions of David are turned into the reasons why the succession of Solomon was so surprising and unexpected.

Most mythology that we know contains a family metaphor. In the Greek myths, we readily describe the relationships between the gods as due to their family relationships. For example, Hera is the wife of Zeus; Athena is his offspring. The metaphor generates a comprehensible and comprehensive order for the stories. Myth also readily combines into groups of related stories, which we call a mythology.

The Israelite principle (which the JE editor, the Deuteronomist, the priestly writer, and the Deuteronomistic Historian take) obviously includes family relationships, as it does among the ancient Greeks. However, the family is a human family, a legendary and mythological form of their ancestors. But that form also includes a very strict historical principle. The stories are related to each other through the course of history. The Deuteronomistic Historian adds the notion that history is strictly governed by God's pleasure or displeasure with the moral behavior of the Israelites. The JE epic may be said to have exemplified much of that in God's direct intervention to make sure each generation was saved and continued the story. But the moral standard was not so clearly articulated, emphasized, and sermonized. And, as we have seen, the early material is often morally ambiguous and puzzling, if not downright mysterious—as in the case of the wife-sister motif.

Prophecies and Deuteronomistic Reworkings

There are some places where the Deuteronomistic history can be seen right beside the earlier traditions. This happens in very important moments. One such moment that can be easily illustrated is the eternal promise made to David by God through Nathan the prophet in 2 Samuel 7:

> 4 But that same night the word of the LORD came to Nathan: 5 Go and tell my servant David: Thus says the LORD: Are you the one to build me a house to live in? 6 I have not lived in a house since the day I brought up the people of Israel from Egypt to this day, but I have been moving about in a tent and a tabernacle. 7 Wherever I have moved about among all the people of Israel, did I ever speak a word with any of the

tribal leaders of Israel, whom I commanded to shepherd my people
Israel, saying, "Why have you not built me a house of cedar?"

(2 Samuel 7:1–17)

The story is well formed. It begins with Nathan offering his opinion to David: "¹Now when the king was settled in his house, and the LORD had given him rest from all his enemies around him, ² the king said to the prophet Nathan, "See now, I am living in a house of cedar, but the ark of God stays in a tent." ³ Nathan said to the king, "Go, do all that you have in mind; for the LORD is with you" (2 Samuel 7:1–3). But that night YHWH comes to Nathan in a dream and countermands his advice with an oracle. Through Nathan, YHWH gives David quite a tongue-lashing.

The speech drips with irony. It reminds David that it was he, YHWH, who produced all this good fortune for David: David was not by his own hand allowed to rise and unify a kingdom. He was, like each of the judges, the most unlikely person to lead. YHWH did it because it pleased him to do it and because it emphasized his own role in the history of Israel. He simply used David to accomplish his ends. This very nicely sums up the theory of judgeship and the kingship of Saul as well. The Lord essentially says that he likes living in a tent and so asks David sharply why he thinks he, David, should make YHWH a house:

> ⁸ Now therefore thus you shall say to my servant David: Thus says the LORD of hosts: I took you from the pasture, from following the sheep to be prince over my people Israel; ⁹ and I have been with you wherever you went, and have cut off all your enemies from before you; and I will make for you a great name, like the name of the great ones of the earth. ¹⁰ And I will appoint a place for my people Israel and will plant them, so that they may live in their own place, and be disturbed no more; and evildoers shall afflict them no more, as formerly, ¹¹ from the time that I appointed judges over my people Israel; and I will give you rest from all your enemies.

(2 Samuel 7:8–11)

Perhaps this is just a way of explaining why it was not David but Solomon who built the Temple. But it definitely also links the history of the people Israel with the story of David. Both are small but were magnified because it pleased God to do so. And it critiques the former, looser confederation of tribes as weak and ineffectual. Indeed it was unable to provide adequate defense against the Philistine invasion of the hill country. It even uses the antique word for king that we find in the story of Saul, *nagid*, which means something closer to military dictator, in this case, a person who arises in a military crisis and whose legitimacy lasts only as long as the crisis lasts. It seems likely that this was the office Saul had achieved. He was unable to overcome the strength of Israel's enemies and died before he could establish his family as an inherited, dynastic king.

But part of the prophecy must also be earlier than Deuteronomy because it essentially promises the throne to David's dynasty forever. Playing on the multiple meanings of the word *house*—a temple, a dynasty, a residence—and completely in character, YHWH then promises David a dynasty that will rule after him. But the fate of David and the fate of Israel seem to be melded in the latter part of the prophecy:

> Moreover the LORD declares to you that the LORD will make you a house. ¹² When your days are fulfilled and you lie down with your ancestors, I will raise up your offspring after you, who shall come forth from your body, and I will establish his kingdom. ¹³ He shall build a house for my name, and I will establish the throne of his kingdom forever. ¹⁴ I will be a father to him, and he shall be a son to me. When he commits iniquity, I will punish him with a rod such as mortals use, with blows inflicted by human beings. ¹⁵ But I will not take my steadfast love from him, as I took it from Saul, whom I put away from before you. ¹⁶ Your house and your kingdom shall be made sure forever before me; your throne shall be established forever. ¹⁷ In accordance with all these words and with all this vision, Nathan spoke to David.
>
> (2 Samuel 7:11–17)

This is an earlier source than the Deuteronomistic Historian because it stipulates that David will never fail to have an heir on the throne of Judah. It is in fact a new codicil in the covenant agreement because it implies a double acceptance formula: "I will be your father, you shall be my son," (2 Samuel 7:14) as part of the language of promise. It shows, perhaps, Deuteronomistic editing in saying that a sinning king will be afflicted with punishments. However, it never says that the promise can be taken away, which is the opposite of what the Deuteronomistic Historian must have thought, since the last editor in the Deuteronomistic Historian's school knows that the kingdom ended when Jerusalem was conquered by the Babylonians. Or, to put the phenomenon in alternative terms, this would suggest that there was more than one redaction by Deuteronomistic Historians, with the later editors reluctant to remove any previous text.

Or perhaps the narrator left the story the way it was to emphasize that the continuing heir to David, perhaps Zerubbabel or Sheshbezzar, will reign after an interregnum. In doing so, it unwittingly adds a great deal to the legend of a future, ideal Messiah. Throughout the Hebrew Bible, up until this point, the "messiah," or anointed one, was the current and present anointed king, priest, or prophet in Israel. There were, of course, bad kings and the hope that one day there might be a wholly good king—Josiah or, after him, a king like him and David. In the Court History most of that language applies to Josiah, who is always the expected king. But afterward it was the return of a scion of David's dynasty. So, for the concept of a future Messiah to gain traction, there first of all had to be a lack of a current one, and that happens for the first time after the exile. Nor does the tradition begin so quickly after the exile. It has to wait for the appropriate social situation of oppression to produce it.

The story of Nathan's prophecy is older than the Deuteronomist because it essentially promises that David's dynasty will live forever on the throne of Judah. Nathan's prophecy is rendered with simple ironies and surprises. At first Nathan tells David to do what he pleases and build the Temple for God. But, that night, God intervenes and gives David a good bawling out: How can you, mortal, make me a house? I have been going around in a tent all these years and am quite pleased to be doing so. Instead, I will make you a house. The narrator plays with the words—*house* can certainly mean "temple," as it does in almost all Semitic languages. But here YHWH uses it to mean dynasty. Instead of David making YHWH a house, YHWH will make David a dynasty. That dynasty will last forever, a statement that must come before the Deuteronomistic Historian because, when it was finally edited, the end of the state, if not the dynasty, would have been well understood.

Moral Meanings Replace Mythic Meanings

The Deuteronomistic Historian, as we have seen, tends to replace previous mythical issues with more directly historical reasoning. We have already seen, in comparing traditions about Jeroboam and the golden calf, that the

DH knows the best argument against Jeroboam and the kind of Yahwism practiced by the northern kingdom is a historical argument about the Assyrian destruction of the north. The earlier argument against them was an elaborate JE comparison between the northern kingdom's calf worship and its heretical nature at Sinai.

This use of a more explicit historiographical argument is clear evidence that the Deuteronomistic material is later than JE and more effective in making its points. It obviously depends on knowing a great deal more historical information, including the outcome of the story of the northern kingdom. As a result, this progress can easily be placed on any number of evolutionary schemes. For example, Deuteronomy counts as the most obvious step forward in Robert Wright's scale, as described in his book, *The Evolution of God*.[2] I suggest this to argue against Wellhausen's judgment that D and P are a step down from the originally more exalted description of the relationship between Israel and God in JE. Of course, JE represents a great mythical saga. But in other ways, D and P are more sophisticated in their pietistic understanding of God and history. So, more obviously, these descriptions of the changes in the way that God and history are described in the Bible are not due to a change in God but rather to a change in the sophistication of human understandings of him.

CHAPTER FOUR

The Concubine of the Levite

A Complete Horror

When There Was No King

Phyllis Trible, in her book *Texts of Terror*, describes the events of the end of Judges as "a world of unrelenting terror."[1] She is right. The book is a catalogue of violence, while the so-called epilogue of Judges outdoes the entire rest of the book for horror. The events almost will not bear describing. The whole passage begins with one of the summary expressions of the book of Judges: "In those days, when there was no king in Israel . . ." or more completely, at the end, when all ambiguity is put aside: "In those days there was no king in Israel; all the people did what was right in their own eyes." Throughout the book, this phrase carries a certain ambiguity because it seems to express nostalgia for the old days. That would mean and does mean that the narrator is speaking of a time long after the events. But by the end of Judges, it is clear that to live without a king is to live like a savage, to live in a world in which tribal warfare rules. It is another little addition from the Deuteronomistic Historian, meant to illustrate life without the law of YHWH and, typologically, a life without the Davidic monarchy. The narrator understands that Ephraim is a northern tribe and the story will have implications for later history. But it takes a lot of development together with other texts to get to the full intensity of the narrator's opinion. As we shall see, the traditions continued in oral form and continued developing alongside other narratives, building the meaning slowly and carefully.

The problem with understanding the narrator's opinion is that it is rarely revealed in ways that we normally perceive it. The narrator rarely stops to editorialize, never expresses the pain that we experience reading these horrendous actions, as a more modern narrative would, and thereby rarely reveals any discernable horror at the situation. We are familiar with this characteristic of Hebrew prose from looking at the story of the matriarchs in distress and the golden calves. Instead, we must learn the attitude of the narrator from the subsequent action and from comparing the action narrated with action imagined in the earlier saga. The narrator describes a God who reveals himself through the events of history, not through the description of internal states and attitudes during the narrative.

Where to Stand?

The narrative begins simply enough with a Levite who takes a lesser wife, a concubine: "a certain Levite, residing in the remote parts of the hill country of Ephraim, took to himself a concubine from Bethlehem in Judah" (19:2). We know practically nothing we might like to know about the status of concubinage among the early Israelites, beyond the obvious implication of her inferior status. The concubine may well come into the marriage without a bride price, giving her a secondary status in rights and privileges. The Levite is from the north, the country, and probably not affluent enough to afford a full wife. So they both appear to be ordinary people of limited means. This sad story starts out as an incident in the lives of ordinary people that quickly escalates into a major tribal war. We know, then, that this is not just a personal aberration. It is a limitation on the whole governmental system. Or, at least, that is the opinion of the Deuteronomistic Historian.

Things go out of balance almost immediately: "But his concubine became angry with him,[2] and she went away from him to her father's house at Bethlehem in Judah, and was there some four months" (19:3). This cannot be good. The reading that she became angry with him, as the more difficult reading, is to be preferred over the alternative "prostituted herself against him." The latter, which is evidenced only in later texts of the story (the Greek version, for example), certainly picks up on an implication of abandoning her husband. To have left his protection in this society might well have been taken as tantamount to prostitution and certainly as a blot on the honor of the husband. Unfortunately, this reading leaves unexplained why the Levite went back to claim the concubine amicably. To turn the concubine into a prostitute is to remove the moral ambiguity of the story. Blaming the concubine (who is in almost every respect the vicitm) for a larger sin beyond abandonment of her husband also explains away the tragic death of the concubine too neatly.[3] Besides, the husband seems genuinely to want his concubine back, and that would be much harder to understand if the wife were guilty of adultery: "Then her husband set out after her, to speak tenderly to her and bring her back. He had with him his servant and a couple of donkeys. When he reached her father's house, the girl's father saw him and came with joy to meet him."[4] This all makes sense if the Levite were acting with supererogatory gentleness. None of this makes any sense if the concubine were guilty of adultery, unless it were possible for a man to forgive adultery by not taking it to the courts.

Evidently, the two men in the concubine's life, her father and her husband, are agreed that the concubine should have a second chance at matrimony. The narrator goes out of his way to demonstrate that there was no rancor on either side in a particularly sensitive situation. We have already seen that the offended Levite seems genuinely to want his wife back. The concubine's father hosted his son-in-law for three days, no doubt making sure that he understood how grateful the father was for the understanding of the offended husband. It is possible that the issue is homesickness, the youth of the concubine, as women were married off even before puberty in those days. Under the right circumstances, as these seem to be, both men could afford to be generous in light of the inexperience of the girl, at least in the more strict moral code of the time.

The extent of his hospitality is implicit in verse 4: "His father-in-law, the girl's father, made him stay, and he remained with him three days; so they ate and drank, and he stayed there" (19:4).[5] The narrative emphasizes the extent of the relationship between the two men and the perhaps obsequious hospitality of the father by describing each day of their meeting. On the fifth day, toward the end of the day, the husband tears himself away from the hospitality of the father and thereby sets in motion the tragedy that ensues almost immediately.

The Tragedy Follows after a Long Introduction

By verse 10 we find the newly reunited couple traveling home, with their sad-dled donkeys, avoiding Jebus (Jerusalem), because it was enemy territory as it had not yet been conquered by David, and instead carefully threading their way in the waning day to the Israelite settlement of Gibeah in the tribal area of Benjamin so that they could sojourn among his own brethren (verse 12). They sit in the open space of the town, but no one takes them in until, at evening, an old man invites them home. The old man, like the Levite, also originally came from the hill country of Ephraim. The old man warns them against spending the night in the open and invites him home to share his lodgings: "The old man said, 'Peace be to you. I will care for all your wants; only do not spend the night in the square'" (19:20). And so he takes them in, providing food for both animals and people, even though the Levite has brought enough for himself and his animals (19:21). The old man provides enough food so that all are sated and allows the Levite to save his provisions for a later day on the trip.

However, there was to be no later day. At that point, the villains, the men of the city, enter the drama. While the old man and the Levite are enjoying their dinner, the men of the city, a perverse lot, surround the house, pound-ing on the door. They say to the old man, the master of the house, "Bring out the man who came into your house, so that we may have intercourse with him" (19:23). The narrator offers no comment, compounding the horror. Instead, the master of the house makes what seems to us to be an almost as terrifying offer, in the name of hospitality: "No, my brothers, do not act so wickedly. Since this man is my guest, do not do this vile thing. Here are my virgin daughter and his concubine; let me bring them out now. Ravish them and do whatever you want to them; but against this man do not do such a vile thing" (19:24). The host offers his own daughter rather than have guests in his household come to any harm. Another horrifying action goes without comment by the narrator; instead the narrator counts on us understanding the old man's action as a superlative act of hospitality, though it certainly raises a different moral question for us. Perhaps the old man was hoping that his own gift would bring the perverse men to their senses by the very extremity of his offer.

Instead the Levite, who cannot allow his host to make such a substitution, sacrifices his own concubine: "So the man seized his concubine, and put her out to them. They wantonly raped her, and abused her all through the night until the morning. And as the dawn began to break, they let her go" (19:26). At break of day, the woman is found at the door of the man's house, with her hand on the threshold, as if grasping for safety. Again, the narrator offers us nothing in the way of explanation of horror.

The Morning After

As morning appeared, the woman came and fell down at the door of the man's house where her master was (19:27). The Levite then says: "'Get up,' he said to her, 'we are going.' But there was no answer. Then he put her on the donkey; and the man set out for his home" (19:28). Again, the narrator offers no help. Why was the Levite so brusque? In this case, we as readers really want to know whether the woman is still alive or dead. The narrator actually goes out of his way to leave the issue unresolved. Instead we are left with the possibility that the tortured concubine actually died sometime on her way back to the Levite's house. By the time he gets home, she has apparently died because he carves her corpse into twelve pieces, limb by limb, evidently a sign to call out the tribal militias, as Saul does with a yoke of oxen (1 Samuel 11:5–7). Thus ensues a punishing tribal war, with many more horrifying events.

But, before we explore the war, let us stop for a moment and catalogue some of the disturbing implications of what we have read. The terror that descends on the host's house has some disturbing implications. First, homosexual rape was considered such an antisocial behavior that raping a daughter seems less terrible? I suppose that we would have preferred that they all go down fighting, in the hope that someone would intervene or help would come. But the text simply does not give us that easy way out. No happy endings are to be found here. God, who should intervene and who did intervene in the case of the matriarchs in distress, is not found here—or, at least, is not found right away.

And so we find lurking under the surface a very disturbing, male-oriented calculus in the worth of types of people. Protecting the men is paramount. Even a virgin daughter is a loss more easy to take than the threatened men, the old man or the Levite. Apparently at the very bottom of the list is our poor concubine, now a victim, the person for whom the Levite had undergone so much trouble to reclaim. In the end, he was forced to allow her rape and death. What a horrible story, and how horrible that our narrator does not react to the terrifying details of the narrative. This is the strangest and most frustrating effect of all, leading many extremely intelligent exegetes of our time to throw up their hands in total despair.

The Destruction of Sodom

In Genesis 19, we find a quite parallel account, this time in the story of Abraham, Lot, and the destruction of Sodom. We need to look at what the Bible describes here. It turns out to offer us another prototype example of what God should have done when he intervened, a mythical reversal of the terrible story in Judges 19.

After reading the famous story in Genesis 19, Judges 19 seems a close, almost but not quite an exact, doublet. This appearance is based entirely on the historical structure of the Bible. After all, the events in Judges would have happened a long time after the events in Genesis, in the chronology of the Bible. But when studying the development of oral traditions in a society with scribal schools and the ability to preserve written traditions as well, things are rarely the way they seem at first blush. In Genesis 19, the synoptic story to Judges 19, we find ourselves again in the story of Abraham. Abraham and Lot separate, and Lot goes down to Sodom to settle. The LORD visits Abraham in the form of three angels who announce the birth of Isaac (18:2). Abraham here serves as the representative of wonderful hospitality, the same function the concubine's father serves in the Judges 19 story and the very opposite of the Gibeonites or the Sodomites. Thinking them strangers in need of hospitality, Abraham picks a choice calf from the herd, asks Sarah to knead cakes, and gathers dairy products for them to eat. Strangely, serving curds with the meat appears to violate the kosher laws given in Exodus. Actually, the Exodus 23:20 only forbids eating a kid in its mother's milk. This has led many scholars to suspect that the prohibition of all meat with any dairy product, which is how the law is interpreted today by observant Jews, is a purely rabbinic interpretation, coming from a much later time. Rabbinic literature itself adds to the same impression by saying that this was before Sinai so Abraham could not have known that particular commandment.

Meanwhile, the remaining two angels come to Sodom with a message for Lot, whom they happened to find sitting in the gate of the city.[6] As Abraham does, Lot rises and bows very low to meet them (Genesis 19:1), clearly the mark of an honorable and hospitable man in this narrative. Lot offers to bring them to his house in the city. But they demur. In the end, they agree to follow him to his house. Lot makes them a feast of unleavened bread. Before they could go to sleep, all the men of the city, both young and old, surround the house with evil intent (Genesis 19:4). The text is very clear that it is *all the men*, young and old, down to the last man, who threaten the guests, which makes the violation of hospitality more obvious and the sin of the Sodomites more terrible.

But the exclamation also relates materially to Abraham's argument with God about sparing Sodom, "lest the judge of all the earth not do justice" (Genesis 18:23–32). It is a somewhat wooden way to answer the question raised by any reader of the previous chapter: "Why does Abraham stop at ten righteous people and challenge YHWH not to destroy Sodom for one righteous person?" After all, it strains credulity to think that even old men and infants were intent on rape and that the women, who are unmentioned in the story entirely, also entirely consented to the crime. A more sensible editing would have Abraham argue with God about one person and God relent even for one person. But this gloss (a statement added later that gets into the text), some verses beyond Abraham's argument, has the advantage of removing all doubt about who is sinful, and it increases the suspense by making Abraham seem less than thorough in his argument with God. It also raises the possibility that the story of Abraham's argument with God was already known to have stopped at ten so it would broach no further tampering. This little gloss, however, after the argument, makes the necessity of Sodom's destruction completely clear. The only people worthy of saving are the family of Lot. The text characteristically leaves out the responsibility of the women, though they presumably are destroyed as well.

Rape Again

The men of Sodom ask the very same horrendous question of Lot that the men of Gibeah ask of the man from the hill country of Ephraim: "And they called to Lot, 'Where are the men who came to you tonight? Bring them out to us, so that we may know them'" (19:5). Lot also answers the same way as the host in Gibeah: "I beg you, my brothers, do not act so wickedly. Look, I have two daughters who have not known a man; let me bring them out to you, and do to them as you please; only do nothing to these men, for they have come under the shelter of my roof" (Genesis 19:7–8). In this version the would-be rapists excoriate Lot as an alien and threaten worse to him than the guests. But it seems clear that the two stories are doublets, the same story being used twice. So we already know to expect that one story will bear on the other somehow. In this case it will substitute a more acceptable ending and add a mythical pattern against which to judge the behavior of the Benjaminites.

The crucial details are not hard to find. Our heroes in Genesis are not hurt, because the angels rescue Lot by reaching out and bringing him into the house (Genesis 19:9–10). The angels then strike the men of Sodom with blindness, from the small to the very great, so that they are unable to find the door to the house (Genesis 19:11). This story supplies "the happy ending" missing in the story of the concubine of the Levite. Heaven has intervened and stopped the horrendous event from taking place. Not that destroying a city is happy. But a God who intervenes in these horrible cases to protect those who worship him is much more satisfactory than a God who ignores the cries of the concubine of the Levite.

In typical fashion the Bible offers no description of the reaction of Lot's family, which must have been quite emotional. Then the angels reveal their plan to destroy the city of Sodom because of the men's rapacious intentions and behavior: "For we are about to destroy this place, because the outcry against its people has become great before the LORD, and the LORD has sent us to do it" (Genesis 19:13). The result is that all homosexual behavior has received the title "Sodomite" on the basis of a typological reading of this passage. It is doubtful that this was the ancient purpose of the story. The ancient point seems to be that, compared to the story in Judges 19, which ends in tragedy and civil war, this story is full of miraculous events in which everyone good and just in the eyes of the narrator is saved from any bad consequences. This is how the story in Judges ought to have ended. And we know that this is a mythical story because, compared to the story in Judges, this story contains exactly the plot we need to provide a happy ending in the concubine case, with little interest in character development beyond the righteousness of those who were saved.

So Lot goes to his sons-in-law, though they first completely disbelieve that the LORD is about to destroy the city (Genesis 19:14). With the morning, the angels hurry everyone out of town, despite their lingering and disbelief (16–17). The LORD's original command through his angels is that they literally head for the hills, but they adjust their orders when Lot wants to head toward Zoar. Zoar will not be destroyed either: "Very well, I grant you this favor too, and will not overthrow the city of which you have spoken" (19:21). By the time Lot comes to Zoar, the sun has already risen. And that is when the LORD destroys Sodom, Gomorrah, and the other cities of the plain, leaving interpreters thereafter with a famous crux of interpretation: "The LORD rained on Sodom and Gomorrah sulfur and fire from the LORD out of heaven; and he overthrew those cities, and all the Plain, and all the inhabitants of the cities, and what grew on the ground" (Genesis 19:24–5).[7]

Then Lot's unfortunate wife, who defies the LORD's orders, looks back and is turned into a pillar of salt (Genesis 19:26). Strangely, after making such a point of dwelling in Zoar, Lot then settles in the hills with his two daughters. It is pretty clear that Lot the character is just running through action after action known to be part of his story with very little attention to uniformity of plot or character. This narrative has the classic marks of myth.

Genesis 19 as Etiology and Happy Ending

So Lot and his now reduced family settle in a cave, where the daughters commit incest by sleeping with their father. Strange that after saving us from one sexual misfortune, the characters wind up in another one so quickly. But that does not take into account the value of the family metaphor as etiology. Their offspring become Moab and Ammon, respectively, two nations lying just east of the Jordan, which Israelite kings always wished to conquer. This polemical myth is a way to justify the conquest of Moab and Ammon. The story admits a relationship between the Israelites, the Moabites, and the Ammonites, by making their ancestors "cousins," but also suggests that they are not worthy of being within the Abrahamic covenant. What is particularly telling is that we cannot find evidence of Moabite and Edomite habitation during the patriarchal period. These stories are not from that period at all. Rather, these stories function in a polemical way during the monarchy, not during the patriarchal period, and they also developed secondary significance during the Persian and Hellenistic periods, where Edom continued to have significance. But they would not have developed then because they were living in an enormous empire when conquest was impossible.

I suggest that they have primary significance during the First Temple period because that is the period during which these individual nations come into being and clash with Israel. We now think that these tribal groupings—

Israel, Moab, and Edom—were at first not greatly differentiated. Indeed, it does not look like Moab and Edom, for example, were even in their places during the supposed taking of the land in the twelfth through the tenth century BCE either. But the nations of Moab and Edom, as well as Ammon, are, significantly, developing at the same time that Israel is developing its own ethnic identity, during the early monarchy. Inscriptions in Moabite, we shall see, come into being at approximately the same time as Israelite inscriptions. And their language and alphabets are closely associated. These stories make clear what the Israelites think are the crucial facts that separate them.[8]

Correction: Happy Ending for Some

The story of the sins of Lot's children function as an etiology, a story that explains or justifies why something exists. This etiology explains why Israel and Judah have the right to dominate their neighbors and cousins to the West—the Moabites, Edomites, and Ammonites—despite the similarity of their language. Similarly, the story of Lot's wife also explains a particularly prominent pillar of salt on the southwest shore of the Dead Sea. Bitumen periodically bubbles up through the waters of the Dead Sea, since it is lighter than the very salty water, and sulphur brimstone can be found on the edges of the sea, where it readily ignites. All these geographical anomalies are explained by the story as well. There is no doubt that the story acts as an etiology for the very stark and unearthly geography and geological features of the area in addition to providing an excuse for the conquests east of the Jordan.

In fact, for the ancients the identity of the Sodomites was a live question. There are ruined cities around the Dead Sea, ruins that existed long before the Israelites came upon the scene. Modern place names on the eastern shore of the Dead Sea, which show evidence of significant habitation during the Early Bronze Age, include Bab edh-Dhra, Numeira, Safi, Feifa, and Khanazir.[9] So, in a very real way, the whole episode is a series of etiologies, explaining why there are Early Bronze ruins on the eastern shore of the Dead Sea. They answer questions of who lived in these ruined cities, and what happened to the inhabitants, which otherwise would have been a mystery to the Israelites. Furthermore, these places are not in biblical Israel during the Second Temple period. They are only part of Israelite territory during the beginning of the monarchic period.

The story relates to another piece of Israelite lore, one we have just begun relating, about the terrible events leading up to the catastrophic tribal war at the end of Judges. Of particular importance is the motif of the homosexual rape of guests, which repeats in these places, Genesis 19 and Judges 19, and only these two places in the whole Bible. It is meant to be the most savage of all savageries; that much is clear from both stories. It seems prudent to investigate how they may be connected.

A great deal of discussion has concerned whether the Sodom story or the concubine of the Levite is older chronologically. Is it the case that an original etiology of the ruins at the Dead Sea served as a counterpart to the story of the concubine of the Levite, showing that the concubine was subjected to the same savagery as the sinful Sodomites?[10] Or did the stories develop the other way around? Is this a case in which the story of Lot and the Sodomites is meant to develop an alternative "happy ending" as a commentary on the terrible story in Judges?[11] It is another example of a pair of stories that bear deeply upon each other. We may not be able to tell which story is earlier, but we see the significance of the deep connection.

Of course, we have seen the importance of oral tradition in doublets like these in oral/written tradition and that both could have developed in tandem for a long time. In a way, it really does not matter much whether the etiology for the ruins at Sodom and Gomorrah preceded the concubine in time. What is clear is that they both grew together for a long time before they were written down. It is enough to see that they grew into bookends for each other, setting the savagery of one against the divine deliverance of the other. The story of the concubine of the Levite surely gives a new significance to the stories of ancient cities overthrown. It tells us that without a king the children of Israel would be condemned to living like those who are outside the covenant. And the story in Genesis emphasizes that God has saved the mythic ancestors of the Israelites in the past and can do the same in the future.

The Matriarchs in Peril and the Rape of the Concubine

Once we see that the primary difference between the Sodom story and the events at Gibeah is the miraculous ending, a new clarity emerges between the three stories of the matriarch in peril (Genesis 12, 20, 26) and the concubine of the Levite: The matriarch in trouble represents another happy ending version of the concubine of the Levite. The Genesis version is again folklore or myth, securing a happy ending for the patriarchal family when God closes off the potential for the matriarch to be violated. But the more realistic story ends much less favorably. In other words, the concubine of the Levite again appears to be a more or less real incident of terrible consequences, while the ability of Abram to save Sarai, of Abraham to save Sarah, and of Isaac to save Rebecca is a truly similar story where fortunately God intervenes and serves as a narrative consolation to the tragedy of the concubine of the Levite. The stories are close enough to be structurally outlined in this way:

GENESIS 12, 20, 26

1. The patriarchal couple must move.
2. The patriarch suggests his wife be disguised as his sister to protect him.
3. The foreign king asks to marry the matriarch.
4. When the truth is discovered, the patriarchal couple leaves enriched and increased.

Outcome: All the children of Israel are purebred descendants of the patriarchs.

JUDGES 19

1. The concubine of the Levite goes home after being unhappy in her marriage.
2. Her husband follows and persuades the father that he still wants his concubine.
3. The couple is brought into danger by terrible outlaw Benjaminites of Gibeah who rape the concubine.
4. The Levite goes home with the dead concubine, which occasions a destructive tribal war.

Outcome: The Israelites suffer a terrible reduction in numbers and the Benjaminites' descendants are put into danger and must appeal to the tribes for increase.

In a way, the repetition of the story of a matriarch in peril three times only underlines the terrible results of the story of the concubine of the Levite. The three stories show the necessary compensation in the imaginative life of the community. The events in the story of the concubine of the Levite get even worse, ending in a completely horrific tribal war. It is the opposite of the patriarchs' leaving the foreign king increased and enriched by the encounter. And, perhaps, part of what was missing in our understanding of the three matriarch in peril incidents in Genesis was simply the extent to which they depend for their existence on this story of the rape of the concubine, a story of such horror that it helped generate many different mythic stories in Genesis. In a way, they are structurally all negative forms of this terrible story.

Comparisons

The coherence of all these stories speaks against the claims of the radical minimalists who say that the whole Bible was written as a fictional account when the Jews came back from Babylon in 587 BCE. Were that true, one would not have expected an etiological story about a Middle Bronze settlement, which is entirely irrelevant to the Second Temple period. And one would not expect so much attention to a tribal war that happened sometime in the eleventh century BCE, when there are no tribal wars in the fifth century BCE. As regards the ruins surrounding the Dead Sea, in the Second Temple period, the inhabitants would not have known one type of ruin from another. And the ruins at the Dead Sea were on the eastern bank and no longer in the state of Judah anyway. The whole connection only makes sense if the narrator is actually situated between the patriarchs and the Second Temple period. Again, that is a relative chronology and short of the kind of accuracy we would like in studying these stories. But it is enough to demonstrate that they are not Second Temple stories.

Moreover, a late date would remove all social significance to the story of the concubine of the Levite, which functions, after all, as an argument in favor of kingship. There was no kingship and no need of a story of kingship in Second Temple times until the days of the Maccabees in 168 BCE. Obviously there are reasons for each to circulate independently. Unlike the story of the golden calf, we can see why each would have its own logic of transmission. Nevertheless, the story of the concubine of the Levite is likely controlling both narratives. It is detailed and exacting. It is, in fact, full of realistic details that are otherwise incomprehensible except for thinking that they must have grown out of an actual historical context, no matter how a folkloric narrator rephrased and augmented them. My opinion is formed too by my analysis of the prior story of the golden calf, in which the story of the calf at Sinai was inserted in the Exodus text to tell us something about the great heresy in the north and that it must have been written before the Deuteronomic layer of the text because after the Assyrians destroyed the northern kingdom, the punishment for the north's sinning was so evident that it was in no need of the story of the golden calf. So too in this case, the story in Genesis is much less detailed and contains an enormous number of miraculous details, as if saying this is how the story of the concubine of the Levite should have ended. It was the happy ending, a desirable ending when God intervened to save the family of Abraham.

But that happy ending was not to happen in the story of the Levite's concubine. In a way, the Abraham story seems much more like a fantasy to affirm that God can intervene to save the Israelite family, even if, as in the case of the concubine of the Levite, no such salvation was forthcoming without a king to ensure it. But the Deuteronomistic Historian and arguably the JE epic before it are effectively putting the story in the context of the rise of kingship, where it becomes the last and greatest reason why the Israelites need a king: otherwise the Israelites will actually begin to act like the Canaanites.

I mention the JE epic because, like Richard Friedman and many others, I see no reason why the so-called "JE epic" should end in the book of Numbers, as the classical documentary hypothesis would have it. It seems to me that the point is to get Solomon on the throne of Judah, ending at 2 Kings 2:46.

The Consequences of the Story of the Levite's Concubine

"Thus shall you say to all the Israelites, 'Has such a thing ever happened since the day that the Israelites came up from the land of Egypt until this day?[12] Consider it, take counsel, and speak out'" (Judges 19:30). This is from the funeral oration of the hapless concubine in the book of Judges. With this cry and the cut-up corpse of the concubine to raise the ire of the tribes, the whole house of Israel comes out against the tribe of Benjamin, assembling at Mizpeh. But it is also the reaction against homosexual rape in the preceding story and the story of Lot in Sodom. The terror is uniform and deeply connected. One immediately senses that this is a rare occurrence, made possible by the sign of the cut-up corpse, just as was the case of the cut-up oxen later in the rise of Saul to kingship.

When the Benjaminites and the other Israelites ask for a justification for such a sudden mobilization of the militia, the Levite tells a version of the story that may or may not represent the reader's view of what has happened. This is a brilliant detail of presentment, as it makes clear that everyone has a different perspective in the drama. We have already seen that the text contains a number of ambiguities, because of omitted information and flat narrative style. The Levite says only that "the lords of Gibeon" raped and killed his concubine and intended to kill him, although the text itself did not tell us that she was dead when the Levite saddled her to the donkey. The response of the people is a formulaic statement that no one will retire from the field before the matter is settled.

Civil War

Meanwhile, back in the book of Judges, the situation has deteriorated to the lowest level: the children of Israel are clearly in dire straights. The tribes have been called out for a civil war, not to defeat an external enemy. The house of Israel goes up against the people of Benjamin. They demand that the Benjaminites give up the criminals, but are rebuffed. Civil war begins in earnest. The battle is carried on by seasoned warriors. Some slingers can hit a hair. Some have the very characteristic that, earlier in Judges, allowed the judge Ehud to conquer Eglon, the obese Moabite king. Exactly what this special gift in combat could be is not clear from the text. Often it is taken as being "left-handed." Perhaps it would be more accurate to say that they could sling left-handed as well as right, an ambidextrous, double threat. Then the expression, which literally means "to be bound in the right hand," would be a reference to a training technique to make the slingers ambidextrous. In any event, it allows Ehud to secrete a short sword on his right side, where no one would expect it, which he uses to kill the Moabite tyrant (Judges 3:15).[13]

The war becomes enormously expensive for both sides. Israel's strategy is to surround the town of Gibeah with the entire force and commit a tenth of the force to the fight, since they so outnumber their enemies. Oracles of the Lord confirm the wisdom of this strategy, yet the people of Israel are defeated twice by the desperate Benjaminites, who presumably have fewer soldiers but commit more of them to battle. This demands a strategic retreat to regroup and muster the forces again. They implore the LORD to give them a better strategy: "The Israelites went up and wept before the LORD until the evening; and they inquired of the LORD, 'Shall we again draw near to battle against our kinsfolk the Benjaminites?' And the LORD said, 'Go up against them'" (Judges 20:22).

Finally, on the third day, they conquer them, supported by an oracle from the ark itself. Nevertheless, they need an additional stratagem to defeat the Benjaminites. They draw the main force away from the city by retreating before them and then cut them off by surrounding the force with men hidden in the rear. The slaughter is terrible: "The LORD defeated Benjamin before Israel; and the Israelites destroyed twenty-five thousand one hundred men of Benjamin that day, all of them armed" (Judges 20:35). The whole city is put to the sword (Judges 20:38). Later, another even more inflated figure is given, probably of those who fled: "Eighteen thousand Benjaminites fell, all of them courageous fighters" (Judges 20:44). Luckily, there is no reason to believe any of these inflated figures in a rural society without a standing army, though it is credible that a small settlement could have been overthrown. Whatever the numbers, the carnage was sickening.

Because of the egregious sexual nature of the crime, Israel had sworn not to intermarry with the tribe of Benjamin (Judges 21:2). Yet, in retrospect, that vow needed to be rescinded because otherwise the tribe would cease to exist. In fact, no such vow has been recorded in any other description of Benjamin, which is, after all, the tribe from which Saul emerged and became king. The story clarifies that the tribal system is no longer viable, even by artificial means, and must be replaced by kingship. It may even suggest that the kingship must have the right and legitimate descent. It must be from the original twelve tribes (as, e.g., Judah), but it should not be from the very reprehensible Benjaminites (as, e.g., Saul).

And the people came to Bethel, and sat there until evening before God, and they lifted up their voices and wept bitterly. They said, "O LORD, the God of Israel, why has it come to pass that today there should be one tribe lacking in Israel?"

On the next day, the people got up early, and built an altar there, and offered burnt offerings and sacrifices of well-being. Then the Israelites said, "Which of all the tribes of Israel did not come up in the assembly to the LORD?" For a solemn oath had been taken concerning whoever did not come up to the LORD to Mizpah, saying, "That one shall be put to death." But the Israelites had compassion for Benjamin their kin, and said, "One tribe is cut off from Israel this day. What shall we do for wives for those who are left, since we have sworn by the LORD that we will not give them any of our daughters as wives?" Then they said, "Is there anyone from the tribes of Israel who did not come up to the LORD to Mizpah?" It turned out that no one from Jabesh-gilead had come to the camp, to the assembly.

For when the roll was called among the people, not one of the inhabitants of Jabesh-gilead was there. So the congregation sent twelve thousand soldiers there and commanded them, "Go, put the inhabitants of Jabesh-gilead to the sword, including the women and the little ones. This is what you shall do; every male and every woman that has lain with a male you shall devote to destruction." And they found among the inhabitants of Jabesh-gilead four hundred young virgins who had never slept with a man and brought them to the camp at Shiloh, which is in the land of Canaan. Then the whole congregation sent word to the Benjaminites who were at the rock of Rimmon, and proclaimed peace to them. Benjamin returned at that time; and they gave them the women whom they had saved alive of the women of Jabesh-gilead; but they did not suffice for them. The people had compassion on Benjamin because the LORD had made a breach in the tribes of Israel. So the elders of the congregation said, "What shall we do for wives for those who are left, since there are no women left in Benjamin?" And they said, "There must be heirs for the survivors of Benjamin, in order that a tribe may not be blotted out from Israel. Yet we cannot give any of our daughters to them as wives." For the Israelites had sworn, "Cursed be anyone who gives a wife to Benjamin." So they said, "Look, the yearly festival of the LORD is taking place at Shiloh, which is north of Bethel, on the east of the highway that goes up from Bethel to Shechem, and south of Lebonah." And they instructed the Benjaminites, saying, "Go and lie in wait in the vineyards, and watch; when the young women of Shiloh come out to dance in the dances, then come out of the vineyards and each of you carry off a wife for himself from the young women of Shiloh, and go to the land of Benjamin. Then if their fathers or their brothers come to complain to us, we will say to them, 'Be generous and allow us to have them; because we did not capture in battle a wife for each man. But neither did you incur guilt by giving your daughters to them.'" The Benjaminites did so; they took wives for each of them from the dancers whom they abducted. Then they went and returned to their territory, and rebuilt the towns, and lived in them. So the Israelites departed from there at that time by tribes and families, and they went out from there to their own territories. In those days there was no king in Israel; all the people did what was right in their own eyes.

(Judges 21:3–21:25)

Even though the kingship should not come from Benjamin, the twelve-tribe confederation must be kept intact, even if it has to be done by a bit of human social engineering. It seems clear that this is being used as an argument against Saul's kingship and for the divine basis of David's rule.

Which Is Earlier? Which Is More Credible as History?

What makes this cycle of stories so striking is the utter futility of civil war. But its functions are clear. It reestablishes the twelve-tribe confederacy, keeping Benjamin intact. Obviously, this is because no matter how small Benjamin was in the time the story was edited, it was still part of the tribal system of the Israelites.[14] And, lastly, it does provide some of the moral meaning for which we have been looking throughout the text. Granted, it has not been entirely missing. Where Genesis 19:8 describes the sexual abuse as a *dabar*, "a thing, an incident," Judges describes it as *hannebala*, "an empty thing," perhaps "an atrocity," and adds the explicit sexual meaning of rape to the story with the words: *we'annu otam* (and they raped them). Still, as we have seen, there is little in the way of moral coloring through the incident itself. But since the story must be read in context and also in parallel or synopsis with the story of the destruction of Sodom in Genesis 19, a great many other aspects of moral coloring appear, because there is moral clarity in the Genesis 19 story. I suspect this is because of the long period of oral development while the written story already existed. Motifs from one story were easily imported into the other, back and forth, so that the full understanding of the significance of the story only emerges by reading both in context. Even the story of Abraham's argument with God to find the righteous in Sodom has ramifications for the story of the concubine of the Levite.

One cannot, in fact, totally dismiss the folkloric aspect of the story of the virgins of Jabesh-gilead. Other stories say similar things—stories like the rape of the Sabines in Rome. On the other hand, it seems likely that there is some kind of historical event in back of both the stories.

In effect, there seems to be a historical core to the Judges 19–20 story, a horrendous incident that caused a great deal of Israelite folkloric or mythical reflecting, which has been built up and ramified by oral traditioning, whereas the Genesis 19 story is obviously at base an etiological myth, full of miraculous happenings, that explains the ancient ruins, the geology, and the geographical features of the southern Dead Sea area. That is not to say that everything in the two-chapter story must be historical. What it does say is that the story of the concubine of the Levite is chronologically earlier than the story of the miraculous rescue of Lot from the men of Sodom because it provides a miraculous ending for Abraham and his family, even though the chronology of the events is completely opposite. For most of their oral life, both stories could have been developing at the same time; only the more troublesome moral issues within the story of the concubine drive the development of both stories, so that is, in a way, logically prior. It provides the great moral dilemma that cannot be resolved within the story. The ending brings not so much justice as exhaustion.

The only satisfactory denouement from the point of view of morality occurs in the mythical story in Genesis, where God destroys the sinners without anyone having to exert any energy and without losing any good people (save the disobedient wife of Lot), yet God has to protect the lives of the matriarchs from such similar hazards. But, in an atmosphere that allows both oral and written traditioning, the issue of origins is moot. They obviously had different origins, but grew together as a commentary on the Judges 19 story.

Besides the moral loading that comes from the punishment of the Benjaminites in Judges 20 and 21, it is also possible that the difficulty of the tribes in overcoming Benjamin reflects the ambiguous moral position of the Levite, whose actions even seem callous to us. The full understanding—that the lack of kingship brought about atrocities like those narrated—is only pointed up more strongly by comparison with the Genesis story. In the Sodomite story the perpetrators are punished with blindness and confusion on the spot and by annihilation by fire and brimstone by God the next morning. In the stories of the matriarch in peril in Genesis 12, 20, and 26, God helps the patriarch and the matriarch exit the situation with no penalty, but with blessings and increase. No such miracle happens in the other, more historically accurate story.

One of the happiest aspects of the Genesis stories is God's continuous direct intervention. Contrast that with the horrifying story of the concubine, in which a countryman intervenes, to be sure, but is little help against the terror of the evildoers. Furthermore, the punishment is hardly direct or equitable. In the Judges 19 story, the punishment is only partial, collective, in that it is the whole tribe that suffers for the sins of a very few; and God's will in the issue is sometimes unclear and even ineffectual. It takes two different oracles, and God seems to be foresworn during the early parts of the battle. It is a description of life as we know it. In short, everyone loses. Because of that, it is easy to see that it is much closer to a historical description.

Get Us a King

By contrast, in Genesis 19 God speaks through his angels, but directly to Abraham. God's will is evident and immediately triumphs. As the book of Samuel claims, and as has been perfectly obvious throughout: "And the word of the LORD was rare in those days; there was no widespread vision" (1 Samuel 3:1). This is just a description of reality as we know it and as the historical Israelites knew it. If we had any historically reliable material from the period of the patriarchs, we would find the same. The easy relationship of Abraham with God and his angels comes from the imagination of the storytellers. It is a mythical fantasy of how evil should be handled in an idealized world. But it is their view of an ideal world, not ours.

The book of Genesis where God intervenes directly, even in bodily form, is simply a literary motif of the Genesis text, a telltale quality that shows the extent to which it serves as the fantasy of a people desperately trying to rise above savagery. It is the folk vision of the Israelites as it developed over time in the First Temple period.

Wherever and however the story of the concubine of the Levite began, it has been placed at the end of Judges to be the final argument in favor of the rise of kingship and against the continuation of the tribal system. It describes the inability of the tribal system to police itself without atrocities. In Judges 17:6 and 21:25, "In those days there was no king in Israel; everyone did what was right in his own eyes" is meant to be the summary critique of the increasing chaos of the period.

But within that critique of past history, one detects the political message of the Deuteronomic Judean editor. This tendentiousness has been noted several times before, most recently by Marc Brettler.[15] The book of Judges has, in general, three sections, all of which show editorializing by the Deuteronomistic Historian. There is a short summary of the conquest narrative, a long middle section that contains the story of the major judges, and an appendix in chapters 17–21 (principally the story of the concubine of the Levite, with the events leading up to it and succeeding it) illustrating the social destructiveness of the tribal system with its theory of charismatic leadership. But the voice of the narrator also extends that critique to the whole northern kingdom, whose kingship system following Jeroboam more resembles a continuation of the charismatic leadership system than it does the dynastic principle of the Davidic kingship.

The south's lack of patience with the rebellion of the north is evident throughout the entire history of the kingship. Not a single king of the north ever receives a good review from the editor of the books of Kings, while only a few southern kings receive good reviews. As noted earlier, the two most successful kings in the eyes of the narrator are David and Josiah. And it looks very much like this tendentiousness is evident editorially in the story of the concubine of the Levite, which is almost always attributed to a southern apologist for kingship some time after Josiah. Now this does not, I think, mean that the story originated then. It shows, as we have seen, a great many facets of a long oral-written history, which accounts for its typological parallels with the Genesis 19 story. So we are talking specifically about the editorial tendentiousness of this section.

The "appendix" to Judges does show a considerable polemic against the north in general and against the Saulide kingship in particular. In Judges 17 the Danites are shown in a pejorative light. The resulting idol constructed from the stolen silver not only shows the moral turpitude of the actors but illustrates the north's religious and moral degradation.

Furthermore, that only two hundred out of the eleven hundred shekels are used to build the image makes the charge of immorality even clearer. Although many different editorial assumptions have been suggested,[16] the one that makes the best sense is that this is a summary critique of the north's independence from the pen of a Josianic and Davidic scribe. Moshe Weinfeld, for example, has convincingly shown the participation of the court scribes throughout this book.[17] It is true that the book is suggesting that those who built heretical shrines during the period of the Judges would repeat the mistake again. But the target is likely to be the whole northern kingdom, and especially the dynasty of Jeroboam, who, we have seen, built the cult place of Dan for the worship of one of the golden calves.

One notes the manner in which the rest of the geographical terms are also used in a typological way. The Levite bypasses Jebus, another term for Jerusalem, because it was still in the hands of the Canaanites, the Jebusites. But, ironically, in the monarchic period, according to the perspective of the Josianic scribal schools and bureaucrats, it is Jerusalem from whence comes the true cult of YHWH and true government.

The Levite and his concubine do stay at Gibeah, which is a town quite frequently associated with Saul, and, indeed, Saul is from the tribe of Benjamin as well. A very obvious criticism of the tribe of Benjamin throughout the narrative would no doubt have been generalized to the dynasty of the king who came from Benjamin, the unsuccessful and heretical king Saul, who consulted a "mistress of ghosts," the famous Witch of En-Dor.

So again, in these synoptic stories of horror, we find a similar pattern. There is evidence that the two stories developed together in combined oral and written form, that they grew together as parallel or synoptic understandings of the same folkloric motifs. But they are each also governed by the editorial tendentiousness of the respective last stages of traditioning, those people who wrote down and organized the story into its current form, in this case, the Davidic-Josianic Deuteronomistic Historian. Since the perspective of this writer is now clear, we can look behind this level, as we saw in previous examples, and see that the stories developed together for some time before editorial perspective was imposed on each passage—in the case of Genesis, we have the JE epic's attempt at polemical genealogy—to distance themselves from the Ammonites and the Moabites. But we also have the longer developing etiology of the geography and ruined civilizations of the southwestern Dead Sea, which was enriched by contact with the story of the concubine of the Levite. In this regard, it is probably futile to try to discover which is chronologically older. The best we can do is to show that the story of the Levite's concubine may have had a historical kernel because of the kind of detail we find in it, while the Genesis story developed from an etiology myth to a myth of foreign tribes punished, finishing the Levite's concubine story in a more satisfactory sense than what actually happened or was retold about it. The parallel synoptic working out of meaning shows that the Israelites eschewed our conventions of narrative commentary and rather preferred to develop their meanings through these synoptic discussions of horror stories in which meaning is developed by layers of traditions and by historical outcomes.

But we can note, no matter which is prior, that the stories in the Pentateuch, in this case the JE epic, were available as a moral compass to those trying to find their way through First Temple times. In this respect, and not gainsaying that they developed in parallel fashion, the stories in the Pentateuch function as the myths of those trying to understand the events of the closer past. In Genesis we find God taking a direct role in the punishment of the evildoers and thus demonstrating how the rather more ambiguous events of the book of Judges should be interpreted. In this respect, the Bible gives us an almost unique historical document. It shows us both what was happening in the political thought of the people, their reflections on government and providence throughout the First Temple period and culminating in the reign of Josiah, and their mythological reflections on the same in the stories in Genesis 19. It offers us quite an unusual and extraordinarily valuable window into their history—first, into the facts of their history, as they understood them (history too is as much interpretation as a chronicle of events), and, second, into the consciousness and attitudes of a group of people that went from savagery to kingship in the course of four centuries. That seems to me to be a unique cultural record, preserved for us by pious scribes throughout the ages who were determined to find a moral meaning to these tales of savagery.

CHAPTER FIVE

THE HORROR OF HUMAN SACRIFICE

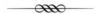

Sex, Intermarriage, and Proper Descent

The Sacrifice of Isaac

If you don't know the story of the sacrifice of Isaac (Genesis 22), this summary of the narrative is hardly going to suffice. It is one of the fastest moving, most powerful, and most horrifying stories in the Bible; it is also justly famous as an example of biblical style at its best. Indeed, its fame has only made it one of the most terrifying stories in all Western literature; at the same time, the moral uncertainties present in the story keep Western authors returning and returning to the text.[1]

Shortly after the birth of Isaac—the son in whom the promise to make Abraham the father of a multitude was fulfilled, according to the Bible, the son produced after years of barrenness and anxious waiting—God decides to test Abraham: "Abraham!" says God. And Abraham answers: "Here am I" (Genesis 22:1). That is the answer of God's obedient servants and the opposite of his disobedient ones, like Adam and Cain, who try to hide from God's gaze.

God then issues this fateful command: "Take your son, your only son, Isaac, whom you love, and go to the land of Moriah, and offer him there as a burnt offering upon one of the mountains of which I shall tell you" (22:2). Notice that God speaks directly to Abraham and requires the most terrible forfeit. This is a good reason, we have learned, to think the narrative is retelling a myth and not the ordinary experience of Israelites living in the land.

The narration moves with even more incredible swiftness, not mentioning any of the inner tensions that Abraham can be assumed to be feeling. This flat, external narrative style is now quite familiar to us; it is, I have claimed, another stylistic characteristic conducive to taking this story as a mythical typology. But one thing is absolutely clear. We know that we must look at the context and parallel discussions to find out how to understand the narrator's voice.

Abraham takes Isaac, the wood, and his men and sets out for the sacrifice, some three days distant. When they reach the destination, identified as Mt. Moriah, we discover that it is later identified with the Temple Mount: "Then Solomon began to build the house of the LORD in Jerusalem on Mount Moriah, where the LORD had appeared to David his father, at the place that David had appointed, on the threshing floor of Ornan the Jebusite" (2 Chronicles 3:1). Hence, we immediately know that we are dealing with a myth that is an etiology for locating the sacrificial cult in Jerusalem. It is normally associated with the E source; if so, the original location of Moriah may well have been somewhere in the north, only afterward being transferred to the south. But there is little evidence to argue any further without speculating.

Abraham and the boy go on alone, one with the wood and the other with a knife and the fire. Isaac asks where the sacrificial victim is: "And Isaac said to his father Abraham, 'My father!' And he said, 'Here am I, my son.' He said, 'Behold, the fire and the wood; but where is the lamb for a burnt offering?'" (Genesis 22:7). He repeats the obedience formula, which makes more understandable his silence: Isaac is aware of and, arguably, consenting to the sacrifice. Abraham answers: "God will see to the sheep for his burnt offering, my son" (22:8). This serves to give the place its other name: God will see/provide (Genesis 22:14). After this brief exchange, they both go on together in silence.

Abraham then lays out the wood, ties up his son, lays him on the altar and stretches out his hand to slay his son. "Then Abraham put forth his hand, and took the knife to slay his son. But the angel of the LORD called to him from heaven, and said, 'Abraham, Abraham!' And he said, 'Here am I'" (22:11). Again we see the repetition of the obedience formula: "Here am I." The text suddenly changes from the word *God* to the word *LORD*, a very difficult textual problem because so far *God* has been the only word used for the divinity. It seems that the story comes mostly from the so-called E, or northern, source, but it has also assimilated the word *YHWH*, if it refers to an angel coming from God. The angel intervenes in the "nick of time"; it must be the definition of the "nick of time." A ram is found in the thicket and becomes the sacrifice in place of Isaac:

> And the angel of the LORD called to Abraham a second time from heaven, and said, "By myself I have sworn, says the LORD, because you have done this, and have not withheld your son, your only son, I will indeed bless you, and I will multiply your descendants as the stars of heaven and as the sand which is on the seashore. And your descendants shall possess the gate of their enemies, and by your descendants shall all the nations of the earth bless themselves, because you have obeyed my voice." So Abraham returned to his young men, and they arose and went together to Beer-sheba; and Abraham dwelt at Beer-sheba.
>
> (Genesis 22:16–19)

The result is that YHWH or his angel (there is some ambiguity here) blesses Abraham and promises him many descendants who will possess the gates of their enemies, a detail that will turn out to be extremely important. And the prophecy of Abraham's legendary descendants starts to be fulfilled immediately:

> Now after these things it was told Abraham, "Behold, Milcah also has borne children to your brother Nahor: Uz the first-born, Buz his brother, Kemuel the father of Aram, Chesed, Hazo, Pildash, Jidlaph, and Bethuel." Bethuel became the father of Rebekah. These eight Milcah bore to Nahor, Abraham's brother. Moreover, his concubine, whose name was Reumah, bore Tebah, Gaham, Tahash, and Maacah."
>
> (Genesis 22:20)

Innumerable Peculiarities Resolved by Seeing the Genesis Story as Myth

At its roots Genesis 22 must be about the rejection of human sacrifice and the substitution of an animal in its place. But we must compare it with a new kind of doublet or synoptic or hypotypical relationship before we can see how cleverly the story functions. In this doublet both stories are related to each other by hypotypicality, they are both prototypes of the mythical rejection of human sacrifice, but they exist in chiastic opposition. A chiasm is when the second story is the negative equivalent of the first. We have seen that the place, Mt. Moriah, is already identified with the Temple Mount in biblical times, so the myth also functions as an etiology.

But to move in strictly moral terms from the story to the prohibition of human sacrifice is difficult. Nahum Sarna, in his commentary on Genesis to the passage, says it straightforwardly: "We cannot evade the fact that the core of the narrative seems to assume the possibility that God could actually demand a human sacrifice."

Sarna's problem is typical of any modern reader: "How can a story that purports to be about the extinction of human sacrifice actually take as its premise the demand for such a sacrifice, plainly stated?" Furthermore, there is the historical problem that during the purported "Patriarchal Period"—1700–1500 BCE roughly, let us say—human sacrifice had already been replaced by animal substitutes in Mesopotamia. The situation is less clear in the first-millennium Levant.

Indeed, even in the Bible, there is certain evidence that God did not expect human sacrifice: "They have built also the high places of Baal, to burn their sons with fire for burnt offerings unto Baal, which I commanded not, nor spoke it, neither did it come into my mind" (Jeremiah 19:5, cf. 7:31). Here Jeremiah says rather peremptorily that God never commanded human sacrifice and that it never even entered his mind, which seems like an obvious overstatement, given what Genesis 22 says.

The idea of human sacrifice certainly enters God's mind, because he explicitly commands it in Genesis 22. It does not seem possible that Jeremiah has not heard the story of the binding of Isaac, even though it is regularly attributed to the E source. Perhaps "entered the mind" means something else to the Hebrews than it means to us. And, perhaps, it is simply an overstatement, meant to be taken with a grain of salt. That seems like the most likely interpretation. But, if that is so, then we need to realize that the Bible cannot ever just be taken at its word. One always has to understand that the Bible is a rhetorical document, using exaggeration, understatement, irony, satire, skepticism, even polemic, and a variety of other tricks.

But I suggest that the reason here is actually that the Bible is narrating a myth. The reason for this risked contradiction with Genesis 22 must be *rhetorical effect*, based on the existence of a Tophet, a place of rumored child sacrifice, near Jerusalem, indeed right outside the walls of the city in the "valley of the son of Hinnom" (Jeremiah 19:6). Human sacrifice was a real possibility and a temptation in the first millennium BCE. In short, what is not possible in expository discourse is exactly the point in relating a myth. One ends up with a prohibition only after trying the opposite. Let us see what is gained by this strange arrangement of arguments.

Two Conceptual Moves (Again)

The answer to this quandary seems to be found in two conceptual moves, which we have been using quite profitably throughout this study: The first is to consider the story of the sacrifice of Isaac (or better named as in Hebrew, "The Binding [*Aqedah*] of Isaac") within the life of the Israelites settled in the land of Israel and the second is to see how it interacts with other stories that have undergone a similarly long oral-written development. In short, wherever the story came from, we shall see that it functions as an etiological myth for the establishment of the cult of animal sacrifice in Jerusalem. This is the first period in its development that we can accurately date. If it is an etiology of the Temple cult, it has to be written down after the building of the Temple in the 10th century BCE.

The biblical record, particularly the Deuteronomist and the Priestly editors, repeatedly tells us about the abominable things the Canaanites do. "They even burn their sons and their daughters to their gods" (also, e.g., Isaiah 59:7, Jeremiah 22:3, 26:15, Psalms 106:38, 2 Kings 21:16, cf. 2 Kings 24:4)[2]:

You shall not give any of your children to devote them by fire to Molech, and so profane the name of your God: I am the LORD.

(Leviticus 18:21)

I myself will set my face against that man, and will cut him off from among his people, because he has given one of his children to Molech, defiling my sanctuary and profaning my holy name.

(Leviticus 20:3)

[31] You must not do the same for the LORD your God, because every abhorrent thing that the LORD hates they have done for their gods. They would even burn their sons and their daughters in the fire to their gods.

(Deuteronomy 12:31)

[9] When you come into the land that the LORD your God is giving you, you must not learn to imitate the abhorrent practices of those nations.

¹⁰ No one shall be found among you who makes a son or daughter pass through fire, or who practices divination, or is a soothsayer, or an augur, or a sorcerer, ¹¹ or one who casts spells, or who consults ghosts or spirits, or who seeks oracles from the dead.

(Deuteronomy 18:9–11)

The last passage lumps a variety of "magical" practices together with the charge that the Canaanites make their children pass through fire, presumably an infant sacrifice by whole offering. "The Canaanites do this; we should not," says the Bible. We understand the polemic. It is an attempt to define an identity by counterexample, a "counteridentity," as we have been calling it. But was it historical?

Ugaritic texts from the thirteenth century on the Syrian coast give somewhat ambiguous evidence that human sacrifice was practiced in Canaanite cities:

> If an enemy force attacks your [city-]gates,
> An aggressor, your walls;
> You shall lift up your eyes to Baal [and pray]:
> "O Baal:
> Drive away the [enemy] force from our gates,
> The aggressor from our walls.
> We shall sacrifice a bull [to you], O Baal,
> A votive-pledge we shall fulfill [viz.]:
> A firstborn,
> Baal, we shall sacrifice,
> A child [an offspring?]
> we shall fulfill [as votive-pledge].
> A 'tenth' [of all our wealth] we shall tithe [you],
> To the temple of Baal we shall go up,
> In the footpaths of the House-of-Baal we shall walk."
>
> "Then shall Baal hearken to your prayers,
> He shall drive the [enemy] force from your gates,
> The aggressor from your walls."[3]

We will leave aside the very real problem of whether Ugarit is part of Canaan or not. Its language, Ugaritic, is Canaanite. The promise that the sacrifice will force the enemy from your gates fits rather well with the promise made to Abraham that his obedience will give his progeny the gates of their enemies. It seems clear that sacrifice and keeping a city safe were associated throughout the whole ancient Middle East. The problem with this passage is that the term for "child" is uncertain. It can just as easily mean a young animal as well, and, in context, it seems that we are talking about a young animal from the beginning. The question is: did they really sacrifice their children, or do we just think that they did, based on the Bible's strong polemic against Canaanites, creating a counteridentity? We shall have to look at the archaeology before we can know for sure.

Jephthah's Daughter

We again find a parallel story of another Israelite forced to offer a child, this time, his daughter, as a sacrifice, this time explicitly to insure a military victory. That is the story of Jephthah's daughter, starting in Judges 11:30. But before we look at the story proper, we must find out who Jephthah was. Like all the judges in this book, Jephthah is an unlikely candidate for the title of judge, though unlikelihood almost seems like part of the job description. All the judges are the most unlikely of people—a woman like Deborah, a womanizer like Samson, a half-breed renegade like Jephthah, even a skeptic like Gideon. It is quite clear that the selection principle behind these appointments is that God chooses the most unlikely of people to glorify his own power, to demonstrate who really brings things to be. We would say that becoming a judge was a matter of charismatic election. The person most likely to beat off the enemy threatening Israel is always the most likely candidate:

> [1] Now Jephthah the Gileadite, the son of a prostitute, was a mighty warrior. Gilead was the father of Jephthah. [2] Gilead's wife also bore him sons; and when his wife's sons grew up, they drove Jephthah away, saying to him, "You shall not inherit anything in our father's house; for you are the son of another woman." [3] Then Jephthah fled from his brothers and lived in the land of Tob. Outlaws collected around Jephthah and went raiding with him.
>
> (Judges 11:1–3)

And Jephthah is certainly an unlikely candidate to rule over Israel, even in time of war. He is the child of an Israelite on his father's side, but, on his mother's side, he is described as the child of a prostitute and a foreign woman. *Foreign woman* would have been enough to get the message across. *Prostitute* may just be a later gloss, like the similar case of the concubine of the Levite. Jephthah will be a negative example; a signifier used to establish a counteridentity. We have seen that correct family and correct offspring is the very essence of the mythology of the Israelites and Judeans. He was cast out by his family, moving out of the country to the land of Tob, where he gathered a militia of dubious moral character. Nevertheless, the children of Israel come to him when threatened by their voracious eastern neighbors, the Amorites, Ammonites, and Moabites. We immediately see the need for the polemical myth about the mixed-breed origin of the Ammonites and Moabites, through Lot and his daughters. Jephthah was able to defeat the Amorites by carefully remaining on good terms with their cousins the Moabites, combined with the ferocity of his battle prowess.

But there was more trouble when he came to the Ammonites. To accomplish this victory, Jephthah makes what turns out to be a very rash vow: "³⁰ And Jephthah made a vow to the LORD, and said, 'If you will give the Ammonites into my hand, ³¹ then whoever comes out of the doors of my house to meet me, when I return victorious from the Ammonites, shall be the LORD's, to be offered up by me as a burnt offering'" (Judges 11:30–31).

So Jephthah goes out to fight against Ammon, and the LORD delivers them into his hands. But when he returns to his house it is his only child, his daughter, who comes out to welcome him in a dance of victory: "And Jephthah came to Mizpeh unto his house, and, behold, his daughter came out to meet him with timbrels and with dances: and she was his only child; beside her he had neither son nor daughter" (Judges 11:34). Needless to say, Jephthah is brought very low, indeed, by her welcome. Fate could not have been worse.

He explains to his daughter that he cannot take back his vow. We are clearly in the realm of myth and folklore here because in real life the vow would be retracted and forgotten in an instant. Or, at least, any penalty from a retracted vow would be less than a sacrificed daughter. Like the Genesis account, the Judges episode is mythological. We cannot claim that one happened while the other did not in this particular pair of horrifying stories. We will see, however, that both are meant to discuss Israelite religious practice and the inappropriateness of human sacrifice. And both are meant to establish the social attractiveness of worshipping in the south, while eschewing the social attractiveness of the northern traditions. Jephthah's daughter, in this mythological, folkloric drama, seems amenable to the sacrifice (her consent is important, just as Isaac's consent was), as much as it saved the country, provided she be granted a certain amount of time to mourn her death with her own virgin friends: "And she said unto her father, 'Let this thing be done for me: let me alone two months, that I may go up and down upon the mountains, and bewail my virginity, I and my fellows.' And he said, 'Go.' And he sent her away for two months: and she went with her companions, and bewailed her virginity upon the mountains" (Judges 11:37–38).

The plain sense of the story is that he sacrificed her. But this is clearly unacceptable, unless we see him as a villain because of his illegitimate birth. In one of the most ingenious interpretations of the rabbis, who take the story literally, they reinterpret some of the words so that he does not actually sacrifice his daughter but only her marriageability, making her a lifelong celibate woman, an Israelite nun. They are deeply disturbed that a story like this occurs in Scripture and they are willing to go anywhere to defuse it. But they are right on the mark in thinking that correct lineage and reproduction is somehow part of this story. The emphasis on her virginity not only suggests that it is a true sacrifice but also signals that all his offspring are at stake.

But there are many stories of this type around the world, most famously the story of Agamemnon's sacrifice of Iphigenia at Aulis to get fair winds for Troy. According to one form of the Iphigenia story, she is sacrificed. According to another, she is saved at the last minute and whisked away to another island, Tauris, where she eventually has to end human sacrifice on that island. These stories show the exact same ambivalence about human sacrifice; they represent the temptation to bribe God for victory, the agreement that one may die to assuage the anger of the divinity in the hope that more offspring may come. Human sacrifice, like all sacrifice, is then a kind of wager. We sacrifice so that we may gain more from the gods. It depends on a magical universe. This seems to be behind all stories of human sacrifice, though it may be valued differently and expressed differently in different cultures.

That is not to say that human sacrifices were not performed. The ubiquity of these stories rather argues that human sacrifice and child sacrifice were performed in many places in the world and given religious sanction. But it also suggests that it was not a normal part of anyone's normal sacrificial system. Canaanite and Israelite statements on sacrifice both suggest it is an extraordinary moment, relating to when the city itself is in danger. Otherwise,

Gresham's law applies to sacrifice, debasing and blunting its effect: If everyone does it, the stories lose their horrifying effect. So the stories are actually expressing a time when the cessation of human sacrifice was the norm. They are polemically arguing for cessation and the substitution of an animal vicitm are significant moral signifiers in the society. In all these societies, Greek, Hebrew, and Canaanite, human sacrifice takes place but in none of them, by the time we read the stories, is human sacrifice valorized without ambivalence. Thus God can argue against human sacrifice while demanding it in this one defining case.

The story of Jephthah's daughter's sacrifice is the basis for another religious ritual, which was apparently celebrated in the northern tribes and was probably another story arguing for the end of human sacrifice. According to the story, Jephthah's daughter founds the ritual of women roaming the hills, weeping for her: "[39] At the end of two months, she returned to her father, who did with her according to the vow he had made. She had never slept with a man. So there arose an Israelite custom that [40] for four days every year the daughters of Israel would go out to lament the daughter of Jephthah the Gileadite" (Judges 11:39–40).

The rite in itself has certain relationships to a more widespread custom in the Levant and perhaps also in Greece. In the summer in the ancient Near East, women lament for Tamuz, the grain god, which probably represents the withering of the grass and grain under the relentless summer sun. In Greece we know of a different ritual involving women roaming the countryside, this time expressing the ecstasy of intoxication for Dionysus or Bacchus—the famous story of the Maenads ecstatically celebrating the wine god Dionysus, whose holiday follows in the fall calendar, by roaming the mountains in frenzy and eating raw meat, which deals with sacrifice and another issue, ritualized cannibalism. But in the Israelite case we have their local etiology, coming from Israel's presumed history instead of from a myth of nature.

The Two Etiologies Compared

We have two separate and quite different mythical etiologies—an etiology of how the sacrificial cult came to Jerusalem and an etiology of why women go out on the mountains to mourn for Jephthah's daughter. In each case we see the dominant source of wealth: the herds of the south and the grain in the north. The stories are being mediated through a southern source because the whole story of Jephthah is treated as a negative example: he has a bad lineage, he makes a rash vow, and his daughter actually does suffer the ultimate penalty.

This is precisely the converse of what we find in the binding of Isaac. But that is precisely the point: the story of Jephthah's daughter is the exact counterexample to the story of the binding of Isaac. The person who has pointed this out most clearly is the anthropologist Edmund Leach. He finds a structural relationship between the two stories, which can be expressed in the following short form:

GENESIS 22:1–18

4. God requires Abraham to sacrifice his only son Isaac as evidence of faith and obedience
3. As Abraham prepares to obey, God imposes a substitution whereby Abraham, in fact, sacrifices an animal in fulfillment of his duty
2. Abraham thus demonstrates his faith and obedience
1. God makes a vow that Abraham shall have countless descendants
Outcome: All the children of Israel descend from Abraham

JUDGES 11:30–40

1. Jephthah makes a vow to make a burnt offering to God after he is granted victory
2. God grants Jephthah victory
3. By implication Jephthah plans an animal sacrifice in fulfillment of his vow
4. God, in the form of chance, imposes a substitute whereby Jephthah is made to sacrifice his only child, his virgin daughter
Outcome: Jephthah has no descendants of any kind[4]

When the stories are represented in this way, it becomes clear that they are also a kind of doublet, but they are a chiastic doublet or a doublet in opposition, with every statement the polar opposite of the previous story. Another way to put it is to say that they are structurally opposite to each other in a binary way, a perfect Lévi-Straussian pair.[5]

Lévi-Strauss thought that all mythical structure was binary. Though a binary structure is not the only possible arrangement, here it works very well.

Abraham is the positive example, yielding holy offspring from a marriage under the covenant with God. Jephthah is turned into the negative example by the south. Even though he is a judge in Israel and can save the people (it pleases God to use the most unlikely people to do his will), he does not have offspring.

Both sides show the advantages of legitimate, endogamous marriages without explicitly saying so. Both stories also legitimate sacrifice—one in Jerusalem, the other in the north, and the Jephthah story also legitimates a further ritual action. So it is possible that both stories, though starting independently, grew together in oral and written tellings or were deliberately edited together to form a pair of meaningful opposites on the topic of sacrifice. Whatever the status of the two stories as myth or legend in their original context, they have grown together into a chiastic or negative model that Lévi-Strauss was so fond of finding, through oral retelling and formal editing, so that they now mediate a single message, not in terms of two reinforcing stories but in two polar opposite stories.[6]

Sexuality, Endogamy, Descendants

On the positive side and in its end form, there is little doubt as to what the message of the two stories is: the covenant made between Abraham and God and reconfirmed throughout Israelite history brings many concrete blessings or gifts to the Israelites. One of the principal ones in this case is offspring—legitimate offspring to inherit wealth and wealth through increase in cattle. One might say quite simply that if you do not sacrifice your children you will have more offspring and God will favor you the more. That seems obvious enough, and the horror of the myths only makes the message more obvious. But more is involved in these stories than that.

For instance, barrenness and fertility alternate in rapid succession in stories that come from the patriarchal period and the period of the settlement. This seems to me to suggest that they existed in a fluid state together and began to illustrate the same message. Barren women like Sarah, Rebecca, Rachel, Leah, Samson's mother, and Hannah all have their barrenness removed as a sign that God's plan will continue through them and their offspring. Fertility is the older theme, but blessings of the covenant seem to be explicitly part of the promise. Offspring, fertility, and blessing are all part of the covenant promise to those who do not sacrifice their firstborn children, as the Canaanites do, but rather only the blood of their son's circumcision and the redemption of the Levite as proof of their steadfastness to the covenant.

It is the blood of the covenant that saves the Israelite firstborn on the night before the Exodus (Exodus 12:12–14). Yet it is exacted of the Egyptians who stand in for all non-Israelites here. The rules against incest and for proper endogamous marriages are clearly explained. The rules against homosexual rape, which we have already studied, are also clearly part of this theme. The Sodomites and the Benjaminites both show the folly of violating them. Such things are not done in Israel. The rules of sexual conduct involve staying away from foreign cults, where sexual rites are performed, as well as staying away from foreign women. Leach brings the following stories to demonstrate the points we have already studied in closer detail in some cases:

1. (Genesis 34) The Dinah story affirms unambiguously the sinfulness of allowing an Israelite girl to cohabit with a foreigner (in this case a Shechemite-Canaanite), even if the foreigner is prepared to adopt the Israelite faith. But the story points out that the enforcement of this principle must lead to political difficulties.

2. (Judges 9) Abimelech is a half-blood Israelite Shechemite by a Shechemite mother. On the death of his father he joins his mother's people, kills all his pure-blooded half brothers except one (Jotham), and is himself killed.

3. (Judges 11) Jephthah is also a half-blooded Israelite by his foreign (and prostitute) mother. On the death of his father, he is chased away by his father's people but is eventually called back to be their leader. His pure-blooded relatives are thereby saved, but his only daughter is sacrificed and he dies without descendants.

4. (Judges 13–14) Samson is a pure-blood Israelite hero who has a series of sexual liaisons with foreign (Philistine) women interspersed with battles against Philistine men. The women are consistently treacherous and finally bring about his downfall. The treachery of the foreign women is here the counterpart of the dishonorableness of the foreign men in the Dinah story.

It thus appears that the positive aspect of the covenant in the story of the Aqedah (which Leach does not notice) is, right from the beginning, undiluted endogamy. The structure of the proper context for playing out this theme of offspring and covenantal obligation is inherent in the editing of the story of the sacrifice of Isaac. God does not want human sacrifice, but the most dramatic way to portray that desire is through the full development and exploration of the theme of human sacrifice. In a mythical universe, it is possible to deny human sacrifice by exploring the possibility that God could in fact demand it. Otherwise, in a countersociety where Canaanites live and do sacrifice human children, the lesson would not be fully learned. For YHWH might easily have accepted human sacrifice, as did Chemosh and the other gods of the neighborhood (Micah 6:7; Jeremiah 7:31).

Apparently, some Israelites thought he had.

Will the LORD be pleased with thousands of rams,
    with ten thousands of rivers of oil?
Shall I give my first-born for my transgression,
    the fruit of my body for the sin of my soul?"
He has showed you, O man, what is good;
    and what does the LORD require of you
but to do justice, and to love kindness,
    and to walk humbly with your God?

(Micah 6:7–8)

The Israelites did occasionally refer to human sacrifice and were even occasionally tempted to sin by making human sacrifices. If Israelites might think that God would require human sacrifice, why would a Canaanite not come to the same conclusion? In fact, several scholars have looked at the archaeological evidence, now beyond a shadow of a doubt, and shown that the sacrifice of firstborn children was a terrible reality in the area of Canaan and Phoenicia. Even Carthage now seems beyond dispute, though, in no case, is there a regular schedule of human sacrifice. It is saved for special crises.[7] The answer from the Bible alone to the question of the practice of human sacrifice would have to be: most likely, even though the reference comes most often in polemic. Ahaz, king of Judah and son of Jotham, is accused of perpetrating the crime (2 Kings 16). It is a polemic, for sure, but unlikely to be merely so. Once archaeology is factored into the equation, it seems likely that in Canaanite, and particularly Phoenician, culture infant

sacrifice was performed occasionally, and in Israelite society the same could
be said.

Now, it is not in every way clear how or when the Canaanite or Israelite
peoples might have indulged in these human sacrifices. Scholars debate as
to how common the practice was, even though it is noted by outside sources
down to the Roman period, when the Carthaginians, a Canaanite people, are
described as participating in this particular savagery.[8] It seems safe to assume that there is no evidence it was practiced every day as part of a regular
cult. But it would not have to be practiced regularly or every day to be noted
in the historical record or met with horror.

A particularly significant event in the Bible shows how the Israelites
thought about these practices, whether they were done regularly or not: "[26]
When the king of Moab saw that the battle was going against him, he took
with him seven hundred swordsmen to break through, opposite the king of
Edom; but they could not. [27] Then he took his firstborn son who was to succeed him, and offered him as a burnt offering on the wall. And great wrath
came upon Israel, so they withdrew from him and returned to their own
land" (2 Kings 3:26–27).

This story demonstrates the power that adhered to human sacrifice during the First Temple period. In the Aqedah story, part of the blessing given to
Abraham, because he was willing to sacrifice his son, is precisely the victory
that Mesha received by sacrificing his son. That explains the Israelite defeat.
And this is precisely the kind of event in which such a sacrifice might take
place. The Israelites, however, get victory by not sacrificing their children.
YHWH promises Abraham's progeny victory for not having performed the
sacrifice, as the Aqedah tells us: "'By myself I have sworn, says the LORD,
because you have done this, and have not withheld your son, your only son,
I will indeed bless you, and I will multiply your descendants as the stars of
heaven and as the sand which is on the seashore. And your descendants
shall possess *the gate of their enemies*, and by your descendants shall all the
nations of the earth bless themselves, because you have obeyed my voice'"
(Genesis 22:16–17; my emphasis).

The Israelites give the account, so there is no Moabite voice in this structurally organized story. As the Israelites tell it, the Moabite victory is assured

because of the "great wrath" that descends on the Israelites. That is a strange phrase to use in context and suggests that the sacrifice itself possessed the special power that defeated them. Otherwise, the context would demand that "great fear" or "anxiety" and not "great anger" descended upon them. The sacrifice itself was believed to have had some important effects. In this case, it gives the Israelites an excuse for losing a battle against their previous possession, Moab.

Keeping the enemy from the gate is exactly what Baal was promising as well, at least in Ugarit, as we have seen:

> Then shall Baal hearken to your prayers,
> He shall drive the [enemy] force from your gates,
> The aggressor from your walls.

I see no reason to doubt that the binding of Isaac was meant to serve in the same stead as the sacrifice of Mesha's son, since that is exactly the comparison that Genesis 22 is making. By not performing the sacrifice, Abraham was conquering the gates of his enemies rather than surrendering to them. It was the obedience of Abraham that gave his surrogate blessing to Israel, without requiring the actual human sacrifice. Even without the sacrifice, the people of Israel will be victorious over the gates of their enemies, as the blessing explicitly states. Again, this is identity formation by opposition.

By the same token, it is fair to say that the Bible's polemic was no help to the Israelite soldiers in the actual incident. It seems rather to explain an otherwise disastrous defeat. As the Israelites were certainly thrown into confusion by the related sacrifice, it had its desired effect anyway: Israel lost one of its most important colonial possessions. One supposes that human sacrifice continued to appeal, even to a people that had been told it was wrong. Unfortunately, from the Bible alone we cannot prove that there was a human sacrifice. All we know is that the story had a strong a role in explaining why the Israelites lost an important battle, resulting in the independence of the previous vassal Moab.

Although this may correspond with standard reports about a child sacrifice, it is not what is described as the standard Canaanite practice of passing children through fire at a Tophet. It may be, but it may also be a different sacrifice, restricted to the crisis conditions at hand. Since the sacrifice was actually effective in relieving the Israelite attack, the Israelites themselves would have wanted the same kind of divine power. The story therefore virtually requires that human sacrifice actually took place at some time and some place. We have seen that Edmund Leach is generally correct in suggesting that Israelite myths and rituals are deeply involved with the theme of fertility. But we have also seen that the issue of sacrifice also is deeply concerned with negotiations of power.[9]

We cannot certify that the sacrifice happened, but we do know that an actual Mesha actually rebelled against an actual Israel. It seems rational to link this event with the story of the Aqedah in Genesis, and it seems quite likely the two events are chronologically related. In exploring these themes, we shall see how much the successful and unsuccessful application of power has been important to this story in both its ancient and modern uses.

The Mesha Stone

This horrendous incident in Israelite history has received an unexpected and seemingly chance historical support.[10] But, as we shall see, it is not exactly historical verification; indeed it is very puzzling and ambiguous in a historical light. But the story is one of the marvels of the rise of modern archaeology. In 1868 an Alsatian priest employed by the Anglican Missionary Society in Jerusalem, F. A. Klein, was told of a fabulous inscribed stone, lying face up at the ruins of Dhiban, about twenty miles south of the contemporary Jordanian capital of Amman and a dozen or so miles east of the Dead Sea. This put it in the center of the area known in biblical times as Moab. There he found a large, thick block of black basalt lying face up on the ground. The stone was some four feet high, twenty-seven inches across, and more than a foot thick, containing a thirty-four-line inscription on its exposed surface. The stone had obviously originally been set up as a monument for public reading, as it was rounded at the top and contained a well-prepared, incised border on the front side. These valuable and rare public monuments have subsequently been known by their classical name as *stelai* (from the Greek, singular *stēlē*), meaning a standing stone, or *stelae* (from the Latin, singular, *stela*), with the same meaning.

When Klein returned to Jerusalem he showed some of his early sketches to J. H. Petermann, a German scholar and consular official. He immediately contacted the Berlin Museum and convinced them to raise the funds to purchase the monument from the Bedouin who lived in the area of Dhibhan.

It also came to the attention of Charles Clermont-Ganneau, another consular official working for France and also a scholar of antiquities, who first sent a representative to look at the inscription, reporting back with a crude drawing of some of the letters, enough to assure Clermont-Ganneau of the inscription's importance. Clermont-Ganneau next dispatched a man named Ya'qub Karavaca to Dhiban to take a full paper squeeze of the inscription, a kind of papier-mâché impression rendering the writing as well as the larger details.[11] While Karavaca was waiting for his squeeze to dry, the local Bedouin became hostile, forcing Karavaca and the horsemen to leave very quickly, one of his horsemen even suffering a spear wound in the leg. The second horseman, Sheikh Jamil, grabbed the squeeze, still wet, from the stone, ripping it into seven pieces in the process. But, even with all that damage to the squeeze, he saved the day by stuffing the pieces into his robe and escaping. The seven pieces of the squeeze were presented to Clermont-Ganneau, who had to place them before a strong light to decipher the letters. The squeeze remains the only evidence of the inscription in its original condition, and for all that a number of ambiguities remain because of tears and rips. Unfortunately, these problems overpowered Clermont-Ganneau, who never published his *editio princeps*.[12]

Further Colonial Intrigue

An unfortunate competition between France and Germany, provoked by the Franco-Prussian War of 1870–1871, led to several more avoidable delays in relocating and deciphering the stone. Then, even further delays ensued when the local Bedouin mistrusted the Turkish authorities with whom the negotiations were entrusted. Since they were the colonial overlords, they could hardly be ignored. But they were also hated by the local inhabitants of the area and universally rumored to be both venal and corrupt.

Meanwhile, the Bedouin themselves had certainly come to the conclusion that the stone was invaluable. For reasons that have never been entirely clear, they managed to crack the stone in several pieces. Apparently they first heated the stone in a fire and then they threw cold water on it. Some speculate that this was to make the stone more valuable because it could be sold in several pieces rather than as a whole. Other scholars think that the division was made to share the proceeds among the various local leaders. Still others believe the idea was to use the pieces as talismans for crop fertility.

Reasonable as this may have been for the canny Bedouin, the actual reason for the fragmentation of the stone is still unknown. The result, however, was a catastrophe for the stone.

Whatever the reason, the large inscription was now in pieces and distributed among a group of local leaders. Eventually Clermont-Ganneau and Charles Warren, the famous British archaeologist of the Holy Land, were able to find approximately two-thirds of the original inscription. The squeeze proved to be a lifesaver because it provided a basis for filling in many of the gaps between the pieces. Since 1875, all the material has been displayed at the Louvre in Paris but the Archaeological Museum of Amman also claims it, while the British Museum has a plaster mold of the face of the stela.

Stone Cold Analysis

The writing on the stone at first seems indistinguishable from paleo-Hebrew, which is to say that it is quite different from today's Hebrew alphabet. It is a stick-figure alphabet more suitable to engraving on stone than today's elegant Aramaic script. The alphabet itself is historically also the basis of Greek and Latin script as well as a variety of other Semitic alphabets that have evolved into forms more suitable for writing with pen and ink on paper, velum, or papyrus. The ancient alphabet of the Moabite stone is well rendered, neatly drawn, and very legible, comparing nicely to the royal inscriptions of the period, especially the less rare Israelite and Judean ones.

The language, as opposed to the alphabet, was puzzling at first because little was known about Northwest Semitic dialectology. It is not Hebrew, though it has many, many close affinities to Hebrew. It is quite similar but also significantly different in grammar and syntax from Phoenician, Aramaic, and even Ammonite, its close neighbor to the north. It is, however, clearly understandable as another Northwest Semitic dialect whose vocabulary is close enough to its neighbors to be decipherable from them. Reading the stone, consequently, was not as difficult a task as deciphering the Rosetta stone, for example, since we eventually gathered knowledge about the many different variations of the Northwest Semitic language.

The stone is a public statement by King Mesha, hence its famous name: the Mesha stone. Furthermore, there are many correspondences with the story told by the Bible, enough to think that it was this king against whom Israel went out to battle accompanied by the prophet Elisha in 2 Kings 3, which would mean the Mesha mentioned in the stone is the exact same one who lived in the second half of the ninth century and whose northernmost administrative capital was Dibon, cognate with the Arabic name of the site where it was found, Dhibhan.

Interpreting archaeological finds as though they are directly relevant to the Bible has been criticized lately for misunderstanding the archaeological record and, often, jumping to the wrong conclusions. Several skeptical scholars would make the case that this is true of the Mesha stone. But there are other reasons to suppose that the nineteenth-century scholars, no matter how shoddy their methods by contemporary standards, actually came upon one of the most momentous pieces of evidence of First Temple Israel. There will be more to say about this very fractious question in the last chapter.

Dhibhan, without doubt the site of ancient Dibon, was also subjected to fairly thorough archaeological excavation, though only its northern section. Situated on the north bank of the River Arnon, it was completely explored by Southern Baptist biblical scholars, who were unabashedly looking for confirmation of the patriarchal period, in the 1950s. They did find some city walls, a large gate, and some other buildings datable to the ninth century BCE—this is contemporary with King Mesha—but very little from the early Iron Age and nothing at all from the Bronze Age, which would correspond with the end of the patriarchal period, when the Israelites were arriving in the land and encountering the Moabites, according to the Bible.

The southern mound is covered by the modern town and is thus unknown territory from an archaeological point of view. On the other hand, it does look like the northern mound was the location of the ninth-century BCE town. The site so far contains no evidence of the events of the book of Numbers, where a victory over King Og, ruler of Bashan (around the Golan Heights) is claimed. Indeed the prophecy against Moab one finds in the book of Numbers is revealing:

> For fire went forth from Heshbon,
> > flame from the city of Sihon.
> > It devoured Ar of Moab,
> the lords of the heights of the Arnon.
> Woe to you, O Moab!
> > You are undone, O people of Chemosh!
> He has made his sons fugitives,
> > and his daughters captives,

to an Amorite king, Sihon.
So their posterity perished from Heshbon, as far as Dibon,
and we laid waste until fire spread to Med'eba.

(Number 21:28–30)

There is little evidence that any permanent settlements were to be found in these cities during the time when the legendary wandering Israelites under Moses were traveling through it on their way from Egypt to the promised land.[13] But there is considerable evidence of settlement during the time of the northern monarchy of Israel. Furthermore, if there were battles in the time of the settlement, the details have been included by people, living in the ninth century or later, who already knew that Moab had developed a city with permanent habitations. This is an argument from silence, but it is the silence of the archaeology, not the silence of the texts. And it suggests that we are on the right track when we seek the historical origin of the stories in the First Temple period, not in the patriarchal period, before we have any evidence of Dibon. And, as we shall later see, it is unlikely to have taken place in the Second Temple period either.

Mesha's Proclamation

I am Mesha son of Chemosh-yat, king of Moab, the Dibonite. My father reigned over Moab for thirty years, and I reigned after my father, (who) made this high place for Chemosh in Qarhoh . . . because he saved me from all the kings and caused me to triumph over all my adversaries.

As for Omri, (5) king of Israel, he humbled Moab many years (lit. days), for Chemosh was angry at his land. And his son followed him, and he also said, "I will humble Moab." In my time he spoke (thus), but I have triumphed over him and over his house, while Israel has perished forever! (Now) Omri had occupied the land of Medeba and (Israel) had dwelt there in his time and half the time of his son (Ahab), forty years; but Chemosh dwelt there in my time.[14]

This is a monumental stele, to celebrate the career of Mesha, and also a dedicatory stone, to commemorate the completion of a "high place" or local shrine to Chemosh, the national god of Moab. It was set up in a place Mesha calls Qarhoh, which may well be the very local place name where it was found, as it is otherwise unknown as a town or city, and we know that the city itself was called Dibon. The name itself might mean "the hilltop," "the high place," or "the sacred precinct of the city." We know very little about the unique aspects of the Moabite language, and archaeology has so far not helped clarify the ambiguity.

This stela, together with the Bible story, shows the war between Israel and Moab to have been a most ferocious border dispute. Note that the theological principle that bad things happened to Moab when its god was angered is parallel with many similar statements in the Bible about the anger of YHWH toward his disobedient people Israel. It appears to have been a common idea of the area. The Israelite enemy king is identified as Omri, but his "son" must be Jehoram, who lost the empire, rather than his literal son, Ahab, who maintained it. The Mesha stone never identifies the descendant as Ahab, but the Bible is more specific that it is Jehoram, and likely the Bible is correct on this detail.

The Mesha stone certainly contains the word *Gad*, the word *Israel*, and, quite plausibly, the word *David*. It is the best reconstruction of the sense of the sentence, though a number of scholars have challenged it, some even quite recently. The stone contains the first use of the term *Israel* within Palestinian inscriptions, though the Merneptah inscription in Egypt mentions "Israel" as a migratory tribe and is datable to 1206 BCE, just as the Israelites would have been settling the land of Canaan. Since the list of conquests in the Merneptah inscription seems to be arranged geographically, Israel appears quite plausibly in the Galilean hills.

A Speculative Reconstruction

In the Moabite stone, the name *Yahweh* can actually be reconstructed, and the full line might well read: "Omri occupied the land of Madeba, and [YHWH] resided there during his days and half the days of his son, some forty years. But Chemosh resided there in my days." If so, and it seems likely that it is so, it would be one of the earliest, clear reference to YHWH in an Israelite/Palestinian inscription. There is, however, an earlier reference again in Merneptah's name, this time his mortuary temple. The reference is to the Shoshu of YHY (the wandering tribes/bandits of YHY).

In the Bible, the region north of Dibon, though it was east of the Jordan River, was claimed by the Israelites and distributed to Gad, Reuben, and half the tribe of Manasseh (see Joshua 13:8). The southern parts of the region, including Madeba and Dibon, were formally assigned to Reuben, but there is some reason to believe that Mesha's inscription is more correct than the Bible when it says that the Gadites occupied the area. Numbers 32:24–26 says that the sons of Gad built Dibon, Ataroth, Aroer, Atroth-shophan, Jazer, Jog behah, Beth-nim'rah, and Beth-har'an, fortified cities, and folds for sheep. Furthermore, Dibon is sometimes called "Dibon of Gad" (as in Numbers 33:45–46). Mesha's account is quite consistent with the Pentateuch's understanding of the place names, though not with the account offered in 2 Kings 3. Again we see that the description of places and events during the settlement period actually describe the ninth century more clearly.

The first thing to note is how many biblical details are corroborated in the Moabite stone. Mesha mentions Israel some half-dozen times. He mentions a biblical tribe, Gad, and a king of the north, Omri. The Bible actually agrees with some of the details of Mesha's description. Perhaps the most striking agreement is that the rebellion happened in the ninth century under the reign of Mesha: "Mesha, the king of Moab, was a sheep-breeder, and he used to bring the king of Israel the wool of one hundred thousand lambs and one hundred thousand rams. But when Ahab died the king of Moab rebelled against the king of Israel" (2 Kings 3:4–5).

The Bible, like the Mesha stone, leaves no doubt that Moab was a vassal who owed Israel tribute in the form of wool and animals, though the figures are wildly exaggerated. The Bible and the Mesha stone both agree that Mesha threw off the domination of Israel. It disagrees with the Bible in many places about the progress of the campaign. A number of scholars think that they actually refer to different campaigns or that the Moabite stone only describes Moabite victories while the Bible only describes Israelite victories. Either may be correct, or neither. There is no way to know. But it is not out of character for a stela only to mention the victories of its subject.

It is significant, moreover, that the Moabite stone does not mention the most dramatic aspect of the Bible's story, the sacrifice of the king's eldest son, "who was to rule after him." If this was done for the reason that the Bible suggests, there would have been no reason for the Moabite stone not to have celebrated it. If Chemosh actually wanted human sacrifice, why would the king not brag about the expense of his sacrifice? This is puzzling for those who want to uphold the value of the Bible as an unimpeachable historical source.

However, we must remember that the Bible is trying to explain why the Israelites lost. Perhaps the inclusion of human sacrifice does that trick for them. We must practice the hermeneutics of suspicion and conclude that the Bible is a source like any other, naturally limited by its own perspective. That makes it a good historical source, but in no way an unimpeachable one.

The inclusion of this story of human sacrifice in the Hebrew Bible might yet be true because to argue that it is not is a relatively weak argument from silence. But, at the moment, it seems much more likely that the inclusion of the story of human sacrifice is Israelite propaganda to explain why they lost the war. It provides a reason why the Moabites, who were destined to be vassals, had in fact thrown off the yoke of Israelite vassalage and reasserted their sovereignty.

In any event, neither Jehoram nor his successors were able to reassert Israelite power over Moab. In the meantime, the story of Mesha's rebellion figures prominently in the theme of YHWH's replacement of human sacrifice with the cult of animal sacrifice. As the real details fade, the story of Mesha's immoral victory would have provided no contradiction to the idea that the armies of God were invincible.

Another Speculative Reconstruction

Most recently, Andre Lemaire proposes reconstructing "the house of David" for one of the most difficult lines in the text, line 31, which would bring the text in line with the more recently discovered Tel Dan inscription. The Tel Dan inscription, another fragmentary black basalt stela, found in the upper Galilee in 1993, contains both references to Jehoram son of [Ahab], king of Israel and [Ahaz]iah son of [Jehoram, ki]ng of the house of David.

It is perhaps best to go through this argument stepwise from its earliest interpreters until today so that the ingenious nature of this reconstruction can be appreciated. In the Moabite stone, line 31 is badly broken; part of the transcription of the letters comes from the stone, while another part has been reconstructed from the squeeze.

After a careful study of the squeeze, Clermont-Ganneau proposed the following uncertain reading at the end of the line: *b[—]wd*.[15] This tentative reading was confirmed by another expert scholar, Mark Lidzbarski, who tentatively identified traces after *b* as part of a *t*.[16] After checking the original and the squeeze in the Louvre, still another scholar, R. Dussaud,[17] proposed to read *bt[-]wd*. Lemaire's examination of the stone and the squeeze, which had by then been restored and cleaned of accumulated dust, confirms that *t* follows the *b*. Now, for the first time, Lemaire reconstructed the missing letter as a *d*.

The result is: *bt[d]wd*, which reads quite readily as the "house of [D]avid."

One problem with this reconstruction is that "house" is spelled *bt*, rather than the usual *byt*, as in standard Hebrew inscriptions and the Tel Dan Aramaic inscription. Missing the yod (the "y") would be practically impossible if the language were Hebrew or Aramaic, as in the Tel Dan inscription. But this is Moabite. In Moabite, "house" was spelled both ways. Indeed, in this very inscription it is spelled *bt* five times (in lines 7, 23, 27, and 30 twice) and only once (in line 25) as *byt*. Inclusion of the *y* may have been an archaic spelling or an optional spelling for Moabite, whereas it is the standard spelling for Hebrew and Aramaic.[18]

After going through the process of fixing the letters of the original Moabite stone, the addition of one more missing letter at the bottom of the Mesha stone yields a very important term, "the house of David," suggesting that this was the way in which Judah was known by its enemies.[19] Though it is speculative, Lemaire's recent suggestion yields an interesting possibility: "As for Hauronen, the hou[se] of [D]avid lived there. . . . And Chemosh said to me, 'Go down [and] fight against Hauronen.' So I went down and [fo]ught against the city and took it, and Chemosh resided there in my days."

Of course, this reconstruction demands that we restore a missing letter, so it must be thought to be a hypothesis, supported but not proven by the term *house of David* in another authentic inscription. It remains a possibility, no more. Whatever one accepts or not about the inscription, it seems most likely that the inscription dates to the death of Ahab around 840 BCE, clearly within the First Temple period. It is one thing to be skeptical of this reading; it is another thing to be skeptical that the Mesha stone in its entirety, or the Tel Dan inscription in its entirety, is authentic. And if they are authentic, then there must be an Israel ruled over by an Omri, who established a dynasty. And there may well have been a house of David. That seems indisputable.

Is the Mesha Stone a Fraud? Is the Tel Dan Inscription a Fraud?

A great many scholars—a huge, vast majority, in fact—have confirmed the authenticity of the Mesha stone, even as they have demurred or accepted one particular reading or another. The same is true of the more recent discovery of the Tel Dan inscription and a variety of other archaeologically confirmed inscriptions. However, there is a specific group of scholars who have refused to accept the relevance of virtually all the inscriptional evidence dated to the First Temple period of the Hebrew Bible. We call these scholars extreme minimalists. Contrary to the consensus in scholarship, these scholars do not disbelieve merely the mythical material at the beginning of Genesis. Most scholars have come to the conclusion that the stories of Genesis 1–11 are literary products developed in Hebrew society and rather similar to, if not directly influenced by, the mythical materials of the ancient Near East.

Nor are they the moderate biblical minimalist who, on the whole, caution against automatically relying on the Bible to judge the results of archaeological digs. These moderate biblical minimalists obviously give first attention to archaeological material and point out how the Bible oftentimes exaggerates or ignores various phenomena that seem present in the archaeological record. There is certainly nothing wrong with skepticism and much to be gained by going over a problem again in the light of new evidence or a new methodology.

One obvious example of this information is what archaeology has told us about worship of various goddesses in Israel and the surrounding area. The Bible cautions against goddess worship. But the archaeological record shows us that goddess worship was far more common than one might expect, even with all the prohibitions and stories in the Bible. In this regard, one must be willing to keep a number of categories methodologically separate in one's mind. For example, to understand what the archaeology is telling us, one must be willing to ignore the Bible and look with unbiased eyes at what emerges from archaeological digs. At the same time, when it comes to writing history, one must be willing to use all sources, even very biased ones, as the Bible often is. Any reconstruction of history that disqualifies a category of evidence for ideological reasons is ultimately going to be unsuccessful as history.

But there is a small group of people whom we should call extreme minimalists. These scholars really accept no report in the Bible at all from the First Temple period and no archaeological evidence that suggests that the

Hebrews or Israelites were ever there. They justify their distrust of the Bible by saying it is a theological document.

Every document, in fact, should be read with the hermeneutics of suspicion, as we have already seen. But they also have a rather strong ideological interest in demonstrating that the biblical record does not furnish any grounds for thinking that Zionists deserve the current state of Israel. Many have, in fact, adopted the very modern political propaganda position that the Israelites were not even in the land in the First Temple period. It is all invented. The Jews were a group of people who arrived in the area after the Babylonian captivity, and they made up the stories of the Bible out of whole cloth as a way of demonstrating mythologically their right to the land. The opposing narrative, and for them it is truly an *opposing* narrative, is that the Canaanites were always in the land and their offspring are the current Palestinians. And a group of Palestinian nationalists have begun to use their findings only because they fit their own understanding of modern history. This is an obvious example of circular reasoning. It is just like using the Bible as an unassailable standard by which the archeological record is judged. In both cases, the desired end of someone's modern political stance is being used as an exegetical key to understanding the Bible and archaeology. This is clearly a bad method with which to read the Bible, and it is a bad way to approach solving modern problems as well.

Obviously this group of scholars takes a completely different point of view about archaeology than the moderate minimalists. The moderate minimalists demand the use of archaeology as primary for their understanding and want it to take precedence over the relatively tendentious perspective of the Bible. They want to reconsider past conclusions in light of new evidence, always a helpful process.

Not so the extreme minimalists. The extreme minimalists actually deny that any of the archaeology done in the land of Israel shows anything about *ancient* Israel that disagrees with their *modern* position. That is because they are in very serious trouble: if there is even one positive artifact belonging to ancient Israel before the Second Commonwealth, then their narrative of Palestinian predominance, a modern narrative projected on the past, is disproven. So they must ad hoc their way through all the positive results of First Temple archaeology, proclaiming them fraudulent or suggesting that misinformed archaeologists interpreted them tendentiously.

Many moderate scholars are actually practicing archaeologists, willing to discuss what is historical and what can be trusted in the archaeology.[20] The radical minimalists are not archaeologists at all, much less paleographers; what unites them is an ethical concern for the modern Middle East. But, not being scholars of the field, there is no reason for them ever to accept any archaeological data as valid if it disagrees with their prior ideological commitments. They are anthropologists or other scholars who sympathize with the Palestinian cause. It becomes an object of faith or, what is the same, ideology.[21] And thus any positive findings gained in previous generations of scholars striving for disinterestedness are sacrificed to a modern political position.[22]

I certainly want there to be an ethical settlement of the modern Middle East. But we are dealing here with scholarship of the past. Misunderstanding the past will not do a thing for the modern world. Rather I see no reason of sufficient gravity not to accept the Mesha stone as historical, in the sense that it is an authentic artifact from the first millennium BCE. Like any other historical document, it has to be interrogated by the historian who must make an independent and autonomous decision about how to weight the evidence. Though its purpose is certainly to magnify the accomplishments of King Mesha, it also sometimes inadvertently verifies the Bible, even if it also disputes the biblical account in 2 Kings 3. Whether it contains the term *dynasty (house) of David* is less probable; it is a possible reconstruction without the same surety that we see in its mention of the "dynasty of Omri." What is more, the Mesha stone does not, in fact, tell us that Mesha sacrificed his son, as 2 Kings reports. Right now, that means to me that one must suspect the Bible is using that story as propaganda to explain away a defeat.

What seems to be demonstrated is that neither the story of Mesha's sacrifice of his son nor the "binding of Isaac" actually speaks directly to the moral question of human sacrifice with the kind of vehemence that the Deuteronomistic Historian would like. The book of Deuteronomy, as we have seen, and the later P source as well, has a quite explicit argument against any form of foreign sacrifice and human sacrifice in general. Neither the E source, the purported source of Genesis 22, nor 2 Kings 3 gives us the kind of categorical denial of the practice that we associate with the Deuteronomistic Historian. In fact, neither Genesis 22 nor 2 Kings 3 argues with the kind of completeness that Deuteronomy would require. God does command a human sacrifice in Genesis 22, though he later substitutes an animal, and the Israelites grant human sacrifice power in 2 Kings 3 by running from the battlefield. Rather they both argue for a period before Deuteronomy and the Deuteronomistic Historian. In that earlier period a mythological and polemical argument against human sacrifice was present in Israelite tradition.

I would argue, therefore, that the core of both Genesis 22 and 2 Kings 3 precedes the Deuteronomic Reform—and probably by a long time. The story in 2 Kings 3 is, in fact, just as interested in justifying the Israelites' inability to prevail in their siege of Dibon as it is in arguing against human sacrifice. It seems to argue against the perception of Genesis 22 that the God of Israel gives the Israelites the same power to conquer and "possess the gates of its enemies" for not performing child sacrifice.

In justifying a retreat, 2 Kings 3 is granting human sacrifice a modicum of power, for sure. It is also giving us evidence that human sacrifice still had a powerful effect on the Israelites. So it is an argument in favor of the necessity of a story like Genesis 22 or the teaching of the prophets and the Deuteronomistic Historian. We know that the question of the power of human sacrifice is a more general one because Greek sources also tell a series of myths arguing against human sacrifice. We know that the first millennium in the Mediterranean basin was struggling with the problem. But we do not know how often it was practiced. What we can tell instead is that there are two polemical uses of myth of human sacrifice in the Bible—one that extolls the Israelites for eschewing it and tells them that they will gain victory by *not* practicing it is contrasted with the converse reports that some Israelites and some Canaanites see it as effective and actually perform it. And they record that human sacrifice continued to retain its power, even among those who were supposed to eschew it, according to Genesis 22. So it is probable that Genesis 22, 2 Kings 3, and the Mesha stone all come from approximately the same time—about 840 BCE. Of course, this is less certain than realizing it must be earlier than Deuteronomy in 621 BCE. But we realize something else important. Sometimes mythical polemic is not enough. It may work for a while, but the book of Deuteronomy takes the prohibition to a higher level.

CHAPTER SIX

WAYS OF A MAN WITH A WOMAN

David and Bathsheba

Women are the victims of terrible crimes all through the Bible: Sarai/Sarah, Rebecca, Jephthah's daughter, the concubine of the Levite. Each story is worse than the previous. To be sure, looking at the portrayal of women has helped us understand how historical events are narrated and how myth is created, even how they evolve together. In the stories about Sarai/Sarah and Rebecca, the matriarchs are interpreted as evincing some virtue in a larger mythical context. They are not presented by the narrator as victims so much as paradigmatic figures, though they must seem to us to be victims of their gender in a crueller time. Even Jephthah's daughter, though she became a sacrificial victim, seems more like Isaac and Iphigenia, mythic figures whose sacrifices endowed a specific ritual in Israelite life. That helps us understand that their stories are folkloric and mythical.

But the concubine of the Levite is presented simply as a victim, even if we need to read the whole passage before we understand how she figures in the tragedy. This suggests to me that there is more of a historical kernel to her story. The Levite's concubine comes to be the symbolic part of a larger tragedy in which the injustice done to her takes on meaning for the entire community. She becomes the poster girl for the need to establish a kingship. Moreover, although almost every woman is externalized in biblical narrative—almost no character is presented as having an inner life until the prophets, women, as a rule, are not only externalized but externalized as objects of men's desire. It has been true of every female character whom we have so far studied. This is certainly also true of Bathsheba, the wife of David, whose story, as we shall next see, is related in 2 Samuel 11. The gaps in her characterization naturally raise a number of frustrating and interesting ambiguities about her character that needed to be noted in the ancient world and by us as well.[1]

Though Bathsheba is victimized, we begin to see different, more active aspects of her character. The narrative is, as usual, very compact, though ambiguous, so that a great many inferences are possible from the text.[2] The ambiguities can also be traced to an important difficulty in the text: Although David and Bathsheba sinned in their adulterous relationship, it was through this relationship that Solomon—the heir to the throne—was born. All subsequent Judean kings are descendants of Solomon. This demands some adjustments in Israel's mythic life as well. The kingship, as improbable as it may have seemed to anyone watching palace intrigues, continued through Solomon and not one of his many older half brothers, all of whom began with a better case for succeeding David. This creates another seemingly moral conflict in which we shall look for mediation in the literature from the primeval period.

David and Bathsheba's story begins with a foreshadowing of trouble. It is the time of year for kings to go out into battle. David tarries at home, though his army is in the field, arrayed against the Ammonites at Rabbah (2 Samuel 11:1). This, one infers, is not the proper behavior of a king, and it soon leads to trouble. At evening, presumably after his summer siesta, David arises from his bed and spies a woman bathing on a rooftop.[3] "She is very beautiful," the text immediately adds (11:2), clarifying that we are looking through David's eyes, or, better yet, the sexually objectifying glance of men. This is the same perspective from which we looked at Sarai/Sarah and Rebecca.

The text does not mention that David is smitten, but, again, we conclude it from her beauty and his subsequent actions. David inquires after the woman, who is identified in standard fashion as the daughter of her father and wife of her husband: "Bathsheba the daughter of Eliam, the wife of Uriah the Hittite" (11:3). There is no longer any necessity to linger on the Bible's lack of attention to women as personages. The Bible identifies so many women only in terms of their relations with men, not even mentioning a name. But this woman receives a name, immediately after we are introduced to her as the object of David's desire. So the Bible approaches her in its normal fashion. But she gains in stature as her history continues.

In this case, it gives us a portrait of Bathsheba as the daughter of one of David's celebrated men of valor and a loyal supporter of David's rise, but also clearly states that she is not available to David because she is already married.[4] Both of these facts ought to have made David pause. But he does not. He rushes headlong into adultery. The language itself expresses David's passion. The facts of their adultery are narrated in two exceptionally action-laden verses: "And David sent messengers, and took her; and she came in unto him, and he lay with her; for she was purified from her uncleanness: and she returned unto her house. And the woman conceived, and sent and told David, and said, "I am with child" (11:4–5). In this very abbreviated and informative report, Bathsheba speaks her only direct line in this incident. It is almost as if the narrator is stressing the brevity of sin while recompense is long.

We have few clues as to what she may have thought about the events that happened to her. David's men took her. That suggests her lack of consent. Yet she did not cry out either, possibly suggesting that she consented to the sex act itself, as Deuteronomy 22 suggests. Films often portray Bathsheba as tempted by David's powerful position. She consents to the act, but the biblical films fall short of the ambiguity of the Hebrew text. In a way, the Bible assumes that she will assent.

In spite of the ambiguities of the central issue in this story, Bathsheba will be the significant love in David's life. Because of the silence of the narrator, motives in the story can appear ambiguous and extraordinarily well mixed. The only sure inference from this passage is that it must have taken some courage to report her pregnancy to the king. We know the parentage of the child because we know that "she was purified from her uncleanness" before she went to David. She is purified and fertile. There is no doubt that the child's father is David, and David has no doubt that it is his.

The detail is crucial for the succession of the kingship. But perhaps it also suggests that, whatever her original feelings about the tryst, she has now become David's ally in dealing with Uriah.[5] And it is understandable because, as a pregnant woman, she is the more vulnerable to being discovered and punished for the adultery, though David might yet escape. But she is loyal to David. She does not publicly designate him as the father and imperil both of them. And, what is more, she does not attempt to warn her husband about David's plan, which suggests that she has been won over by David's personality or his power or simply that she knows she has only one practical choice now.

But, more importantly, David is also loyal to her. Moreover, it is David alone who plays the active role in the conspiracy against Uriah the Hittite, although both David and Bathsheba are trying to escape being publicly charged with the sin of adultery. He sends his most loyal servant, Joab, to bring Uriah to him, asking about how the war progresses, feeding him a good meal, and then bidding him take the evening at leisure, wash his feet, and enjoy his wife's company. Washing one's feet may be a euphemism for cleansing oneself for sexual congress. But Uriah foils David's plan by refusing to break his vow not to have sex with his wife, while the army is encamped against Ammon. This appears to be a more general practice of the elite fighters, since David himself later reports a similar regimen: "And David answered the priest, and said unto him, truthfully, women have been kept from us about these three days, since I came out" (1 Samuel 21:5). In this case, Uriah's spotless and unsuspecting nature serves as a foil to David's deviousness.

David tries once again, deliberately getting Uriah drunk, but to no avail (11:11). Does this impugn Uriah as not being man enough for his beautiful wife, because even when he is drunk he will not forget his vow? Perhaps the text means us to understand that, but, as usual, it says nothing explicitly. It seems more likely the text is portraying Uriah as a very good soldier who refuses to break his battle vows of celibacy, even with the permission of the king. But there is surely something sadly comic in this scene of David's unsuccessful attempt to seduce Uriah into having sex with his own wife to hide David's sin.

After that incident, however, the comedy is finished. David will not be able to pawn the child off as Uriah's. Now the story takes a darker turn. David must take decisive, quick, and concerted action against Uriah, his most loyal and innocent of soldiers, else Bathsheba's pregnancy will alert everyone to their deed. Though David is the monarch and Uriah his subject, it is David who plays the role of a traitor. The irony emphasizes the chain of sins that David sets in motion. Whatever Bathsheba may have felt, we clearly know what David feels about her because of the undertakings he plans and the magnitude of the sins he subsequently commits.

Although Uriah is too good to become David's dupe, the scene will still end in Uriah's death. Not only is Joab to arrange that Uriah will be in the front line, but he is to connive the rest of the troops to retreat when Uriah is in the heat of the battle, thus ensuring Uriah's death. Uriah, like an ancient version of Rosenkranz and Guildenstern, carries the letter sealing his doom from David to Joab (14–15). The narrative, as it does typically, explains the plan in the letter and then repeats it when it happens, adding to the horror of the murder.

After Uriah is dead, Joab instructs the messenger to return to David with news of the battle. In the midst of this is an analogy that places blame on Bathsheba as well as on David. Joab makes reference to the story of Abimelech's demise at the hands of a woman. He was killed by a mill stone (rolling pin size), thrown from the walls of Thebez, which crushed his skull (Judges 9:53). This Abimelech is the one who was well known to have been inadvertently and comically killed by a woman.[6] Although Bathsheba is not portrayed as participating in this sinister plan, Joab evidently is blaming her for being so attractive to David and therefore responsible for Uriah's death. Uriah is, in the eyes of Joab, another victim of Bathsheba, while we would naturally see the situation as reversed. We should describe this ironic position as Joab's perspective, because, in the story, it is uniquely his. The important question is: is this what the narrator wants us to understand about Bathsheba and women from this story? Does he want us to remain with Joab's jaded and cynical view of women as sinister distractors of men, or is there another position from which to appreciate Bathsheba as a person who did not cause the events at all but who had only a few practical choices to make in this male-dominated world?

Joab's instructions to the messenger include the request to answer any of David's questions justifying the loss of so many valiant men, ironically, with the news that David most wants to hear. "And the messenger said unto David, 'Surely the men prevailed against us, and came out unto us into the field, and we were upon them even unto the entering of the gate. And the shooters shot from off the wall upon your servants; and some of the king's servants died, and your servant Uriah the Hittite is dead also'" (22–24). Never revealing his secret relief, David sends back another coded message to Joab through the unsuspecting messenger, comforting him for his loss of men and counseling him not to despair for the loss of even very good men like Uriah. No doubt the audience is taking some pleasure now in being party to the secret. Joab, who is entirely aware of what is happening, is now as guilty as David is, which is underlined by the messenger's lack of understanding.[7]

With Uriah out of the way, David is seemingly free to do as he pleases. The rest of the chapter quickly resumes the story, recounting how Bathsheba mourns, how David marries her after her mourning is over, how she takes up residence in the palace, and, at her appointed time, bears a son. We might think that David has gotten away with his plan, but the very last line of the chapter tells that it is not so: "The thing that David had done displeased the LORD" (27).

David and the LORD

We know justice must be coming. In the end, all the secrecy, in which the audience had participated as well as the characters, was no protection. Secrecy did not bring about safety. The LORD will punish the wrongdoers, even if it is the king himself who hid the deeds.

The LORD sends Nathan to David with an unpleasant task (2 Samuel 12:1). Nathan must tell the king that he has committed a terrible sin. He picks a very clever way to do so, avoiding the ire of the king. Nathan tells David a parable about a poor man and his beloved lamb. A poor man has but one lamb, which he treats as his pet, while his rich neighbor has a large herd. Yet the rich man kills and serves the poor man's lamb to a guest rather than supplying one of the many lambs of his herd. Asked by the prophet to judge wisely, David angrily rules that the rich man should die and that the poor man should be compensated four times over. At this point, the prophet intervenes with the judgment from God:

> 7 Nathan said to David, "You are the man! Thus says the LORD, the God of Israel: I anointed you king over Israel, and I rescued you from the hand of Saul; 8 I gave you your master's house, and your master's wives into your bosom, and gave you the house of Israel and of Judah; and if that had been too little, I would have added as much more. 9 Why have you despised the word of the LORD, to do what is evil in his sight? You have struck down Uriah the Hittite with the sword, and have taken his wife to be your wife, and have killed him with the sword of the Ammonites. 10 Now therefore the sword shall never depart from your house, for you have despised me, and have taken the wife of Uriah the Hittite to be your wife. 11 Thus says the LORD: I will raise up trouble against you from within your own house; and I will take your wives before your eyes, and give them to your neighbor, and he shall lie with your

wives in the sight of this very sun. [12] For you did it secretly; but I will do this thing before all Israel, and before the sun."

(2 Samuel 12:7–12)

Nathan's parable is meant to be the ironic counterpart to the secret subtext of the messenger. David completely misses the true meaning of the parable until it is made plain to him. The prophecy warns of evil within his own house and that the punishment will be public because the sin was so private. David immediately admits his sin and repents, which (in the eyes of the Deuteronomistic Historian) slakes God's anger and saves his life: "And David said unto Nathan, 'I have sinned against the LORD.' And Nathan said unto David, 'The LORD also hath put away thy sin; thou shalt not die'" (verse 13). But, instead, the first son David and Bathsheba conceived together will die. This is not a solution we would consider just, but these were different times.

And this is what happens without delay. We see David grieving over his sickly firstborn son from Bathsheba. David mourns and prays in the house of the LORD, while the child is alive. But, after he dies, David takes off his sackcloth and returns to his palace. His explanation is a good summary of the wisdom and resignation of the ancient Israelites in the face of death: "While the child was yet alive, I fasted and wept: for I said, Who can tell whether GOD will be gracious to me, that the child may live? But now he is dead, why should I fast? Can I bring him back again? I shall go to him, but he shall not return to me" (22–23). For the Israelites and many Near Eastern cultures, wisdom was primarily gained in the contemplation of life and death. One senses, perhaps, some anger as well as resignation in David's voice. But no one in the story questions that the LORD can take away a child for the sins of the parents. The Bible eventually affirms that God will stop punishing children for the sins of the father. But that comes several centuries later, when the Israelites are facing exile, and the oracle of God's change of mind comes from prophetic sources (Jeremiah 31:29, Ezekiel 18:2). It is safe to assume that this story precedes those prophets.

The Perspective of Joab

Joab continues to show himself David's loyal subject. To him belongs the honor of taking the city of Rabbah from the Ammonites. But he forebears and lets David strike the last blow. He is David's loyal henchman. The victory signals that God's ire is past, and it also ironically underlines that David himself, as the result of his sinning elsewhere, really deserves no credit for the victory because of his infatuation with Bathsheba:

[26] Now Joab fought against Rabbah of the Ammonites, and took the royal city. [27] Joab sent messengers to David, and said, "I have fought against Rabbah; moreover, I have taken the water city. [28] Now, then, gather the rest of the people together, and encamp against the city, and take it; or I myself will take the city, and it will be called by my name." [29] So David gathered all the people together and went to Rabbah, and fought against it and took it. [30] He took the crown of Milcom from his head; the weight of it was a talent of gold, and in it was a precious stone; and it was placed on David's head. He also brought forth the spoil of the city, a very great amount. [31] He brought out the people who were in it, and set them to work with saws and iron picks and iron axes, or sent them to the brickworks. Thus he did to all the cities of the Ammonites. Then David and all the people returned to Jerusalem.

(2 Samuel 12:26–31)

The gaze of the narrator has left Bathsheba, with all the ambiguities of her character unexplained, and has been transferred to Joab. Joab, too, has an ambiguous position because he both serves David and goes beyond what is ordered. Later we shall see Bathsheba successfully conniving with Nathan to seat Solomon on the throne of Judea over those who favored Adonijah, Solomon's older brother by Haggith, one of David's other wives. Joab is rightly in favor of Adonijah, supporting the dynastic principle and the more mature candidate. But Adonijah is the loyal servant of the king, and perhaps he reasons that Adonijah was the expected older brother and legitimate heir to David. Joab always represents the simplest logic of realpolitik. He upholds the dynastic principle (i.e., Adonijah is Solomon's older brother). Joab's support underlines that Adonijah is the better choice on the face of it. Unfortunately, our story takes a strange turn, and Joab, the ruthlessly loyal servant of David, pays with his life when Solomon ascends the throne. But what is important to understand here is what Joab knows. Again he knows the whole design, as we do, but he seemingly sees his job as protecting the king from his own mistakes. He lives in a world of ferocious ironies, especially about women. He clearly feels that David's dalliance with Bathsheba has endangered the kingdom, but he keeps quiet about it.

All this becomes clear when Joab mentions that Abimelech died at the hands of a woman too. This perspective externalizes women and makes women guilty of seduction when it is the desire that men feel toward women that is the actual motivator. That is, of course, not the only way to see this story. It is only Joab's ironic view. But it quite likely is a point of view that could have been widely shared in the society. The text leaves Bathsheba's role somewhat more ambiguous than Joab's irony. But does the narrator actually make a point that women are independent persons, not just objects of desire?

One clue that it does comes from Joab's fate. Joab, the villain and hatchet man who is the loyal servant of the king, is a puzzlement. Does he represent the Bible's last word on the motivation of Bathsheba, a moral condemnation? Or is there another perspective as well, one that goes beyond the knowing irony of Joab? The perspective of Joab is never directly affirmed, but it is never denied either. It must be given its due. We can trace the fortunes of Joab and see whether we end with a condemnation of Bathsheba's enticements with which she distracted the king. There seems to be an element of this position in Joab's understanding of the events. He was a villain, but a loyal empire builder too, which is hard to justify in any simple moral tone of the former prophets:

> 28 When the news came to Joab—for Joab had supported Adonijah though he had not supported Absalom—Joab fled to the tent of the LORD and grasped the horns of the altar. 29 When it was told King Solomon, "Joab has fled to the tent of the LORD and now is beside the altar," Solomon sent Benaiah son of Jehoiada, saying, "Go, strike him down." 30 So Benaiah came to the tent of the LORD and said to him, "The king commands, 'Come out.'" But he said, "No, I will die here." Then Benaiah brought the king word again, saying, "Thus said Joab, and thus he answered me." 31 The king replied to him, "Do as he has said, strike him down and bury him; and thus take away from me and from my father's house the guilt for the blood that Joab shed without cause. 32 The LORD will bring back his bloody deeds on his own head, because, without the knowledge of my father David, he attacked and killed with the sword two men more righteous and better than himself, Abner son of Ner, commander of the army of Israel, and Amasa son of Jether, commander of the army of Judah. 33 So shall their blood come back on the head of Joab and on the head of his descendants

forever; but to David, and to his descendants, and to his house, and to his throne, there shall be peace from the LORD forevermore." ³⁴ Then Benaiah son of Jehoiada went up and struck him down and killed him; and he was buried at his own house near the wilderness. ³⁵ The king put Benaiah son of Jehoiada over the army in his place, and the king put the priest Zadok in the place of Abiathar.

(2 Kings 2:28–35)

Joab is abandoned and Benaiah serves as commander-in-chief in his stead.

Solomon knows that Joab is not his ally and immediately acts to remedy the situation. But Joab's death was not merely the result of a blood feud. He was a very loyal and effective servant of David, just not an ally of Solomon. The text is anxious to show that the shedding of blood in the manner of Joab is now over. But it also seems clear that no such culmination is possible in this society. Benaiah now is the commander of the Kerethites and Pelethites, the position Joab held, and thus he is the commander of the palace guard.

Contradictory Evidence and the Objectification of Women

The story of David and Bathsheba is an unavoidable and very sensitive conflict for the narrator. If Bathsheba had not been the mother of Solomon, the next king, the tone of the story could have been more condemnatory, or the whole sordid history could have been devalued as an unsavory side chapter in the history of the Judean monarchy. Indeed, the narrative of David's life in the books of Chronicles does exactly that. It completely omits the adultery between David and Bathsheba from the story. This presents us with an excellent argument for seeing the narrative in 2 Samuel as being from the First Temple period; clearly later historiography can safely recount uncomfortable facts with impugnity.

But Solomon succeeds David, so Bathsheba, as queen mother, is too important for the narrator in the former prophets to ignore. She is actively involved in the palace intrigues of the succession narrative (or SN, as it is often called).[8] As we have seen, if the contradiction cannot be ignored, biblical text will create a mythical way to surmount the contradiction. One of the functions of myth is to mediate these contradictions, as we have repeatedly seen.

Presumably the narrator is a southerner; the narrator must deal with Bathsheba and must deal with her completely and yet present her in a complex power setting when it comes to the succession. As in the case of David, the narrator must be both adulatory and critical by turns. As it is, the narrator flatly relates their relationship in 2 Samuel 11, leaving many gaps to mystify us, and in the next chapter, 2 Samuel 12, supplies some of the missing moral significance by relating the effects of YHWH's anger, even as it appears that David and Joab have succeeded in covering up David's crime with Bathsheba. It does not end a whole series of ambiguities created by the gaps in the texts, but it provides a strong moral compass missing in quite a few of the stories we have studied. To account for this unexpected result, the narrator creates the new theme of David's penitence.

But we, the readers, are clear about one thing. The LORD knows and punishes even secret crimes. The reader's perspective shares a bit with Joab, since we and he are both privy to the terrible ironies of David's adultery, while most of the other characters in the drama are not. His perspective on desire includes the thought that many men are victimized out of desire for women. But it is a cynical perspective because he recognizes that men's desire objectifies women and, in fact, blames women for men's dependence on them. This is certainly a perspective that can be seen all over the world, even today. But it is important to note that this is the perspective of Joab, who is no center of moral significance. Joab is David's henchman and cleanup team, and for him David's romance is nothing but a difficulty.

Judah and Tamar

Gary Rendsburg and several other scholars have pointed out the deep structural relationship between the story of David and Bathsheba and an incident in the patriarchal period, one that is otherwise difficult to explain: the story of Judah and Tamar in Genesis 38.[9] This is a completely different Tamar from the daughter of David mentioned in 2 Samuel. This Tamar is the daughter-in-law of Judah. The difficulty between Tamar and Judah depends on an unexplained problem. But it begins with a marriage that should not have taken place:

> [1] It happened at that time that Judah went down from his brothers and settled near a certain Adullamite whose name was Hirah. [2] There Judah saw the daughter of a certain Canaanite whose name was Shua; he

married her and went in to her. ³ She conceived and bore a son; and he named him Er. ⁴ Again she conceived and bore a son whom she named Onan. ⁵ Yet again she bore a son, and she named him Shelah. She was in Chezib when she bore him. ⁶ Judah took a wife for Er his firstborn; her name was Tamar. ⁷ But Er, Judah's firstborn, was wicked in the sight of the LORD, and the LORD put him to death. ⁸ Then Judah said to Onan, "Go in to your brother's wife and perform the duty of a brother-in-law to her; raise up offspring for your brother." ⁹ But since Onan knew that the offspring would not be his, he spilled his semen on the ground whenever he went in to his brother's wife, so that he would not give offspring to his brother.

(Genesis 38:1–9)

We know from the beginning of the story that this will be an intermarriage between an Israelite man Judah and a Canaanite woman who is the daughter of Shua. Her name might even be said to be Bathshua, because she is the daughter (*bath*) of Shua, making the names Bath Shua and Bath Sheba nearly identical. Indeed, in Chronicles 3:15, David's wife Bathsheba is called Bath Shua, as if to make the analogy even closer. We also know that nothing good is likely to come of this story because the Bible does not favor intermarriages. Of course, David is from the tribe of Judah and so they are directly related characters. But David and Judah are closely associated structurally as well. They are both heads of families, and they are both shepherds who tended their flocks during their youth. They both go to live in Adullam (Genesis 38:1 and 1 Samuel 22:1). Judah has a Canaanite friend, Hirah (Genesis 38:1), while David forms an alliance with Hiram, king of Tyre (2 Samuel 5:11).

There are more connections to discuss. Judah's first child with the Canaanite woman Shua is Er and the second is Onan. Tamar is selected by Judah as Er's wife. But then Er is executed by God for an unnamed but terrible crime—possibly sexual in nature, because lack of sexual responsibility is the leitmotif of the story—and Tamar is given to Onan to raise children from the deceased Er. Onan refuses to live up to the standard terms of the Levirate marriage because he feels the children would not be his. What precisely this means is not clear. At this point in the story, we might suspect that Tamar is not staying true to her husband. But once Onan refuses to raise children after his deceased brother, because he fears the children will not be his, it becomes clear that she is staying true to her marriage responsibilities to raise up children from her husbands. She wants Judah to perform the rite of the Levirate, giving her the status she deserves as a mother in Israel.

The Tamar story becomes a kind of sexual comedy. She disguises herself as a prostitute, entices Judah into intercourse from which she conceives a child, and walks off with his staff and signet. When her pregnancy is discovered, instead of being burned as an adulteress, she brings out Judah's property and explains that she tricked Judah into performing the duty of the Levirate. Thus Judah has unknowingly committed a sin—the sin of sleeping with his daughter-in-law—but at the same time fulfilled the law by raising up children to memorialize his sons. He acknowledges that Tamar has tricked him into performing his duty.

At the same time, this story puzzles us. You mean the Bible is suggesting that a widow should have sex with her father-in-law to satisfy the Levirate marriage? Exactly. That seems like incest or at the very least a very exceptional use of the Levirate marriage, which normally concerns only brothers.

Even the standard Levirate marriage seems a lot like incest. Eventually, it was such a problem that the early rabbis reversed the performance of the commandment. In their estimation, not performing the Levirate marriage (*yibum*) but releasing (*halitzah*, meaning a ritualized release of a sandal) became the superior ritual. But this story goes to the other extreme, explaining that Tamar actually surpassed Judah in making sure that her husband's seed continued through a son.

One supposes this is a story that basically explains how Levirate marriage should work, at a boundary condition, when a son refuses his responsibility. Structurally, it occupies the place of the story of the sin of David and Bathsheba. If so, it is suggesting that the sexual irregularity is necessary under these special conditions, which would create an exculpatory environment for David and Bathsheba. There are a number of lesser convergences as well, which have been mentioned. David loses two of his sons to internecine fighting. Judah loses two sons too. Judah, the ancestor of David, whose daughter-in-law has a very similar name to Bathsheba's, has committed a great (but in this case inadvertent) sexual sin and then is tricked into admitting his guilt. The same is true of David, though his sin is very intentional.

One wonders whether this analogy or typology is meant to be political satire or a justification for the Davidic monarchy or both at the same time. Perhaps it's best to assume the story is meant to do both. It satirizes Judah and David, but it also begins from the notion that these are the kinds of foibles that victimize men. It also valorizes Tamar by showing that she has the intelligence and gumption to trick Judah into doing his duty toward her. It explains David's sin by saying that David is only reenacting the prototypical sin of his ancestor, Judah, who comically commits incest but actually winds up doing what he was supposed to do toward his daughter-in-law. So it both justifies and criticizes Judah and David too by means of the prototypical example. This is a primary function of myth according to Claude Lévi-Strauss and Edmund Leach. So we ought not to wonder that sometimes we cannot tell whether a story is trying to legitimate an action or serve as a political satire. A mythical story can be simultaneously polemical and legitimating. So we must take a look at the primeval sexual comedy—the story of Adam and Eve.

The Garden of Eden: A Comic View of Human Sexuality and the Objectification of Women

The most obvious prototypical argument justifying David's behavior comes from the story of Adam and Eve. Unfortunately the biblical creation tradition has often been interpreted as entirely negative about women. This is, in large part, because later interpreters have taken an excessively negative view of women. But, I believe that this is just as wrong as interpreting Tamar as a villain. She is actually a heroine. The Bible itself is not entirely cynical about women's role. Rather the Adam and Eve story also takes a more positive view of women's roles and a more comic view of men's inadvertent mistakes—just like the Judah and Tamar story. Certainly, one finds many interpreters who take Joab's ironic cynicism as the final word on women's role, but, if one looks at the story of Adam and Eve, I believe the Bible is offering an ironic but comic rather than cynical view of the relationship between men and women, just as with the story of Judah and Tamar.

Though Bathsheba and David lose their first child, neither suffers any further punishment. Indeed Bathsheba stands up for her son Solomon, as we shall see. Adonijah does not become king after David, though he is dynastically the next in line; Solomon does. Indeed, because Solomon inherits the kingdom, many different cases of ultimogeniture are emphasized in the patriarchal narrative. The perspective of Joab does not prevail. There is another idea operant about the way in which men and women interact. That perspective about men and women can be traced all the way back to the Garden of Eden, and, in biblical tradition, women have some amazingly positive and active roles to play.

To be sure, the Garden of Eden story can easily be understood to mean that men are victims of women's sensuality, which would essentially mean that women are being blamed for being a projection of men's desire. It is a classic case of the objectification of women. That is the dominant interpretation of Christianity and Islam and certainly a prominent interpretation of rabbinic Judaism as well. But, once the connection with David and Bathsheba is clear, we can see that there is a subtler perspective to appreciate, one that does not blame a single character as much as illustrate the whole human comedy of sexual desire and its fulfillment.

In the story of Adam and Eve in the Bible, it is certainly Eve who is the active character. The actual story of Adam and Eve, seemingly so different from the dominant interpretation in our society, provides us with a parallel case to the later depiction of Bathsheba by describing an even more deliberately well-formed woman. Though the gaps we have grown accustomed to appear in the Genesis story as well, we do get a much more well-rounded picture of Eve. In a way, it is Eve's characteristics and personality that gives us license to understand Bathsheba's active role in Solomon's succession as a positive role. It is hard to find anything precisely like this story in any other royal archives of the ancient Near East. Just as the story of David and Bathsheba begins in a tragedy of desire and murder but leads to a continuation of the Davidic dynasty, the story of Adam and Eve begins in comedy and ends in life as we know it. After huge distress, we all manage to carry on successfully.

This drama of everyday life is very different from the creation story that we find in chapter 1 of Genesis—the six-day creation story—in which God himself is the only creator, having control of every event, organized on a seven-day week, and ending with the creation of humanity. The whole creation is pronounced "very good." It is God who sets up the cosmos. Though we think that the seven-day week and the Sabbath are part of culture, this story reads them into the fabric of the universe.

But the comic story of Adam and Eve starts over in chapter 2:4b and discusses a drama with many competing forces at work at once. The Eden story begins with a true moment of paradise. When the water wells up from the ground, creating what amounts to a desert oasis, the grasses begin to sprout, and then the Lord God plants a garden for the man he has just made (Genesis 2:5–6). Every tree grows pleasing to the sight and good for food, with the tree of life in the middle of the garden (8–9). We are in a fabulous imagined landscape, like the Mesopotamian myth of Enki and Ninhursag, which is the Sumerian myth of the loss of paradise. In Sumer "Eden" was called Dilmun, a place where Enki, the water-drawer god, is allowed to eat eight magical plants. So there is a cultural context for the fabulous plants and the first of the two critical trees, the tree of life.[10] The second tree, seemingly its polar opposite in terms of the story, is "the tree of the knowledge of good and evil" (16–17). These two trees represent the two poles of movement in the story. The narrative takes us from paradisical amorality and immortality with the tree of life to awareness of good and evil within the limited, mortal world that we all know; the fantasy gives way to our familiar reality.

Indeed, this description of paradise is a Middle Eastern pastoral land-scape, familiar to us from the Arabian Nights, as well as its many ancient antecedents.[11] The garden is filled with the great rivers of the world, includ-ing the small spring, the Gihon, that waters Jerusalem, with the great river valleys of the Fertile Crescent.[12] The tone of fabled paradise achieved at the beginning is furthered with legendary gold (*zahav*, 2:11), incenses (*bdellium*, 2:12), and precious stones (*even shoham*, 2:12), however inexactly we can identify them. The lyrical, pastoral tone continues uninterrupted with the first speech of God: "Of every tree of the garden you are free to eat; but as for the tree of knowledge of good and evil, you must not eat of it, for as soon as you of it, you shall die" (2:17). Though the fabulous description continues, the seeds of the drama are just as surely planted as the trees.

The Lord God then creates the man, as a potter might build a clay figure, but he breathes his spirit (*ruaḥ*) into him (2:7). He places the man in the gar-den "to till it and keep it" (2:15), carefully chosen words to show that Adam is not actually working in the garden, but caring for it as if it were a hobby. That is because "work," as we know it, is a punishment for disobedience. *Keeping* the garden (which he did not plant) is more like tending the garden. That makes his work sound more like play. The man needs companionship, so God creates animals that the man names, showing Adam's superiority over them, who cannot name themselves. Again, Adam's tasks are more like play than work. After creating the animals (again in contradistinction to the first story), the woman is created, one who is to be a helper. In Hebrew "helper" is expressed much more mordantly as a "help corresponding to him," literally a "helper like/opposite him" (2:18). The whole subsequent drama between Adam and Eve is cleverly expressed in the word used for the woman's role

WAYS OF A MAN WITH A WOMAN

as a helpmeet and helpmate. Even though the narration already shows the woman to be his helper, not the other way around and not as equals, we shall see that the woman has a great deal of independence in the narrative because she is much smarter than the man. The institution of marriage is justified by the first speech of the man. It is very likely an oath or recognition of kin of some sort:

> This one at last
> is bone of my bones
> And flesh of my flesh.
> This one shall be called Woman
> for from man she was taken.
>
> (Genesis 2:23)

Certainly this language expresses a publicly ratified relationship, as it seems to in 2 Samuel: "And say to Amasa, 'Are you not my bone and my flesh? God do so to me, and more also, if you are not commander of my army henceforth in place of Joab'" (2 Samuel 19:13). But that does not make it good poetry. It shows that the man we know as Adam is not very articulate, he is just animated dirt. Unlike man, taken from the ground and always a kind of clod, the woman is made of flesh and blood and her intelligence is prodigious. The woman forms complicated and very sophisticated sentences. She has much more to say even than Bathsheba. Yet she shows herself in the next chapter to be so fully articulate that her own words trip her up. The fact that man achieves mastery over her is a kind of primal joke.

The mood of innocence is maintained even though the couple are married and must be functioning sexually. The narrator is taking care to use words economically but exactly: "The two of them were naked, but they were not ashamed" (Genesis 2:25). In biblical description the man and his wife are adult children—a fact brought out more strongly when we notice the Bible's frequent pairing of the images of children, nakedness, and innocence in the sense of not knowing good from evil (e.g., Isaiah 7:16). The latter "knowing good from evil" is a phrase that describes human development. Adults have it; children do not. On the other hand, this is a dangerous state of innocence. It cannot last. They are as yet merely children in a sheltered garden, even though they have distinct personalities. In the Adam and Eve story, it is comedy that keeps the drama of blame from becoming a tragedy of desire, as it is in the story of David and Bathsheba.

The inherent imbalance of the paradise is brought out by wordplay, placed exactly when the mood changes abruptly. Just as they are naked (*arumim*, Genesis 2:25) so is the snake the most shrewd (*arum*, Genesis 3:1) of all the animals. The words for *naked* and *shrewd* are homonyms, but their meanings could not be more opposite because *naked* is part of the innocent world, but *shrewd* is part of the adult world where one has to be able to recognize temptation. Adam and Eve are babes in the woods by comparison to the snake.

The snake is the antagonist in the drama. He asks the woman: "Did God really say: 'You shall not eat of any tree in the garden?'" (Genesis 3:1). She answers bravely and articulately, beginning a dialogue of misunderstandings: "We may eat of the fruit of the trees of the garden; but God said, 'You shall not eat of the fruit of the tree which is in the midst of the garden, neither shall you touch it, lest you die'" (Genesis 3:2). This is a long complex sentence that even hints at indirect speech. So we know that Eve is a very intelligent person. But, like Adam, she has no moral sense.

This raises at least two interesting problems: 1. The Lord God did not give the command to Eve directly, rather to Adam; how did she know what the command was? 2. Nor did he forbid either of them to touch the fruit. All this ambiguity arises in two short verses. The story never stops to explain. It moves quickly to the snake's next statement, which is an ironic truth: he tells them that they will not die if they eat. Rather their eyes will be opened and they will become like gods, knowing good and evil (Genesis 3:4). Ironically, that is the exact truth. They do not die when they eat of the tree, and they do become like gods, knowing good and evil. As with the ancient Near East, wisdom and death are related. In Mesopotamia, wisdom is often the result of understanding our mortality. Death itself comes later. Animals have life; humans have life and wisdom; but only gods have immortality. Humans have lost immortality but can develop wisdom through their mortality. The purpose of the many stories that deal with these themes is to explain how that came to be. This one is no different.

The final damage comes when the woman sees how appealing the fruit is: "good for food" . . . "a delight to the eyes" . . . "and desirable to make one wise" (Genesis 3:6). These are meant to underline the woman's sensuousness and sensuality as well as her intelligence. Certainly she is the better-equipped intellectually of the two characters. But she is also more sensuous—altogether a better-realized person. That sensuality as well as her intelligence is her undoing. She eats and gives the fruit to her husband who eats as well, without any further dialogue, again depicting his lack of intelligence.

It may be that the story is blaming the woman alone for the sin of dis-obedience, but there is hardly anything in the story to make that clear. She is sensually attracted to the beautiful fruit, as well as clever enough to be outwitted by the cleverer snake. She is the more clearly articulated and de-picted character of the primal couple. But is she any more to blame than her husband? That does not seem obvious if the man's lack of articulation caused her to mistake the command to begin with. Adam is likely standing next to her throughout her conversation with the snake, and he can think of noth-ing to say. He just obeys his wife. If Eve is beguiled by the snake, Adam is beguiled by Eve's obvious intelligence and sensuousness. He is just as much to blame as she is. His inarticulateness and guilelessness have gotten him into this fix. To think that Eve is more to blame than Adam is to fall victim to the objectification of women. It is to affirm the perspective of Joab in the creation story. A fuller understanding of the situation is surely a comic one, in the sense that it tells us something true and enduring about the human condition through humor.

Adam, of course, has a few more pratfalls to show us. Not even the fruit makes Adam smart. What they get from the tree is not "intelligence"; their IQs are unaffected by the change. Adam is still rather slow and Eve is still smart and sensuous. When God asks where he is, Adam answers that he is hiding. I would say that that is literally the oldest joke in the world, except that Adam's seduction by Eve is even older. But they do not fall; to be exact, there is no fall in the story, except to say that they lose their childhood inno-cence. Rather, their capabilities are increased. What they get is "knowledge of good and evil," which is meant to signify moral discernment, for they are now ashamed of their nakedness, showing us that they have matured, and so find leaves to dress in. The relationship between knowledge, in the sense of wisdom, mortality, and human nature cuts across the myths of the entire ancient Near East.

In any event, neither Adam nor Eve is a good tailor (Genesis 3:7). God eventually has to help them design clothes: nakedness can be innocent in children, but in adults it violates moral sense. So good clothes, perhaps even the knowledge of textiles in general, are a kind of divine gift (Genesis 3:21). Clearly, these are culturally determined moral judgments that make more sense to the Hebrews than they would to, say, the Australian bushmen. But the story just builds them into God's promise. Adam's and Eve's newly won moral discernment also accounts for their guilt feelings, expressed by their hiding from the presence of the LORD God (Genesis 3:10).

More than two decades ago, the prolific literary critic Harold Bloom suggested that the author of this story was a woman. That was a sensational suggestion, very inspirational to the women's movement, and just what a professor of religion at a women's college (but part of a major university) would have liked. But the suggestion, upon reflection, seems far-fetched, and not just because attendance at a scribal school was a men's occupation. After all, God punishes Adam "because you have listened to the voice of your wife" (Genesis 3:17). It is hard to imagine that any woman could have written that phrase—even ironically. To make a cogent case for a woman's authorship, one would have to explain this phrase.

It is always possible, of course, but there is nothing inherent in the story to make a woman author or narrator necessary. In this culture it would have been hard for a woman not to leave easily readable marks on the story; a female narrator is even apt to leave grammatical signals in the text in Hebrew, since Semitic languages can easily distinguish the gender of the speaker. And there are a number of ironies that suggest the narrator is taking Eve's perspective very seriously but is having a little fun at her expense, just as he is having some fun with Adam's character. As we have seen, Eve is the innately more intelligent of the two characters, but the result of her intelligence is that the two of them get into trouble. One wonders if we are not to believe the same about David and Bathsheba.

The ironies I for one feel here are not that of a woman writer's having fun at a man's expense, as Harold Bloom has too blithely assumed, but, unfortunately, another kind of not so innocent fun designed by men—in fact, men joking with each other in a very male-dominated ancient social world. Even when men are in charge, they reflect ironically on the power that women hold over them because of sexual attraction. Since men want sex, they do agree to provide things that women want. This is part of the objectification of women, but it is also part of the comedy of life. It is Eve who has both intellect and is also the object of Adam's desire. They represent the sexual politics of their contemporary life well and see the inherent comedy in marriage by imagining (what is to them) an unstable form of it, with a very intelligent woman and a slow and easily beguiled man.

This is the stuff of comedy worldwide. Our mistake in the modern world is that we do not expect comedy from the Eden story because we are sure that this story, of all stories, must be earnest and serious. And also we do not find anything to laugh at in this view of man and women. We are victims of the later moralizing we have all heard about this story, and a great many of us cannot separate the story from the concept of original sin. But what mitigates the objectification of women in the Bible is this sexual comedy in Genesis. To understand the comedy is to realize that Eve is the far more capable person and that her punishment is exactly ironic: she needs to be mastered by her less intelligent spouse.

For all its fabulous wealth and fertility, Eden is meant to be a topsy-turvy world, emphasized for comic effect. I do not mean that in real life men are smart and women are not. I mean that the story implies that women naturally have the advantage to men in the sexual comedy of life because men desire them. God reversed the original and comic order of nature because of the disobedience of the pair (this is punishment for both characters), but the result is the world as we know it. It is a comic vision—many other ancient Mesopotamian creation myths are equally comic—that objectifies women, though it obviously does a similar job on men as well.

When I say that it is a comic vision, I do not mean that it has no serious purpose. But I do mean to say that to valorize and essentialize Adam's position as superior is to miss the point of the story, to fall victim to the later tradition that moralizes sex as bad and essentializes the story as a lesson in male superiority. Adam is duped, which makes him just as guilty as Eve. I see no reason to think that the Hebrews blamed the woman any more than the man, nor to think that human life was therefore considered depraved. Adam and Eve sinned because of their curiosity; Eve was too smart for her own good, Adam the converse. The same is true of Bathsheba and David. Bathsheba gets her share of the blame. Their sin was terrible, but there was no unatoned guilt. Once the sin is atoned, it is over. And the story is still funny, just as the Babylonian stories are funny.

This better theory of sexual relations has a similar effect in discussing the story of David and Bathsheba. After their sin, which appears to be mutual, they get on with the business of raising their family without further prejudice. Like Adam and Eve, they lose some of their progeny through sibling rivalry. And ironically a curse follows both couples. The curse that follows David is that there will be no peace within his family. Through a series of terrible accidents seen as providential by the narrator—the rape of Tamar by her brother Amnon, the rebellion and theft of the harem by Absalom, the usurpation of the kingship by Adonijah—Bathsheba waits for the moment to present her son, Solomon, as heir to the throne. And, through a patient political campaign, she succeeds in putting Solomon on the throne in David's old age.

Ordinary life, as we know it, is also a punishment in the Genesis story. But there is no suggestion that there is a modicum of unatoned guilt in it. Indeed, if anything, the punishments to Adam and Eve are already extreme, way beyond "measure for measure." The story merely explains how we got into this fix called mortal life and why we do not live in an Eden, though we can all imagine a paradise. In short, like Voltaire in his work *Candide*, the authors of the Bible think we do not live in the best of all possible worlds. Like Voltaire, too, the narrators pick an ironic way to get that message across. Indeed, even God must fight continuously to preserve his initial act of creation. Finally, like Voltaire, the Bible finds that knowledge and wisdom are better than naïveté, a principle that it illustrates with a picaresque view of the original couple. The Eden story was not written for us; it was written for the people of that period.

Taking for granted the enormously unbalanced punishment for a seemingly innocuous offense, the dialogue that follows in the Genesis story is a witty exercise in trying to find ironic punishments for the appropriate crime. The Lord God strolls in the garden during the cool part of the day, as any householder might do, to take his ease after the sweltering heat of a Mediterranean summer at noon, a very human pleasure, even today. He asks the man where he has hidden himself and concludes from this that Adam has disobeyed. The man blames his wife and God for having given the woman to him—another obvious joke. The woman blames the snake, making the avoidance of guilt into a running gag.

The woman accurately reports that the snake has enticed her. Clearly, this charming dialogue—which puts God, humans, and snakes on the same level—for comic effect surely—contains one more reversal. The reversal concerns what is missing in the story. The Lord God does not ask the snake why he did this evil deed. Possibly he already knows, because we do. And so we see that, unlike the story of Pandora's box, the Eden story is not about how evil came into the world.

Instead, the Lord God hands out punishments, which underline how the weaknesses of each character interacted to produce life as we know it, all of which we have just seen exemplified in the dialogue: The snake is punished for arrogance by being forced to crawl on its belly. The woman, who innocently looked for the pleasures of the eye and knowledge and whose articulateness made her the natural superior to her husband, is forced to endure pain in childbirth and the domination by her not-too-bright husband.

The punishments get more severe as they go along, and seemingly more undeserved. The simple man will return to the ground from which he came. He will always be a clod. The earth will no longer yield itself to him freely; instead of tending the garden, he will have to work the land and risk collective starvation, failing sufficient effort to feed the family. Of course, the result of this casual, childlike, disobedient credulity is terrible, until we realize that this punishment merely defines life as we know it. Though sin is clearly disobedience, the result is not the lack of immortality, which we can only imagine as an infantile fantasy, but only the basic human predicament.

Now we see the effect of the comedy. The story comically implies that if the issue were native intelligence we would be living in a very different world, one in which women ruled. The reason that women are subject to men is that otherwise women would continuously lead unsuspecting men astray by their intelligence and seductiveness. This is meant to be humorous in their society; but it is a man's humor, not a woman's. And it should be unacceptable to us. Under the humor is a ferocious and discriminatory irony, but it is appropriate to the time and the writers of the text. The final effect of the story is misogynistic after all, much like the position of Joab. But not entirely so. The story gently pokes fun at everyone and was written in a society that assumed women were subject to the command of their fathers and husbands, not the society in which we want to live.

But, to put the problem in terms of the Bathsheba story, it is not a complete victory for Joab's irony either. What makes this a comedy while the story of David and Bathsheba is a tragedy is that Adam is innocent and gullible where David and Joab are canny and conniving. We are misled when we think that Eve received the greater punishment. Their punishment is life as we know it. The same is true about David and Bathsheba.

It turned out that Solomon succeeded to the throne and Bathsheba's descendants ruled throughout Judah's entire history, so the punishment of Bathsheba perforce has to be seen as limited. The story could not be made up, as many scholars have thought, because it is much too complicated to explain. As we shall see, Bathsheba takes a very active role, even to the point of misleading David. Descendants and blessings, we have already seen, are the center of the mythology of Genesis and Exodus, just as they are in the Bathsheba story. In the Adam and Eve story, the presence of evil is merely adult experience, which is merely the interference of God in another form. The snake, in short, cannot be Satan or even a satan, even if he is not just a snake.

But *our* purpose in looking at the story is to see what (if anything) it implies about the Hebrew view of the moral of the story. Some things are more obvious when we reflect on what we already know about the Hebrew notions of the afterlife: it is this life that is important, blessing, land, and offspring, as we have already seen and will see again. The story of the succession to David, and that it is Bathsheba's offspring that succeeds to the throne, is a story of a surprising blessing and offspring. The land will not remain united forever, but responsibility for that secession is never laid at Bathsheba's feet.

More intriguing yet is the question of why the snake enticed the woman, if he is just a snake and not a simple cipher for Satan. It turns out that there is no Satan in the Hebrew Bible, no person with the name Satan who is captain of the forces opposing God. Even *the satan*, who appears in Job, is only God's court official, who can do nothing without God's explicit command. Satan is not this character's name; it is his occupation—opposer or "prosecuting attorney." An evil Satan is the invention of the Second Temple period. Identifying the snake with a figure like Satan, the interpretation of a later time, does clarify the moral ambiguity of the story. That is why it occurs to so many church fathers, Muslim scholars, and not a few rabbis. The one thing the West's identification of the snake with Satan does is clarify all the motivations in the story: Satan's presence would say right from the beginning that we live in an eternal struggle between good and evil, present even in these childlike people. And it would say that Satan is stronger than God because he forces God to make people mortal, evidently opening up the rich possibility for a hell. That is the dominant interpretation of Western Christianity. But it is enormously tendentious. There is not a trace of this interpretation actually in the story, when read properly, with that doctrine in the background. Then why did the snake commit the crime?

The snake commits this crime because he is a loyal servant of God. A later text in the Bible sequentially, but perhaps one written around the same time, seems to suggest something rather more profound about the ways God picks his agents:

Then Micaiah said, "Therefore hear the word of the Lord: I saw the Lord sitting on his throne, with all the host of heaven standing beside him to the right and to the left of him. And the Lord said, 'Who will entice Ahab, so that he may go up and fall at Ramoth-Gilead?' Then one said one thing, and another said another, until a spirit came forward and stood before the Lord, saying: 'I will entice him.' 'How?' the Lord asked him. He replied, 'I will go out and be a lying spirit in the mouth of all his prophets.' Then the Lord said, 'You are to entice him, and you shall succeed; go out and do it.' So you see, the Lord has put a lying spirit in the mouth of all these your prophets; the Lord has decreed disaster for you."

(1 Kings 22:19–23)

The scene on earth is the court of the evil Ahab where we hear the true prophecy of Micaiah ben Imlah, a historical prophet who unfortunately has left us no writings. Ahab has called this court session to convince the southern king Jehoshaphat to accompany him into battle. But Micaiah's is a powerful, very effective, and very complicated prophecy. After trying to mislead Ahab into a mistake that will cost him his life, Micaiah reveals a more exalted court, God's heavenly throne room where God has also deliberately misled all the other prophets in Ahab's court in order to accomplish his well-deserved death. God has done so on the advice of one of his courtiers, a nameless spirit, who is then appointed "the lying spirit" for the specific purpose of misleading the prophets, just as *the* satan (proper names in Hebrew do not have definite articles) in Job apparently has the specific role of adversary in God's court. In that case, the existence of *the* satan implies nothing more than that God used an assistant, his prosecutor. In this case, it implies the same.

All the prophets have told Ahab that he will win if he goes out to battle for Ramoth Gilead. The Bible tells us that he lost and that he died there. The Bible offers an example of revelation as a flashback. God has previously set up the situation as a trap. The verb for what God's prophets do to Ahab is *entice* (21, 22), not exactly the same word for *entice* that is used of the snake in Eden but a quite similar notion. Interestingly, the "enticement" of Eve has sexual connotations while the "enticement" of Ahab has the implication of being played for a fool.

This is a particularly sharp irony against Ahab, who is portrayed as more stupid than Adam here, though he acts in a shrewd way by interrogating the Judean king Jehoshaphat. He clearly does not know how he is being played, while Jehoshaphat, the southern king, is a model of wise circumspection. Furthermore, the God of our Bible is quite capable of using both forms of enticement to point out the foolishness of those whom he wishes to ruin. That God presents Adam and Eve with temptation in Eden seems innocent comedy by comparison.

The situation between Ahab and the primal couple is similar in that both are restrospective tellings of the facts of a situation in which God's actions seem equivocal. Ahab is a great sinner but he clearly has the upper hand in this story; he is the powerful and successful king, while the wise Jehoshaphat is merely his vassal. And the ironies in the latter case are far more savage. Ahab will be killed terribly and without mercy; both he and his Queen Jezebel will die, and their spilled blood will be lapped up by dogs, forbidden even a decent funeral. It means to warn us of a death equally ugly to all those who would insult the majesty of YHWH by playing the harlot to other gods.

In this case, as in Eden, the Lord God must do something that appears wrong in our eyes in order to accomplish his greater plan. He must deliberately mislead his prophets in order to trick Ahab to go out into battle and die. If the same concept of enticement is being used in both cases, the next question must be why it should be in God's interest for Adam and Eve to eat from the tree. The answer appears quickly enough. Discernment of good and evil, the mark of mature human thought in the biblical text, is a positive notion throughout that text. Had Ahab exercised moral discernment, there would have been no need for a special emergency session in the divine throne room. He is rather like Eve, but infinitely more demonic. He is a smart character who uses his intelligence rather than his moral discernment and winds up operating only for his own evil benefit.

The story says first of all that moral discernment gives us a divine nature, equal to YHWH in our ability to confront him, though our intelligence operating without moral discernment is only a trap. In the case of Adam and Eve, the scene is played for laughs. In the case of Ahab, it is played as a revenge tragedy, an earnest moral tale. And, though we think we have the upper hand, we are totally outclassed when we try to defeat YHWH using our intelligence. It also says that God favors the kingdom of Judah, at least sometimes, and he always hates the kingdom of Israel, even though they are far richer and more advanced.

And there is more to say than that. Not only does the ability to discern good from evil mark a mature human being, but there is a funny way in which the garden story is developmental in character. Like children, the primal pair learn right from wrong by being told to obey a rule, transgressing it, and getting the punishment. The story is based on a simple observation about how we teach our children to learn the same discernment. Such is the genius of myth worldwide.

This connection between Adam and Eve on the one hand and David and Bathsheba on the other shows us another way in which myth and "history" interact. We have already seen in the case of the concubine of the Levite versus Lot and the Sodomites a clear distinction—there was some historical truth, some awful remembrance that the events happened, behind the Levite's concubine story, and in the Lot story we see a more idealized and acceptable outcome. God strikes the Sodomites blind and then destroys them outright the next day. But the outcome of the Levite's story is a terrible war. The Israelites preferred the Lot story among the Sodomites, with its literal deus ex machina ending, to a story that ended in a cruel civil war that was fought to a standstill before "right" triumphed.

So too the story of Adam and Eve is a kind of idealization and mythologization of the story of a man with a woman. It is, if you will, a kind of astute political commentary on the royal marriage between David and Bathsheba that produced Solomon. It prominently displays the male as somewhat slow, while the woman is both sensuous and intelligent. This is one clear understanding of the Bathsheba story. We have called it "Joab's perspective." But it is taken up into the overall discussion of the Deuteronomistic Historian. And the Deuteronomistic Historian wants to emphasize the covenant relationship.

But that does not stop the Adam and Eve story from being an ancient story, begun before the events in the succession narrative. Similar stories of coming to knowledge are found in Gilgamesh. In one story, the wild man Enkidu is shown learning from a prostitute, who effects his estrangement from the animals. In another story, the wise man Adapa is misled into giving up immortality after being tricked by rather secondary gods. The Bible has obviously inherited a number of stories from Babylonia and elsewhere and tailored them to its own task. The Bible, by comparison with Gilgamesh, is not interested nearly so much in the issue of immortality. Instead it emphasizes the issue of coming to moral discernment. It does so because its main themes—one God and covenant—are furthered by this treatment. Monotheism and protection against idolatry lead to the deemphasizing of alternative religions and their possible opponent divinities. There can be no realm of the dead in a monotheistic system, unless that realm is squarely within the power of God. So it appears to me that wherever the story began, it very much also contains a message for a society that surely knew of the story of David and Bathsheba and wondered about what this might mean about their descendants.

Even more important, the covenant theme of the Hebrew Bible demands that humans have moral discernment. The covenant is a formal agreement between God and humanity. It demands that human beings enter into the agreement of their own choice. Here is one clear example of the covenant, as understood by the book of Deuteronomy:

> See, I have set before you today life and prosperity, death and adversity. If you obey the commandments of the Lord your God that I am commanding you today, by loving the Lord your God, walking in his ways, and observing his commandments, decrees, and ordinances, then you shall live and become numerous, and the Lord your God will bless you in the land that you are entering to possess. But if your heart turns away and you do not hear, but are led astray to bow down to other gods and serve them, I declare to you today that you shall perish; you shall not live long in the land that you are crossing the Jordan to enter and possess. I call heaven and earth to witness against you today that I have set before you life and death, blessing and curses. Choose life so that you and your descendants may live, loving the Lord your God, obeying him, and holding fast to him; for that means life to you and length of days, so that you may live in the land that the Lord swore to give to your ancestors, to Abraham, to Isaac, and to Jacob.
>
> (Deuteronomy 30:15–20)

Here is a classic example of the choice presented by the covenant of God with Israel. In order to enter the covenant, one needs moral discernment. It is absolutely necessary for the task. Thus the story of Adam and Eve, far from being just the story of how we lost immortality, is more aptly titled the story of how we can live well, having received the critical faculty of moral discernment, and become eligible for the covenant. Notice that the reward of this obedience in Deuteronomy is length of days, a long life.

CHAPTER SEVEN

No Peace in the Royal Family

Tamar and Amnon Redux

The explicit punishment meted out to David for the crime against Uriah the Hittite and against God is that David would have no peace in his family:

> ⁹ Why have you despised the word of the Lord, to do what is evil in his sight? You have struck down Uriah the Hittite with the sword, and have taken his wife to be your wife, and have killed him with the sword of the Ammonites. ¹⁰ Now therefore the sword shall never depart from your house, for you have despised me, and have taken the wife of Uriah the Hittite to be your wife. ¹¹ Thus says the Lord: I will raise up trouble against you from within your own house; and I will take your wives before your eyes, and give them to your neighbor, and he shall lie with your wives in the sight of this very sun.
>
> (2 Samuel 12:9–11)

The LORD's curse begins immediately after the story of David and Bathsheba with the rape of Tamar by Amnon. Amnon is the half brother of Tamar, daughter of David, and full brother to Absalom, David's son. But the tragedy ensues when Amnon falls in love with Tamar (2 Samuel 13:1). He desired her so much that he became physically ill for want of her (13:2). Though he was as lovesick as Romeo, he was not above feigning a physical sickness to try to seduce Tamar; when that fails he rapes her (13:14), as we have already reviewed in a previous chapter. None of this would be invented by a public relations firm. Its very distastefulness almost guarantees that there is a historical kernel in the story.

The seduction is suggested by his friend Jonadab, so it is both deliberate and well planned. The scheme is based on Amnon's request to his father, David, to have Tamar bake his favorite cakes in his presence. When she does so, he grabs hold of her, but she rebukes him: "No, my brother, do not force me; for such a thing is not done in Israel; do not do anything so vile! As for me, where could I carry my shame? And, as for you, you would be as one of the scoundrels in Israel. Now therefore, I beg you, speak to the king; for he will not withhold me from you" (2 Samuel 13:12–13).

We have looked at these words before. It is always possible that Tamar says these words only to distract Amnon from his terrible intent and that it is her feeble attempt to escape, contrary to all fact and experience. After all, we have already seen that marriage between half siblings is forbidden, because Deuteronomy and the holiness code state it (Leviticus 18:9, 18:11, and 20:17; and Deuteronomy 27:22). Tamar's exact words are lost to us. But her words do make sense if her desperate delay is a completely legal possibility when the events took place and was remembered as such. We already have some evidence that the law forbidding marriage between half siblings is from a later time. If so, that would suggest the Court History—and this story in particular—precedes both D and P and is begun by an ancient, if not an eyewitness narrator. That seems to be true on other, independent grounds anyway. Otherwise, it is hard to imagine that David could have allowed such a union when it is so explicitly forbidden by law or that Amnon might be dissuaded from his deed.[1]

In any event, Amnon does not wait for permission; he rapes her. And then, presumably because of his guilt or her rejection (though that is not explicit), he hates her just as fervently as he previously had loved her (13:15). If this had been Shakespeare, we might have been treated to a psychological drama. But that is not the point of the story. The mysteries of love and their relationship to hate are left unexplored in the story. The point of the story, at least from the narrator's point of view, is that this is the beginning of the punishment of David for his sinning with Bathsheba. Yet, in the end, it is their son, Solomon, who inherits the kingdom, so the story of punishment must be limited by the final success of Solomon. Palace politics, in the end, governs the narrative.

It is significant that Tamar's words are almost a direct quotation of several other moments of great danger. We also know that parallels are one way that the Bible explores these themes. The most obvious is the statement of Lot at Sodom, "I beg you, my brothers, do not act so wickedly" (Genesis 19:7), and of the Levite among the Benjamites, "'No, my brothers, do not act so wickedly. Since this man is my guest, do not do this vile thing'" (Judges 19:23), and again at the beginning of the tribal war, "Thus shall you say to all the Israelites, 'Has such a thing ever happened since the day that the Israelites came up from the land of Egypt until this day? Consider it, take counsel, and speak out'" (Judges 19:30). Let us explore the hypotheses that oral traditions growing more and more parallel lie behind the earlier material we have seen in Judges and Genesis and are here melded by the voice of the editor who sees the inherent similarity between the cases and uses one to reflect on the other.

Obviously, we also know that the curse is as much the narrator's explanation of subsequent history as a prophecy. So we know that logically it must have been written after the events. But the narrative needs to be a reasonable understanding of what people remembered. Otherwise, there would be no reason for this explanation because an incestuous rape within the royal family is much too defamatory to be invented. In short, there is no reason to suppose that the writer is making things up out of whole cloth. The narrator already knew how unpleasant the story of David's dynasty was and was explaining it as well as he could.

This story does not easily fit the Second Temple period. Why would a hypothetical narrator trying to establish the identity of a group in Second Temple times make up such a terrible story about his ancestors? Scribal schools carrying and reformulating historical traditions that date back from the tenth and ninth century is therefore not an outrageous hypothesis, though we need to find more supportive evidence before concluding that it might be true. The voice of the editor is especially obvious in Judges 19:30, but the best hypothesis for the conventional speech in these similar rape situations is that the formulation is due to a school of scribes who imposed more and more a written form on oral traditions.

We have already studied the matriarch in distress theme, which appears three times in Genesis. There, we discovered that in one of the versions of the story Abraham and Sarah admit that they are married half siblings. Perhaps marriage between half siblings were once legal and later rescinded during the time period covered in the Bible, after all. There is yet another story in the Bible that assumes it is possible for a man to marry a woman after having raped her and that the arrangement would heal the breech.

The Rape of Dinah by Shechem

This story is from Genesis 34 and it represents a countertradition to Amnon and Tamar, a story in which the raped woman is Israelite, her attacker Canaanite. Instead of furtive rape and public revenge like the 2 Samuel story of Amnon and Tamar, Genesis 34 becomes a story of public rape and furtive revenge. It will return us to the theme of the trickster yet again, with a difficult moral issue that bothered them as well.

The story of Dinah, too, begins with a female relative in distress. Dinah goes out to visit with the girls of the neighborhood. She is spied by Shechem who rapes her but then decides that he likes her and wants to marry her. He asks his father to negotiate a marriage for him. His actions represent the structural converse of Amnon's: "Now Dinah the daughter of Leah, whom she had borne to Jacob, went out to visit the women of the region. When Shechem son of Hamor the Hivite, prince of the region, saw her, he seized her and lay with her by force. And his soul was drawn to Dinah, the daughter of Jacob; he loved the girl, and spoke tenderly to her. So Shechem spoke to his father Hamor, saying, 'Get me this girl to be my wife'" (Genesis 34:1–4).

Shechem's father Hamor is named for an ass—that is, his name means *ass*—even though he is a prince. This can hardly be taken as an innocent detail and it cannot be a friendly epithet. Like Jezebel's name, it is meant as an insult. But there may be more to the insult since Genesis 33:19 refers to the Shechemites as *běnē ḥǎmôr*, "sons of a donkey,"[2] and there is at least a possibility that the animal foundation sacrifice found at Shechem was of a donkey. Hamor at first seems as cooperative as Amnon is unbending. He agrees with Jacob to a marriage contract, even requiring all the Shechemites to be circumcised. In return, they agree that their two families will intermarry, share women and wealth, and, in short, become one people: "Then we will give our daughters to you, and we will take your daughters for ourselves, and we will live among you and become one people" (Genesis 34:16).

It seems as if the children of Jacob and the Shechemites will become one people. But that is not to be. The Israelite fear of being swallowed by the larger, more powerful group is underlined by the Canaanites themselves. When the Israelites are not there, the Shechemites reason: "Will not their livestock, their property, and all their animals not be ours? Only let us agree with them, and they will live among us" (Genesis 34:23). The Canaanites are not openly deceptive, but they understand relations of power: they will predominate in any agreement with the Israelites. They know that if they allow the Israelites to live among them freely, eventually, they will become one people and that people will be Shechemite. Consequently, we know that the Israelites are in a power deficit where the trickster motif makes sense.

Dinah's brothers trick Shechem into thinking all is well (and trick us too, since we do not know their plan until it is launched). The narrator cues us in verse 13 when he says that the sons speak deceitfully. In a surprise change of tone and events, we discover that while Shechem and the men of the town were suffering from their circumcision operations, Simeon and Levi went through the town, killing all its men and taking all their property as booty (34:27), a ferocious surprise to us and a lethal surprise to them. This is not a story that teaches cultural pluralism or any moral value we would recognize. It is certainly as terrible a story as anyone could find in the Bible. Instead it suggests that correct genealogy is much more important, illustrated by the negative example.

But the Israelites and the Bible do not have a single mind about the event. Jacob's family council afterward represents both sides of the issues: "And Jacob said to Simeon and Levi, 'You have troubled me to make me to stink among the inhabitants of the land, among the Canaanites and the Perizzites: and I being few in number, they shall gather themselves together against me, and slay me; and I shall be destroyed, I and my house.' And they said, 'Should he deal with our sister as with an harlot?'" (Genesis 34:30–31).

Jacob realizes that he is in a difficult situation, being a small family of sojourners in a large and organized Canaanite society. The end of the story offers an unambiguous moral through hothead sons Simeon and Levi. Yet the story does give more than one understanding of correct behavior. Even Jacob, the ultimate trickster of the patriarchal period, is wary of offending the Canaanites around him, but his sons insist that the price of honor must be paid. The story reflects both sides of this difficulty and tries to represent them both before making its moral known. It obviously cannot advise both, but it rather explores both and represents a real social problem in the society. Jacob counsels caution and at least a modicum of acculturation, while his sons Simeon and Levi are determined that they must enforce their own counteridentity against the Canaanite majority. Whatever happened, it is functioning as myth to legitimate a hard boundary between Israelites and their neighbors and certainly no intermarriage.

This moral is characteristic of the early Second Temple period as well. Under the directorship of Ezra and Nehemiah, intermarriage was flatly forbidden. But the ambiguity—that maybe the marriage is appropriate, which Jacob brings up—would not have been tolerated in the Second Temple period. The story, traditionally ascribed to E, is actually earlier than the P or D source and is certainly earlier than the editorial perspective of the Second Temple period. To the priests of the early Second Temple period, marriage with a person outside the group was never an acceptable solution, even if the stranger represents himself as friendly and a willing marriage partner. There was no need to discuss it. Rather our story seems very analogous to many of the myths we have studied in the Bible: it reflects on both sides of an issue.

At the same time, the violence in Jacob's blessing of Simeon and Levi in Genesis 49 might well evince the same ambiguity: "[5] Simeon and Levi are brothers; weapons of violence are their swords. [6] May I never come into their council; may I not be joined to their company—for in their anger they killed men, and at their whim they hamstrung oxen. [7] Cursed be their anger, for it is fierce, and their wrath, for it is cruel! I will divide them in Jacob, and scatter them in Israel" (Genesis 49:5–7).

We cannot know whether the "blessing" of Jacob of Simeon and Levi is referring to the Dinah incident. But we can say that the blessing itself is quite often understood as an early example of Israelite poetry and so it too has a strong chance of being preexilic and a decent chance of being quite old even within that category. This suggests again that there was some ambiguity in the early community about whether one should accommodate strangers or automatically suspect them and fight with them. The issue is linked, as it quite often is, to the issue of marriage and correct offspring.

Like many of the stories we have seen, the beginning is that a female relative is caught in a distressing situation (though in this case she appears to consent to the marriage). But we must note that here the outcome is that the Shechemites are murdered in response to their rape. In any case, the trickster motif seems to be a way to explore both sides of the paradox. Furthermore, this story makes clear that the trickster motif assumes that the trickster is not the powerful character in the drama but is, instead, the less powerful character. This was an unemphasized part of the matriarch in distress stories in Genesis 12, 20, and 26. If Abraham had been more powerful, he would not have had to employ the elaborate ruse and would not have needed God's intervention. But here the powerlessness of the trickster seems impossible to deny.[3] And it emphasizes for us that the issue of power and powerlessness was in back of the story of the wife-sister. Abram/Abraham and Isaac were the inferior partners to Pharaoh and Abimelech. The stories depended not only on knowing that Abraham or Isaac was inferior, having to use a daring trick to escape the superior monarchs, but that by trust in God all turned out well.

Although both stories—Tamar and Amnon, Shechem and Dinah—concern rape, they are very different stories. Both cases deal with vengeance after the occurence of a rape, of course. But one story is about a dysfunctional royal family, while the other is about the consequences of rape for group identity. In a way, the more dangerous case is the less severe one not mentioned in either of the two stories. I am thinking of the much more common case where two youngsters from different cultures meet and wish to marry with or without parental consent. Since marriages are only undertaken with parental consent, these stories really suggest that parental consent should best never be given in the case of intermarriage and that meeting without chaperones is a kind of statutory rape.

Shechem in Biblical History

Shechem was the locus of a great deal of conflict. It is the very place where the Bible says: "the Canaanite was still in the land" (Genesis 12:6), a phrase that argues against the five books of Moses being revealed all at once. Apart from the passage's admission that there was a past before the time of the narrator, it also testifies that the Israelites did not control Shechem. As one might expect, then, Shechem has a long history both in biblical text and in archaeology. Archaeologically, it is a site with over twenty layers of settlement. We have letters in Akkadian written to the the famous Amarna pharoahs from Shechem by 1350 BCE. We know from biblical description that there were times when the city was under Canaanite domination and other times when it was the Israelites who controlled it, even if we cannot always separate the periods archaeologically.

In such a much contested place, one might expect several Israelite traditions claiming ownership. It was a place where, as the Israelites narrated it,

Abraham built an altar to God (Genesis 12:7). A tradition of sacrifice attempts to establish ancient rights of the Israelites to control the area. An even more significant tradition associated with Shechem is that Jacob bought a piece of land near the city from King Hamor (Genesis 33:19). In fulfillment of Joseph's deathbed request (Genesis 50:25, 26), the Israelites carried with them the bones of Joseph (Exodus 13:19) when they left Egypt and buried them in this plot of ground, which Jacob had bought (Joshua 24:32).[4]

Since Shechem is the very place on which the Israelite conquest converges, according to the book of Joshua, we may suspect that these stories explain that conquest and try to justify it, even though the land is often in the hands of the Canaanites. We must suspect that the story of the altar and implied sacrifice, with its very real promise of possession of the land, as well as the story of Shechem and Dinah, function as myths to establish Israelite ownership of the city as well as mediate issues of tolerance and intolerance. In view of the continuously vexing changes of power between Israel and Canaan, the mention of God's promise of the land and the presence of a relic as important as Joseph's bones is particularly significant as a mythical claim for land possession.

It is no surprise that Shechem was both a strong city that resisted Israelite domination and one in which Joshua brought the people to swear a covenant renewal oath (Joshua 24). It was a city the northern tribes thought they might be able to conquer, though it was in the plain and not in the hill country. Nevertheless, in spite of the stories in Joshua, in the time of the judges, Shechem remained a Canaanite city for some time, featuring at its high place the temple of Baal-berith ("Master of the Covenant"). There is some evidence for destruction during the settlement period about 1000 BCE. A narrative of its destruction is present in Judges.

Stories like this will always continue to be meaningful to an ethnic group, but it is not particularly important to the Second Temple period, where all is subject to the Persian state, which governed the area. Furthermore, Shechem itself was no longer within the borders of Yahud, Judah, during the Persian period, so it is unlikely that the story was born in Persian times. But it certainly was a familiar theme to the threatened small Jewish community of that time.

But the point of the story is that it does reflect conflict in First Temple times. Shechem was rebuilt, according to 1 Kings 4, and probably served as the capital of the tribal holdings of Ephraim. According to the idealized tribal allotments in the book of Joshua, it is right on the border between Ephraim and Manasseh (Joshua 17:2, 7). It was a Levitical city, a city of refuge where people could go to avoid blood feuds (Joshua 20:7, 21:21, 1 Chronicles 6:67).

In the book of Judges, Shechem is also involved in the rise of kingship. Gideon's son Abimelech (Judges 9:4), whose mother was a Shechemite woman, pursuaded the men of the city to make him king (Judges 9:6, cf. 8:22–23) there. This Abimelech was an unsuccessful and illegitimate contender for kingship, according to Judges, without any relationship to the Abimelech whom Abraham encountered.

Eventually the Israelites did conquer Shechem, and eventually it became a city of significance in the conflict between Israel and its neighbors. In short, it was a city that Israelites fought about and worshipped at throughout their First Temple history. Perhaps this checkered history best explains a local difficulty between Israelites and Canaanites in the Shechem area, the associated story taking us back to the mythical patriarchal period. Perhaps it commemorates an actual skirmish from the distant past, which has picked up mythological coloring. But, in its current form, its moral is not merely to prevent mixing between Canaanites and Israelites; at the same time, it also includes the other side of the issue, that killing Canaanites and treating them high-handedly will lead to further strife and bloodshed. It seems to me that this story expresses the deep difficulties that converge on the site of Shechem because of the meeting of cultures there.

Samson and the Border with the Philistines

The well-known story of Samson explores the issues of fertility and right lineage, intermarriage and tolerance as well, but in the southern areas of Judah, on the border with Philistia. Samson's exploits center around the town of Beth-shemesh ("[33] Naphtali did not drive out the inhabitants of Beth-shemesh . . . ," Judges 1:33). Samson continuously asks his father to get him a Philistine women, which he does, after a great deal of parental remonstration. Delilah, only the last of several foreign women, is the cause of his downfall. In the end, he regains enough of his strength to wreak vengeance on the perfidious Philistines. This is not a story that makes much sense in the Second Temple period; it is a far more fitting story of the First Temple period, with its weak understanding of statehood. Indeed, there is little difficulty with the Philistines in the Second Temple period. During the Second Temple period, the issue is first the Persians and very quickly becomes the culture of the Hellenistic Greeks, and the documents of the period have no trouble expressing them exactly as they are. Of course, the story of Samson must have continued to resonate in the later periods as well. But the issue here is its origin, and that seems to be within the mythic fabric of the First Temple.

The story of Samson is often understood by scholars as based on a borrowed mythical motif, sometimes actually thought to be taken from Greek Mycenaean (Philistine) culture and reunderstood as an Israelite hero. So, it is a prefabricated example of the mythological story put to Israelite use in the First Temple period. Even Samson's tribal background, from Dan, sometimes is understood as derived from the Greek tribe the Dannaioi.

The myth, wherever it came from, has certain undeniable solar aspects. Samson's name is related to the word for "sun," as is a place he inhabits, Bethshemesh. Samson's blindness may be understood as eclipse or sunset, and his lover Delilah's name seems related to the word for "night." His recovered strength can symbolize the return of the sun.

What is seldom noted in the encyclopedia and dictionaries of the Bible is the new Israelite use of that myth. It is no longer about the sun at all; instead it has developed an Israelite interest in correct lineage and fertility, intermarriage, and endogamy, interests that appear to be shared with other tribal peoples in the area. The adventures of Samson show us life on the border between the Israelite and Philistine areas of settlement. The archaeology of the area allows for the possibility that the stories surrounding Samson have significant social credibility to any time in the First Temple period. In short, the stories describe the same conflict of culture we can recapture by archaeological study as early as the rise of kingship in Israel. So here is an example of a mythological structure than can be placed in the actual world of preexilic, even premonarchic, Israel. It may be that the stories continue to develop for generations after this period, so, as usual, there is no way to date stories with long oral developments. The best we can do is present evidence for when it reached written form.

Samson and his personal war against the Philistines might be the earliest, most certain example of a mythological cycle used to explain and mediate cultural uniformity and correct lineage, since Samson's stories may have been borrowed from another culture. The Philistines were one of several "sea peoples" who migrated from the Aegean to settle a broad swath of coastline from Egypt to the coast of Anatolia in the early twelfth century BCE, more or less the same time that the Israelites were arriving to colonize the land of Israel.[5] In Canaan the Philistines invaded the seacoast, settling quintessentially in the five Philistine coastal cities: Ashdod, Ashkelon, Gaza, Ekron, and Gat, and eventually giving the name Palestine to the whole area, courtesy of the Romans. In the former prophets they are the quintessential "others," the greatest, implacable enemies—enemies to the core—a feature made even more raw by the Philistines' early mastery of iron. The Israelites had to rely on the Philistines to sharpen and work iron implements (1 Samuel 13:19–22). The Philistines, archaeologists find, raised hogs, and we find pig bones prominently in the animal remains of their rubbish dumps. Israelites, by contrast, did not. Eating pork is an ethnic identifier that separates Israelite from Philistine from the earliest of times, not merely in Persian times.

The story of Samson emphasizes the issues of cultural contact and legitimate offspring, as usual in biblical literature, by use of the negative examples. Samson has a series of battles with Philistine men, all of which demonstrate the judge as a hero saving Israel from foreign oppression, interspersed with intrigues with Philistine women in which the equally strong forces of attraction are featured. The myth must express both sides of the approach-avoidance dilemma, especially if it is going to argue that the best sense is to avoid Philistine women. In between are many different kinds of material, including prayers, etiologies, victory songs, and riddles.[6] They are separable oral units that can themselves be quite ancient. And, of course, Samson is a great trickster, solving riddles and keeping solutions secret for a time, even if he is too thick really to keep the secret of his great strength.

Samson desires Philistine women, so he must come into contact with Philistine men. He fights with the men and beds the women. The women, as it turns out, are as perfidious as the men. They constantly conspire with the men to learn the solution of Samson's riddles or the secret of his strength. But Samson, no matter how strong, is never depicted as very clever. He constantly wants what he should not want and eventually, for seemingly no reason, actually does give away the secret of his strength.

The result is a personal tragedy, which lands Samson blinded in Philistine Gaza in prison. Though he regains his strength, he prays for nothing more than that he should die with the Philistines: "[30]Then Samson said, 'Let me die with the Philistines.' He strained with all his might; and the house fell on the lords and all the people who were in it. So those he killed at his death were more than those he had killed during his life" (Judges 16:30).

Obviously, the story of Samson was constantly of interest to the Judeans and Israelites of First Temple times. Within it one finds an easy way to criticize Solomon for his foreign entanglements, especially with the Pharaoh Shishak of Egypt, whom we have already seen was later to come to pillage the south and remove the glorious golden implements of the Temple. It also continued to be of interest when the city of Beth-shemesh was ceded back to the Philistines during the reign of Ahaz in the eighth century.

Since this kind of issue is always relevant—who is close enough to marry but not too close to be incest—we might think of the stories of the offspring of Jacob as the mythic blueprint for the borders of the people. They are close enough to marry, but not so close as to commit incest. Though the patriarchal stories argue that all the tribes are descendants of Jacob, it is hard to know how early this kinship between tribes actually is. We shall see, in the next chapter, that there is a certain amount of evidence that the tribes did not all arrive at the same time and take up residence in the places that the book of Joshua assigns them. If not, a covenant ensuring relationship during an "intermarriage" is certainly a logical ritual to perform. Even without it, the myth that a tribal relationship unifies all the people of Israel as the descendant of Jacob does much the same thing. These stories of the patriarchs seem best, therefore, to have originated in the First Temple period, not a story of Israel living in imperial Persian times. We will return to that issue in the next chapter.

Myth in an Environment of Competing Values

The stories of Dinah and Samson represent an exploration and idealization—in short, a mythologization—of what the normal behavior between peoples should be, in particular by their marriage rules. Our minds are repelled by the thought that the correct response to this situation could be the typological use of the Dinah story—stealthy plans, lying, followed by murder, then followed after that by regret and remorse, followed again by certainty. We may more appreciate the story of Samson, who becomes a tragic figure for giving in to his desires. The moral is the same. But the stories do explore all the conflicting possibilities of relationship between the Israelites and foreign cultures. One might say they are meant to be a mythical typology of how to maintain identity by opposition to one's neighbors. In short, it is an exploration of the conflicts and difficulties of the First Temple period and little suits the social situation of the Second Temple period.

These are not stories that once happened so much as stories that were happening all the time. They are not stories that express everything that could happen: they purposely disallow the possibility that an intermarriage could have a happy ending. And yet we have other stories illustrating that these "intermarriages" did occur. The dominant ideology of the Bible is that no mixing of the two peoples should occur.

The ideal and prescription of the Bible, even in the First Temple period, is not to allow any intermarriage. There is little in the archaeology that can demonstrate or disprove that relationships between these groups were as separate as the Bible wants. But many things, including the text of Judges, suggest that there was far more cultural contact between these different groups. The material culture of Canaanites and Israelites is very similar, often so similar that we cannot tell the difference, with only a few crucial ethnic identifiers separating them. Burial practices, for example, are very similar. It looks as though, again, the primeval and patriarchal period provides the prescriptive mythic structure promising legitimate offspring to those who refuse to intermarry. But the situation on the ground is far more ambiguous.

We have noted that myths mediate between perceived contradictions in this society. These stories do have the same conflicting issues in mind and so we can think of them as myth. Fertility is always emphasized, but the competing value of correct descent is actually just a strong motivator of family planning. And the issue of power and control over marriage and even the city is just as important. These stories can be viewed as myth not for the conclusions that they come to alone but because they explore the issues and suggest that there are multiple possible outcomes that must be mediated. The proper prescribed behavior for Israelite men would be not to allow anyone, male or female, to intermix with the Canaanites, but the archaeology seems to suggest that the Bible's prescription was not particularly successful in First Temple times.

In any event, these stories point up the difference between a prescriptive text like the Bible and a more strictly descriptive text. Every prescriptive text makes a strong case for avoiding or performing a behavior. If so, the story makes clear that intermarriage is to be treated with the same ferocity as rape. This is not exactly what one hopes for in a biblical text, but that is what it says.

The story relates to the theme of proper genealogy; and this, one supposes, takes parental intervention in all cases. As Edmund Leach says in his essay "The Legitimacy of Solomon," "On the one hand, the practice of serial endogamy is essential to maintain the purity of the faith, on the other hand, exogamous marriages may be politically expedient if peaceful relations are to be maintained with hostile neighbors."[7] Leach, in spite of his great anthropological credentials, expresses himself in a theological way. Perhaps "purity of the faith" should be reunderstood as ethnic solidarity, by means of those symbols, rituals, and myths that established Israelite counteridentity in the time of the kingship. The stories are mythical because they are being backdated anachronistically into the time of the patriarchs.

Back to the Royal Family: Absalom and Amnon

All this is written large in the fortunes of the Davidic royal family. We remember that Amnon has enticed his half sister to his rooms and raped her. Though the story is hushed up, we know that the truth will out, just as in the story of Bathsheba and David's sin. David's troubles are not over because the story of Amnon's shameful behavior can hardly be kept secret. Tamar is herself brought to shame. She rips her court garment, knowing that her court days are over, and pours ashes on her head in mourning (2 Samuel 13: 18–19). First, Absalom and then David find out; neither is at all pleased by Amnon's behavior. But both hold their tongue. Absalom keeps Tamar in his household without bringing forth a report, cautioning her not to speak about the issue. David does nothing further, which spurs Absalom to action. This is an exact typology with Jacob, who does nothing further about Dinah, which spurs Simeon and Levi into action. One supposes that the Dinah story suggests that we should expect a painful outcome in the case of the rape of Tamar, even though the royal family is involved. In this way, the Jacob story is indeed prototypical.

Absalom too has some of the most wily characteristics of the trickster. He is inferior to his father David, so he accomplishes his aims by deception. He is just biding his time until the right opportunity arrives (13:20–22). That turns out to be two years later at a sheep shearing in Baal-hazor, where Absalom's herds are grazing beside Ephraim. Absalom invites all the king's sons (13:23). After some negotiation, the brothers go; meanwhile Absalom plans an ambush for his half brother Amnon, just when he is most merry with wine at the festival (13:28). The plan is successful; Amnon is murdered, and the conspirators successfully escape. And so do the rest of David's children, who flee back to Jerusalem on donkeyback.

But the report comes to David that all his children were killed. When he learns that only Amnon is dead, he is relieved (13:30–33), as the text gives us a very explicit description of the nervous waiting period before David's remaining sons return. As usual, the text rarely discusses internal feelings and contents itself with key outward appearances. Unlike Shakespeare's *Hamlet*, the Bible is long on objective correlatives and short on soliloquies. Absalom, however, runs away to Talmai, the son of Ammihud, king of Geshur, a foreign king, and stays out of his father's sight for some three years.

Meanwhile, David's anger and mourning are healed over time, and he yearns for his son Absalom. "David mourned for his son every day," says the text, again concentrating on the outward behavior and not on the grief itself (37–38). Seeing David's state of mind, Joab engineers a change in the king's decree by means of the wise woman of Tekoa (2 Samuel 14:1). She pretends to be a widow and tells David a very sad story of the death of her husband and the subsequent death of one of her two sons by fratricide, though possibly an unintentional one. She pleads with the king to spare the remaining son, though her relatives want to kill the son in forfeit for the brother's life. David sides with the woman. And, eventually, when the story is revealed as a parable, David apparently decides for himself that he can allow Absalom to return for the same reason.

In any event, Joab goes to Geshur and convinces Absalom to return home (2 Samuel 14:23). Wisely, Absalom stays away from the court for some two more years. After two years, he wants to approach Joab to let him see the king. Joab refuses to come to see Absalom until his men set Joab's fields on fire. Then, finally, he agrees to let Absalom see the king. In the end, David and Absalom are reconciled (2 Samuel 14:33).

Cain and Abel

The story of Absalom and Amnon cries out to be understood in terms of the primeval history of Adam's children, Cain and Abel. It is the wise woman of Tekoa—not the ground—who does the crying out. The wise woman of Tekoa, though she is dissembling, takes up a story of a fratricide in which the surviving son needs to be protected for the lineage to survive, though he killed his brother. But that is exactly what happens in Genesis 4–5, if God is given the role as parent, and one suspects that it is a mythic illustration of the principle adduced by the wise woman of Tekoa, who must have been speaking the prescribed answer of their culture. Furthermore, in both stories, the murder takes place "in the field" (a word that occurs in Genesis 4:8 and the speech of the wise woman of Tekoa in 2 Samuel 14:6).

The story of Cain and Abel has a good mythical background in the story of Enkidu and Dumuzi, which goes back to Sumer. Like Cain and Abel, Enkidu and Dumuzi are farmer and pastoralist, respectively. They argue about which occupation is better. Usually it is Dumuzi, the pastoralist, who picks the argument, as the farmer is satisfied with his place and often refuses the argument. But, in all the versions found to date, they always resolve the argument in peaceful ways.[8] Perhaps, then, more local issues are driving the outcome of the Israelite version, which ends in the murder of the pastoralist Abel by Cain, the farmer. So, at one level, it seems likely that the story of the murder of Amnon by Absalom has influenced this story.

More often than not, the relationship between siblings in the Bible is conflictual, and very often it is the younger child who wins. We will now see why. It has everything to do with the age of Solomon when he ascends the throne.[9] The mythological story of Cain and Abel also mediates these values. Eve bears first Cain then Abel. She names Cain because he was produced with the help of the LORD. The etymology of Abel's name is not given. Abel was a shepherd, while Cain was a farmer, a tiller of the ground (Genesis 4:2). Both bring offerings to the LORD, who accepts Abel's but is critical of Cain's. The Lord offers a statement to Cain that makes more sense on a mythical level—a generalization for all behavior—than a specific explanation for Cain. There is nothing in Cain's behavior until the moment to warrant this: "If you do well, will you not be accepted? And if you do not do well, sin is lurking at the door; its desire is for you, but you must master it" (Genesis 4:7). It is ambiguous and without specific reason, but it becomes the basis of a murder and thus a pattern representing a mythical explanation. Its exact meaning is, however, quite obscure.

Cain asks his brother to go out in the field, where he kills him. The LORD then says to Cain: "Where is your brother Abel?" Cain responds, "I do not know; am I my brother's keeper?" (Genesis 4:9). His answer is like Adam's when he is hiding from the Lord God. It is the very opposite of God's loyal servants—people like Samuel and Moses, who say "Here I am." Cain's desire to hide from the LORD is enough to incriminate him. Cain's punishment is like Adam's. He is cursed from the ground, which will no longer yield its produce easily, and, like Adam, he is forced to flee to the east. Cain says that his punishment is greater than he can bear. "Then the LORD said to him, 'Not so![10] Whoever kills Cain will suffer a sevenfold vengeance.' And the LORD put a mark on Cain, so that no one who came upon him would kill him" (Genesis 4:15). Like the story of Adam and Eve, these initial stories are meant to have the generality of referring to all humanity but the connection to the affairs of David's state cannot be missed.

Just as the story of Adam and Eve tells us the comedy of human married life, this story tells us something far more serious: the first death in the Bible is a murder and the first murder is a fratricide. Perhaps this is meant to demonstrate that all killing is a kind of fratricide. But it is hard to imagine that the writer did not have the events in the royal family in mind too. One can imagine the punishment for anyone making a statement so openly against the royal prince, the heir to the throne. So the myth functions as an oblique attack on a person against whom one cannot offer a direct criticism.

It is not just the generality of the story that alerts us to the mythical quality of the story. We all know this story is a myth because of the question everyone who reads this story asks: "Who in the land of Nod, in which Cain settles, could have killed him, since he is the only child left on earth and the only person beyond Adam and Eve?" It does not make straightforward narrative sense. But it does tell us something far more important about the issues of marriage and legitimacy in First Temple Israel.

We thus have two stories of fratricide—one in the period of the monarchy and another in mythical prehistory—but they do not line up in a straightforward way. In effect, they seem to be converse and contrasting stories. This has been diagrammed structurally by Robert C. Culley:

1. Cain's offering displeases YHWH
2. YHWH makes clear that Cain has done wrong and announces his punishment
3. Cain points out what the dire consequence of such a judgment for him will be
4. YHWH acts to prevent such a consequence
5. Cain leaves to live out his punishment
Outcome: Though a sinner, Cain has descendants[11]

This can be compared to the story of Amnon and Tamar:

1. Amnon wrongs Tamar (and hence David and YHWH)
2. David does nothing, and so no punishment is announced
3. Absalom devises a trap to judge Amnon

4. All the royal heirs are in danger from Absalom's revenge
5. All are spared except Amnon, who should have been punished to begin with

Outcome: Amnon has no descendants, but the monarchy continues through David's other sons[12]

Stitch Words or Leading Words

These narratives have been designed to meet certain structural features of Israelite society. One does not need to be a folklorist to see it, because Israelite writing turns on a very limited vocabulary that functions to unify the narrative. One of the most adept scholars at seeing and expressing how repetitious vocabulary underlies the narrative action is Michael Fishbane, especially in his first book, *Biblical Text and Texture: A Literary Reading of Selected Texts*.[13] The verbal structure (German Bible scholars call this phenomenon *Stichwörter*, words that serve as *stitches* to unite the narrative, or *leitwörter*, leading words) shows that there is an underlying interest governing the primeval history. Perhaps the best way to describe them in English is as *thematic words*:

GENESIS 4:3–16	GENESIS 3
1. "Then the man knew [*yada'*] his wife, Eve"	"and they knew [*va-yede'u*] that they were naked"
2. temptation dramatized through coiled, serpentine sin	temptation dramatized through the serpent
3. "its [the serpentine-sin's] urge [*teshuqato*] will be toward you"	"your [the woman's] desire-urge [*teshuqatek*] will be toward your husband"
4. "but you can dominate [*timshol*] it"	"but he will dominate [*yimshol*] you"
5. "Where is ['*ay*] your brother?"	"where are you [*'ayeka*]?"
6. "Be you cursed by the earth ['*arur 'atta min ha-adamah*]"	"cursed be the earth ['*arura ha-'adamah*] because of you"

7. "when you work the earth [*ta-'avod et ha-'adameh*] it will no longer give its yield to you"	"briars and thistles will sprout for you to work the earth [*la-'avod et ha-'adamah*]"
8. "you have banished [*gerashta*] me"	"He banished [*va-yegaresh*] the man"
9. "I will be hidden ['*essater*] from your presence [*paneka*] Elohim"	"then the man and his wife hid [*va-yithabbe*] from the presence [*pnei*] of YHWH"
10. "eastward of Eden [*qidmat 'eden*]"	"eastward of the garden of Eden [*miqqedem la-gan 'eden*]"

As Fishbane pointed out, there is a narrative structure that connects the Genesis stories. Although they do not tell the same story, they have the same underlying structure, dramatized by exactly the same thematic vocabulary. As I read it, the "fall" is not nearly as drastic as the Western canon has read it. But we already know that. Rather the second cycle of the pattern, the Cain and Abel story, describes a far worse story of murder and mayhem. But that only points up the mythical nature of the Genesis narrative. Both stories contain a pattern of sin and punishment that requires desire, acted upon in an unacceptable way.[14]

So too Absalom and the son in the story of the wise woman of Tekoa live theoretically to continue their lineage. (Absalom, however, comes to grief in the next story.) And it is like the tribe of Benjamin at the end of the terrible civil war at the end of Judges. These are equally the concerns of a tribal society—offspring and lineage to carry on the tribe—and a royal family. But like all issues in which myth is concerned, power to carry out one's desires is the center of the issue. Eventually and inevitably, the ability to reproduce and to guarantee one's legitimate offspring is a direct expression of power. It is that power that makes a Davidic dynasty possible and real.

So it seems to me that the story of Cain and Abel must be seen as a First Temple story. It is structurally similar to the Adam and Eve creation story, clearly part of the same literary effort from the same scribal school. We learn this from the very thematic words upon which the narrative depends. Fishbein has shown us this connection, though he left out the significance of the phenomenon for oral traditioning and the process of scripturalization in scribal schools. Also we know that the story has a mythical past in the background of the ancient Near East. Furthermore, we know that the Israelites made unique changes in the standard "farmer and pastoralist" myth, which bring it more in line with the fratricidal issue in the succession narrative. All these things make it more obvious that the story of Cain and Abel must be a First Temple story.

Just as Rebecca Aids Jacob, So Too Bathsheba Aids Solomon

But Absalom was not to be king after the death of David either. Ironically, he spends so long trying to get back into his father's good graces, only to rebel against him in the end. He too dies in trying to force the succession. He rebelled successfully enough to force David to leave his throne in Jerusalem and flee (2 Samuel 15:14). He went so far as to use his father's abandoned concubines sexually (2 Samuel 16:11). In the end, however, he was defeated in battle (2 Samuel 18:7); he himself was killed by Joab after he was caught in a tree by his hair (2 Samuel 18:14). Joab kills Absalom for the good of the kingdom, as David never would have allowed his son's death.

That leaves two sons of David in contention to succeed him. The issue comes to a head in David's old age. The narrator dramatizes David's old age by relating the story of Abishag the Shunamite. She is brought to David's bed not for carnal knowledge, the text tells us, but for her ability to minister to him and to warm up his body. The story quickly tells us that David is no longer able to govern as effectively as before because his mobility is greatly restricted.

It is then that Adonijah began to assert himself as king. The text does not give us a radical reason at first why he should not:

> 5 Now Adonijah son of Haggith exalted himself, saying, "I will be king"; he prepared for himself chariots and horsemen, and fifty men to run before him. 6 His father had never at any time displeased him by asking, "Why have you done thus and so?" He was also a very handsome man, and he was born next after Absalom. 7 He conferred with Joab son of Zeruiah and with the priest Abiathar, and they supported Adonijah. 8 But the priest Zadok, and Benaiah son of Jehoiada, and the prophet Nathan, and Shimei, and Rei, and David's own warriors did not side with Adonijah.
>
> (1 Kings 1:5–8)

Everyone who has read this story has wondered whether it was Solomon's supporters rather than Adonijah who actually did the revelling. It seems clear that Adonijah is a good man, next in line for the throne, though apparently an impatient one in this retelling. The court divides into factions supporting the two candidates, Adonijah and Solomon, all this seemingly without the knowledge of David. Adonijah's first action is to have himself declared king at En-rogel, with the appropriate sacrifices of a king and appropriate princely titles for his brothers, certainly a ritual exercise of ascribed power. But the text reiterates who was left out: "But Nathan the prophet, and Benaiah, and the mighty men, and Solomon his brother, he called not" (1 Kings 1:10). Clearly power has not been completely consolidated behind Adonijah, and that was a fatal miscalculation.

Nathan then tells Bathsheba that her life and that of Solomon's are in danger and that David does not know of these maneuverings by Adonijah (1 Kings 1:12). The narrator makes no secret of their collusion. They plan to back each other up, confirming the story that Solomon should be king. The implication, therefore, is that they are conspiring together. It is possible that David had no such plans to advance Solomon's career or that he only spoke with Bathsheba on the subject. But it seems evident that David has not yet made his wishes known publicly, though he may possibly have made the promise privately to Bathsheba. In any event, there is no reason why the rest of the court should not assume that Adonijah is the rightful heir. He certainly seems to be the next in line by primogeniture. Yet he does not rule; Solomon rules in his stead.

Bathsheba quickly brings the issue to the point, asking David for his judgment on the matter while emphasizing Adonijah's rashness. And, while she is speaking, Nathan comes in on cue, arguing that the kingdom should go to Solomon. Apparently, Bathsheba has exited the room while the men confer, though we know that Bathsheba and Nathan have previously conspired to present the issue together. When Bathsheba reenters, David offers his judgment that Solomon should succeed him: "The king swore, saying, 'As the LORD lives, who has saved my life from every adversity, as I swore to you by the LORD, the God of Israel, Your son Solomon shall succeed me as king, and he shall sit on my throne in my place,' so will I do this day" (1 Kings 1:29–30).

So the succession is decided upon the younger son Solomon, though the text gives us plenty of room to consider that Adonijah was robbed of the throne. Once it is clear that the succession is Solomon's, Bathsheba bows down low to the ground in thanks for David's having designated Solomon his successor. Only then does she exclaim her praise for the king: "Then Bathsheba bowed with her face to the ground, and did obeisance to the king, and said, 'May my lord King David live forever!'" (1 Kings 1:31). It also qualifies Bathsheba as a very successful "trickster," a person with only ascribed power who manages to manipulate the situation to her advantage. So it was with women in this society. They had no direct power, but they could manage to manipulate the family situation to their advantage.

Since this settles the succession in the face of David's senescence, the statement has a certain resonant sadness. Clearly, after long years at court, Bathsheba is portrayed as having developed her own voice and considerable diplomatic skills. She certainly knows how to intervene at exactly the right (and the last) moment. But it is set against an aged king who can surround himself with beautiful women but cannot use them sexually.

The text, however, fails to convince us that this outcome was David's original and uncompromised wishes. Instead it leaves us with the impression that David was in his dotage and was easily manipulated by Bathsheba. Again, this irony is an insider voice; it is an ironic perspective like Joab's. But it is not Joab himself; he is on the losing side and has already forfeited his life. Instead, it is a narrator who can characterize either or both sides in knowing ways.

The difficulty now is to make sure that David's wishes, no matter how manipulated, are respected, for David's express vow has changed the balance of power completely. Solomon is brought out to the Gihon Spring and anointed as king; Adonijah's support evaporates once it is clear that Solomon is David's choice. Perhaps the reason is that Solomon also had the support of David's personal guard, the Cherethites and the Pelethites. Perhaps Adonijah was practical enough to see his bid had been neutralized or even clever enough to see that indirect opposition might bring him the kingdom when direct action did not. In any event, Adonijah begs forgiveness of his father.

One might well pause for a moment and reflect on this choice. Although there had never been a father-to-son succession in this young kingdom, the dynastic principle not having been tested, it is arguable that the kingdom, by rights, should go to his oldest surviving son, to Adonijah. That is certainly what Adonijah thought, as the text is quite clear that Adonijah was a worthy candidate for kingship. Furthermore, that is the clearest principle to establish in this case. There is a great deal of evidence that this is the principle that was followed hereafter. So this incident, the succession of Solomon, represents a very real crisis in the Davidic line, both because it comes first and seems to contradict a rule that exists thereafter.

And, quite surprisingly, with the help of Bathsheba, the queen mother, the succession goes to Solomon. Solomon is not the elder; he is the younger of the two remaining sons. But he is David's son through Bathsheba. And now we see the implication of all the younger children inheriting, in spite of their older siblings, most obviously in Jacob and David himself. If one were making up a story from scratch, would the throne have gone to the offspring of an adulterous union, which is one of the basic rules of the society? But the point of view of the teller is again a very knowing "inside" person like Joab. Since Joab dies in the story, it is unlikely to be him personally. Perhaps it is even a person who thinks that the kingdom should have passed to Adonijah. But it is again a jaded and practical courtier or scribe who knows cynically that women do affect the outcome of succession narratives because men are subject to them in affection, though women themselves rarely have. I do not want or think it can be identified except to say that it is likely to be a close witness to the events. Otherwise, there would no reason to risk the ire of the Davidic monarchy.

Jacob and Rebecca

The story of Jacob's stealing of the birthright is so close to the pattern established by Solomon's ascent to power that it should be considered a doublet. As such, it establishes Jacob as the most successful of all the tricksters in the Bible. It is no accident that he is a prototype for Solomon. As a mythic commentary on the events of Solomon's ascent, it might even be read ironically as a political satire. We have seen that the narrator is not altogether convinced that Solomon's rise to power against Adonijah is just because the audience with David is too carefully planned by Nathan and Bathsheba: "Then while you are still there speaking with the king, I will come in after you and confirm your words" (1 Kings 1:13). Perhaps the story of Jacob's birthright helps bring about the surety and assent that the 1 Kings 1–2 story does not provide. But it also emphasizes the trickery.

The story of Jacob stealing the blessing from Esau is also an etiology, because Jacob becomes Israel, the ancestor of the whole Israelite nation, while Esau is the ancestor of the Edomites (Genesis 36:1). In a way the story hints that the Israelites took the good land of Canaan from the Edomites, who had to settle in Seir, even though the Edomites have a claim to priority. The earliest extrabiblical reference to Edom appears in a late thirteenth-century BCE Egyptian papyrus, which reports that some Bedouin tribes from Edom stopped at one of Pharaoh Merneptah's forts.[15]

The story begins with the old age of the patriarch and words that sound something like David's mordant statement recognizing that he is going the way of all flesh: "When Isaac was old and his eyes were dim so that he could not see, he called his elder son Esau and said to him, 'My son'; and he answered, 'Here I am.' He said, 'See, I am old; I do not know the day of my death. Now then, take your weapons, your quiver and your bow, and go out to the field, and hunt game for me'" (Genesis 27:1–4).

After the meal, Isaac intends to bless Esau with the birthright. As soon as Esau leaves, Rebecca hurries to tell Jacob that there is a chance to steal the birthright from Esau, just as Solomon steals the kingship from Adonijah. They slaughter a kid and make Isaac's savory meal. To fool the nearly blind patriarch, they dress Jacob in the skins of the animals so that Isaac will feel Esau's arms—for Esau was a hairy man—instead of Jacob's presumably hairless arms. All goes according to plan, even though Isaac is suspicious.

So Jacob went up to his father Isaac, who felt him and said, "The voice is Jacob's voice, but the hands are the hands of Esau" (Genesis 27:22). Jacob receives the blessing meant for Esau. But, of course, it is the perfect blessing for Israel (Jacob) over against Edom (Esau):

> So he came near and kissed him; and he smelled the smell of his
>   garments, and blessed him, and said,
>   "Ah, the smell of my son is like the smell of a field that the
>   LORD has blessed.
>   May God give you of the dew of heaven,
>   and of the fatness of the earth,
>   and plenty of grain and wine.
> Let peoples serve you,
>   and nations bow down to you.
> Be lord over your brothers,
>   and may your mother's sons bow down to you.
> Cursed be everyone who curses you,
>   and blessed be everyone who blesses you!"
>
> (Genesis 27:27–29)

NO PEACE IN THE ROYAL FAMILY

Almost as soon as Isaac gives this generous, mostly agricultural blessing to his younger son, Jacob, Esau comes back looking for his blessing. The ruse is discovered, and yet Isaac has only a lesser blessing for Esau. This fantastical world, in which blessings are a zero-sum, fixed quantity to be apportioned and used up, a folkloric theme that is just accepted as fact, is another sign of the mythological rendering of the events:

> Esau said, "Is he not rightly named Jacob?[16] For he has supplanted me these two times. He took away my birthright; and look, now he has taken away my blessing." Then he said, "Have you not reserved a blessing for me?"
> Isaac answered Esau, "I have already made him your lord, and I have given him all his brothers as servants, and with grain and wine I have sustained him. What then can I do for you, my son?"
> Esau said to his father, "Have you only one blessing, father? Bless me, me also, father!"
> And Esau lifted up his voice and wept.
> Then his father Isaac answered him:
> "See, away from[17] the fatness of the earth shall your home be, and away from[18] the dew of heaven on high.
> By your sword you shall live, and you shall serve your brother;
> but when you break loose,[19] you shall break his yoke from your neck."
>
> (Genesis 27:36–40)

Instead of the blessing of agricultural abundance received by Jacob, Esau is only promised that he will be a desert raider, living by his sword. This is, of course, an etiology of Israel and Edom; their blessings describe the land they possess and the power that one exercises over the other. Israel took the majority of the fertile land between the Jordan and the Mediterranean and some to the east of the Jordan too, which gets more and more fecund in a northerly direction. Edom (and Moab too, for that matter) settled in the arid desert land to the east of the Jordan and, what is more important, east of the rain shadow from the Judean hills. What secures this inheritance for the Israelites is, of course, their military power. But it is good to have a myth justifying it. Furthermore, Esau did serve his brother Jacob, as indeed Edom served Israel for many years. And Edom did in fact break free from Israel. All of this is prophesied, but the latest narrator of this story at least must surely have known the history of Israel later than 845 BCE to have gotten so much right.[20] In the Bible, Edom is closely linked to the region called Seir, where Esau dwelt (Genesis 36:8–9, Deuteronomy 2:4–5, 22, 29; by the time of the book of Deuteronomy Edom was no longer a vassal).[21]

One other important connection to consider, however, is the role of the mother in both Jacob's and Solomon's rise to power. In the case of Solomon, after Bathsheba had intervened on Solomon's behalf so strongly, his first test as monarch still lies in front of him. And it is Solomon, not the older and more capable Adonijah, who gets to rule the kingdom. Perhaps, in the end, the trickster motif is exactly relevant to the intrigues of the royal court as well.

Jacob's Dream at Bethel

In this particular place, the most interesting comparison, as we have seen, is with Jacob and Rebecca. For Jacob, Rebecca's help is both needed and potentially harmful, just as it was in the case of Solomon. Jacob is certainly not a hero from the beginning of his story. He is a trickster figure; he tricks his brother and his father-in-law Laban (who represents the Arameans), and, in turn, is victim to their tricks and ire as well. And his reliance on his mother is suspect in his case just as it throws a shadow over Solomon. Rebecca herself expresses this ambiguity when she tells Jacob, "Let your curse be on me, my son; only obey my word, and go, get them for me" (Genesis 27:13). But Jacob agrees to the scheme of his mother, and it is successful.

On the other hand, like Solomon, he must eventually prove himself. This he does in many subsequent episodes, when the LORD recognizes him and chooses him to be Israel. As in the court narrative, the chance to prove himself an independent player comes immediately after his stealing the blessing from his brother Esau.

The story of Jacob's dream at Bethel is, in fact, confirmation of YHWH's choice. YHWH there gives Jacob all the land and resolves the mysterious events of the previous chapter. It directly parallels Solomon's trip to the north for acceptance. Just as Solomon was fated to rule, no matter who else tried to make claim to the kingship, so Jacob deserves the blessing of Isaac. The promises of YHWH will be fulfilled through him. He also is an astute bargainer himself. Not only does he see (the angel of) YHWH at Bethel, but he also receives the major promise that, in return for the tithe, God will remain with him, eventually giving the land to him and his seed, and that his descendants will spread out in all directions. Jacob himself swears to this covenant, which is conditional on YHWH's largesse: "Then Jacob made a vow, saying, 'If God will be with me, and will keep me in this way that I go, and will give me bread to eat and clothing to wear, so that I come again to my father's house in peace, then the LORD shall be my God, and this stone, which I have set up for a pillar, shall be God's house; and of all that you give me I will surely give one tenth to you'" (Genesis 28:20–22). This promise is at last finally made safe with the ascent of Solomon to the throne and his building of the Temple, which confirms YHWH's control of the land.

An editor quite like the editor of the Court History has also been active in Genesis, because in the story of Jacob's vision at Bethel he goes out of his way to identify the manner in which the place is to be identified: "He called that place Bethel;[22] but the name of the city was Luz at the first." While this is not as good a demonstration of the role of the editor as the Deuteronomic phrase "and the Canaanite was then in the land" (Deuteronomy 12:6), it does clearly make a distinction between the time of the events in the story and the narration. They do not have to be the same narrator, because there were a number of different redactions in the course of Israelite history—perhaps as many as three—the original, the Deuteronomic, and the postexilic.

The Transfer of Abishag

The test of Solomon's mettle happens soon enough, when Adonijah asks Bathsheba for the virgin Abishag the Shunamite, the beautiful but chaste companion of David's old age (1 Kings 2:17–18). Bathsheba sees nothing wrong with this request as a consolation prize for Solomon's half brother and so asks Solomon herself for this boon for Adonijah. But Solomon apparently sees in it Adonijah's last attempt to rehabilitate his (legitimate) candidacy for the kingship. True to his word in 1 Kings 1:52, Solomon treats Adonijah as a rebel: "If he will show himself a worthy man, there shall not an hair of him fall to the earth: but if wickedness shall be found in him, he shall die." This is quite similar to the voice of the LORD in the Cain and Abel story. And that is no accident.

Solomon acts decisively and wisely, according to the narrative, in having his brother put to death. But the question remains as to why this request

seals Adonijah's doom. It is always conceivable that Bathsheba tricks Adonijah to his death, knowing it to be his death, but the text does not imply it. It
seems more like even savvy Bathsheba sees no offense.

Most scholars suggest that possession of the "harem" was one of the pre-
rogatives of the king; therefore Adonijah's request kept his bid for the succession alive. It certainly seems to be so in one other episode in Court History,
in regard to Absalom (2 Samuel 16:21). In the case of Absalom, the context
gives us more complete information: "²⁰ Then Absalom said to Ahithophel,
'Give us your counsel; what shall we do?' ²¹ Ahithophel said to Absalom, 'Go
in to your father's concubines, the ones he has left to look after the house;
and all Israel will hear that you have made yourself odious to your father, and
the hands of all who are with you will be strengthened.' ²² So they pitched a
tent for Absalom upon the roof; and Absalom went in to his father's concubines in the sight of all Israel" (2 Samuel 16:20–22).

To us, this seems like incest.[23] Indeed, it is the converse crime that Judah
commits with Tamar in Genesis. And it too becomes incest in Deuteronomy
and Leviticus, two later texts. Again, we have some evidence that what is
defined as incest changed over the five hundred years of Israelite history.
So we do not understand everything that we want to understand here. But
it does look as if there is material in this narrative that is earlier than the
Deuteronomic and priestly redactions. So too, in the case of Adonijah, Absalom could easily have been continuing his campaign to secure the throne
for himself. If that is true, Bathsheba did not see it at all or consider it as that
important a request. But Solomon did.

The motivation is hard to understand exactly; perhaps Solomon was in
love with Abishag himself. In view of his many marriages, that seems unlikely.
Perhaps he was jealous of giving anything to an older brother. No doubt he
was looking for a pretext to get rid of a rival, in any case. And perhaps the dying wish of his father David was but a pretext to kill Joab, who had sided with
Adonijah (1 Kings 2:5). But, in the context of the succession narrative, these
ferocious acts show that Solomon is able to rule in a savage environment.
It shows that this is the role that God assigned to him from the beginning.

Solomon's Dream at Gibeah

Solomon's rule begins with an alliance with Egypt, enforced by a marriage
with Pharaoh's daughter (1 Kings 3:1). This is certainly a very bold move,

knowing what the Bible has to say about intermarriage, easily interpreted as a new sin. But Solomon gets a provisional pass from this DH narrator for the moment. He then journeys to Gibeah to offer sacrifice there. When he does so, God appears to him in a dream and accepts him as heir to the throne, in spite of the messiness of his succession and his marriage to Pharaoh's daughter (1 Kings 3:5). Even in the story, the only witness for this acceptance is Solomon himself. God asks Solomon what he wants. Solomon's answer is very Deuteronomic. No doubt, it has been supplied by that editor:

> [6] "You have shown great and steadfast love to your servant my father David, because he walked before you in faithfulness, in righteousness, and in uprightness of heart toward you; and you have kept for him this great and steadfast love, and have given him a son to sit on his throne today. [7] And now, O LORD my God, you have made your servant king in place of my father David, although I am only a little child; I do not know how to go out or come in. [8] And your servant is in the midst of the people whom you have chosen, a great people, so numerous they cannot be numbered or counted. [9] Give your servant therefore an understanding mind to govern your people, able to discern between good and evil; for who can govern this your great people?"
>
> (1 Kings 3:6–9)

The language is Deuteronomistic *enumerate*, and the dream would be hard to confirm since no one else is involved. There is no prophetic guarantee of this blessing. But, in the eyes of the DH, it certainly shows that God accepts Solomon's rule, indeed is very pleased with it, and decides to give him the wisdom, understanding, and discernment that he has asked for, but also the wealth that he has not asked for. And then he supplements all of it with long life (verses 10–14). Besides the vocabulary, the Deuteronomistic Historian's perspective can be seen in the knowledge that Solomon lived and reigned a long time, which could not have been known at the beginning of his reign. This aggrandizement of Solomon is very much the product of the DH.

So Solomon needed to act independently to end the various threats against his surprising rise to power. He establishes his wisdom to rule with his quick action in getting rid of Adonijah. Solomon's wisdom is a theme that is sounded strongly thereafter in many ways, even though his sin of marrying foreign wives is never ignored or forgiven. Thus the text continues to articulate a measured ambiguity about Solomon. Despite his own luxuriousness and marrying foreign women, the very issues incorporated into the patriarchal stories, the opinion of Solomon remains fairly high. Without a prior sense of the difficulty of marrying out of the tribe, the criticism of Solomon would be incomprehensible. But there is no getting around this ambiguity, the simultaneous approval and disapproval of Solomon in his text. In many ways, Solomon is one of the principal heroes of the Court History, but he never reaches the status of David, his father, or the piety of Josiah, his descendant. There are many ways to explain this phenomenon, but the usual one is to say that there is more than one editing of the material or that the Deuteronomistic Historian is different from the editor of the JE epic (Rje) and that their perspectives differ. What is being propounded here, and throughout this chapter, are mythological stories of the patriarchs, and, as we shall see, also Samson, used to fill in moral meanings against the royal family when the narrator of the DH seems unwilling to express critique.

At least one other editing must surely have been undertaken by the Deuteronomistic Historian, and, in this version, it is Josiah who takes over the role of greatest king and hero of the Judean people, and he is described as the equal of David, not Solomon. As we have seen, in many ways Josiah is portrayed as superior to David and Solomon. Before the final Deuteronomic editing, though, the patriarchal stories of the descent of the Israelite family mediated all these complicated and ambiguous stories.

Telltale Ziklag

While the editors have helped put together these stories, there are perhaps as many as three different and separate editings in the succession narratives, or perhaps this is a shorthand for the constant process of glossing that may have gone on over the centuries. We know that the phrase "The Canaanite was then in the land" (Genesis 12:6) assumes that the narrator is speaking at a later period, but since we do not know when the Israelites were able to remove the Canaanites completely from their state, there is no way to fix an absolute date from this statement. We do know, however, that the narrative implies a historical present when Canaanites were no longer in the land, contrary to some very contemporary interpretations of biblical history. That is important to emphasize. So the phrase "the Canaanite was then in the land" gives us two very important pieces of information or the narrative would not command authority. Unfortunately, we do not yet know which two periods the narrator has in mind.

There are a number of other phrases in the text that have the same effect of opening up a gulf between the writers and the historical present. Several times we find the phrase "to this very day" or some other phrase to that effect. So there is no doubt these phrases are all due to a relatively long period of traditioning, editing, and glossing, giving us both a historical past as well as a historical present to define in the text. While we can see that there are two levels of historical perspective in the text, it is not easy to define what they are in absolute terms.

There is, however, one place where we have some further hints as to the earliest possible dates of the core tradition. That is in 1 Samuel 27:6, where the text states that "Ziklag belongs to the kings of Judah to this very day." The context is the reward for David's service to the Philistine king Achish. "Then David said to Achish, 'If I have found favor in your sight, let a place be given me in one of the country towns, so that I may live there; for why should your servant live in the royal city with you?' So that day Achish gave him Ziklag; therefore Ziklag has belonged to the kings of Judah to this day. The length of time that David lived in the country of the Philistines was one year and four months" (1 Samuel 27:6–7).

The story tells us that David was a valued mercenary in the hire of Achish and that he was rewarded for his service with the gift of the town of Ziklag. That is a very interesting story in that it tells us that David's rise to power involved a stint as a mercenary in the hire of the Philistines. This suggests perhaps that Israel was not so firm that it prevented a great chieftain from enlisting in an army that could fight against his own people. Nor is it a particularly easy story for those scholars who want to maintain that Israelite ethnic identity was born in the sixth century BCE. But it is a painful and hence realistic detail when placed in the tenth century BCE, except that we are naturally skeptical about such early dates. Unfortunately, we cannot be sure where Ziklag is or how long it remained in Israelite hands.

Unlike the previous examples, we can, however, make a good guess. Ziklag must be in the south, in or at the border of the Negev, to put it close to the Philistine heartland. And we know that all such lands were taken by Egypt shortly after Solomon's death, when Shishak (Shishonq) invaded Judah and Israel and took away both land and riches: "In the fifth year of King Rehoboam, King Shishak of Egypt came up against Jerusalem" (1 Kings 14:25).

Since this takes place at the beginning of Rehoboam's reign, it would have to be describing the situation sometime before the end of the tenth century BCE. This gives us the first hint that we could have some absolute dating that actually goes back to the end of the united monarchy, though a great deal of the writing must, nevertheless, come from a later period.

Fertility and Well-Being

The main issues of both the Pentateuchal stories and the great Court History are understandably the correct and legitimate succession and the resultant fertility, which overlaps with the covenantal stories as well. Obviously, different aspects of fertility are at stake in the succession narrative. But we might just as easily think that the royal family is an ordinary family writ large. Certainly, issues of fertility and survival are more or less equal in both. So we can see how issues in one group of stories will have echoes in the other. We can see this plainly, for example, in the attention given to barrenness in the patriarchal stories. In both sets of stories, barrenness and curse is placed against fertility and blessing. And the result of the blessing is many children, long life, and also the land. Barrenness is a characteristic of all the favored matriarchs before they become the favored mothers of the chosen child:

> But Sarai was barren; she had no child.
>
> (Genesis 11:30)

> And Isaac entreated the LORD for his wife, because she was barren.
>
> (Genesis 25:21)

> And when the LORD saw that Leah was hated, he opened her womb: but Rachel was barren.
>
> (Genesis 29:31)

But the same stories are told about the births of Samuel and Samson:

> He had two wives; the name of the one was Hannah, and the name of the other Peninnah. Peninnah had children, but Hannah had no children.
>
> (1 Samuel 1:2)

> And there was a certain man of Zorah, of the family of the Danites, whose name was Manoah; and his wife was barren, and bare not.
>
> (Judges 13:2)

In each case, the result of the barrenness is the birth of a special child, for whom YHWH opens the womb. It is a phenomenon from the natural realm; traditional literature is full of stories of people who were barren and who conceived after long trial. It is very much like the story prohibiting human sacrifice that begins by commanding one. The result of the barren woman story, in the Israelite case, is the birth of a special child. So too in the Bible; only God is always the person who provides. For Sarah, the special child is Isaac; for Isaac's wife Rebecca, it is Jacob; for Jacob's wife Rachel, it is Joseph; for Manoah's wife, it is Samson, and for Hannah it is Samuel. That is the pattern. The point is that the barrenness of each matriarch is relieved by YHWH, who changes the curse into a blessing, which brings forth a savior for Israel.

The Ironic Case of Rachel

In the case of Rachel, the story is especially ironic. Jacob worked seven years to get Leah, as it turned out, and then seven more years for his favorite, Rachel. But Rachel was barren, while Leah was fertile: "When Rachel saw that she bore Jacob no children, she envied her sister; and she said to Jacob, 'Give me children, or I shall die!' Jacob became very angry with Rachel and said, 'Am I in the place of God, who has withheld from you the fruit of the womb?'" (Genesis 30:1–2).

The plight of Rachel is inherent in her spoken line and it, ironically, seals her early death as well. More explicitly, it gives the narrator a prototypical justification for her early death. But it also establishes very quickly that it is YHWH who provides fertility to overcome barrenness, blessing to overcome curse, and gives Rachel the role of a trickster in trading time with her husband to get with child. In this context, it must mean that it is YHWH and not any of the other gods of Canaan who orders events and allows Rachel to conceive. The chapter continues the process of naming the sons of Leah: in addition to the handmaidens Zilpah and Bilhah's tribes, we are told of Zebulun and Issachar, and finally of Leah's daughter Dinah, who is not given an etymology (verse 20).

The story of the mandrakes, if that is what *dudaim* are, suggests that Rachel outsmarts Leah (verses 14–16) as a trickster would. She trades one night with Jacob for the plant that will allow her to conceive Joseph (verses 22–25). And, of course, she hires out Jacob in a way that balances Jacob's hiring himself out to her father Laban for what turns out to be fourteen years.

Finally, Jacob triumphs over Laban through his trick of making the goats produce the kind of marked offspring that will go to Jacob and not to Laban. It is parallel to Rachel's use of the mandrakes to conceive Joseph. The birth of Joseph does indeed bring increase, as Joseph's name implies. The result is that Jacob becomes very rich in sons and herds: "Thus the man grew exceedingly rich, and had large flocks, and male and female slaves, and camels and donkeys" (Genesis 30:43). That is the secret of the trickster. He holds divine power and so can turn any losing situation into a winning one. With all the difficulties that Jacob and his wives go through, the LORD is with them and blesses them with land, natural increase, and many children. These stories have universal appeal, but they must also be specially appealing to Israel, a pastoral and agricultural people who seek to govern a land of Israel in the face of jealous neighbors.

Jacob and Laban

Of course, Laban is a distant relative of the Israelites, but Jacob and Laban do not always act like family to each other. Their relationship very much recapitulates the relationship between Israel and the country of Aram or Syria. Archaeological discoveries have contributed much information to the understanding of the Jacob-Laban narratives. Scholars have seen in the relationship between Jacob and Laban some parallels with the adoption and marriage customs practiced in northern Mesopotamia, as recorded in the Nuzi tablets, although the view has been challenged by van Seters (1969),[24] who thinks that the key to the Laban stories is to be found in the Second Temple period. Not withstanding van Seters's theory, Morrison (1983:156) has said that the agreement between Jacob and Laban, sealed by these marriages, bears "a strong resemblance to Old Babylonian herding contracts."[25] The basic element of this contract was Jacob's promise to work as a herdsman for Laban in return for his two wives and certain types of livestock.

After twenty years with Laban, Jacob became a very rich man. Just as in the stories with the wife-sister motif, Laban and his sons "did not regard him with favor as before" (Genesis 31:2). For this reason, Jacob flees with his wives, his children, and his flocks to return to the land of Canaan. When Laban hears that Jacob has fled (with the household gods hidden in Rachel's personal effects, Genesis 31:19), he pursues Jacob as far as Gilead (Genesis 31:25). God appears to Laban in a dream (Genesis 31:24), admonishing him not to harm Jacob. So Jacob and Laban instead enter into a covenant. The covenant is sealed by an oath when Laban calls on the God of Nahor and Jacob calls on the God of Abraham, the gods of their fathers (Genesis 31:53) as their witnesses to the covenant. A monument celebrating the event was erected. Laban calls it, in Aramaic, Jegar-sahadutha (*yĕgar śahădûtā**) and Jacob calls it, in Hebrew, Galeed (*gal*ēd*). Both phrases mean a "heap of witness."[26] No doubt, this story establishes the social and geographical limits between Israel and Syria in the tenth or ninth century BCE.

We have now found another stela in the north, in Dan, in which the Aramean king has nothing so friendly to say. It is a victory stela. The unknown Aramean king says instead that he beat the house of David back and killed their king in battle. Evidently, this is a later exchange between the two peoples. The Bible only recognizes a more friendly encounter in its mythological level. And it includes trying to prevent intermarriages:

> [43] Then Laban answered and said to Jacob, "The daughters are my daughters, the children are my children, the flocks are my flocks, and all that you see is mine. But what can I do today about these daughters of mine, or about their children whom they have borne? [44] Come now, let us make a covenant, you and I; and let it be a witness between you and me." [45] So Jacob took a stone, and set it up as a pillar. [46] And Jacob said to his kinsfolk, "Gather stones," and they took stones, and made a heap; and they ate there by the heap. [47] Laban called it Jegar-sahadutha: but Jacob called it Galeed. [48] Laban said, "This heap is a witness between you and me today." Therefore he called it Galeed, [49] and the pillar Mizpah.
>
> (Genesis 31:43–49)

The heap of stones or stela is supposed to serve as a boundary stone and a witness that both sides will keep the terms of the agreement, even if the principals of the covenant are not there to police it. It is clear from this event and its strategic location that Laban represents the Aramaic state to the north and east of Israel. And since Laban seems to represent the Aramaic state, it also perhaps suggests something about Israel's relationship with the Arameams in which both peoples prospered for a while but eventually needed more freedom. No more will the two peoples intermarry. It does present an alternative, not often stressed depiction of times in which the Israelite tribes gained from living in the presence of their neighbors.

Jacob's covenant with Laban again shows the importance of right and legitimate offspring. Jacob gets to keep his wives and maidservants and their children, the twelve tribes, but Laban imposes on Jacob the duty to treat Laban's offspring well and not to take any wives in addition to Leah and Rachel: "⁵⁰If you ill-treat my daughters, or if you take wives in addition to my daughters, though no one else is with us, remember that God is witness between you and me" (Genesis 31:50). These rare moments of agreement have their natural limitations. The stela that we actually found shows a much more ferocious relationship between the two peoples, one in which the Aramean king was the obvious winner. The Syro-Ephraimite Wars, however, are eighth-century wars, and therefore the Bible's discussion of the more peaceful period should precede it.

Rachel and the Mandrakes

The covenant between Laban and Jacob was a rare exception, not the rule in this part of the world, as the Israelites and the Arameans entered into several long wars that were only extinguished by the arrival of the Assyrians on the scene.

However, this is not the end of Rachel's saga either. She bears a second son, Benjamin, and, in giving birth, tragically dies:

> Then they journeyed from Bethel; and when they were still some distance from Ephrath, Rachel travailed, and she had hard labor. And when she was in her hard labor, the midwife said to her, "Fear not; for now you will have another son."
>
> And as her soul was departing (for she died), she called his name Benoni; but his father called his name Benjamin. So Rachel died, and she was buried on the way to Ephrath (that is, Bethlehem), and Jacob set up a pillar upon her grave; it is the pillar of Rachel's tomb, which is there to this day.
>
> (Genesis 35:16–20)

There are several ironies in this section. Rachel's own desire for offspring leads to her death. The story, it seems, is at bottom an etiology of the pillar of Rachel's tomb, which was a known place in the time of the narrator, and of course, marks a spot in a settled land. None of this quite prepares us for the irony of the midwife's statement: "Fear not; for now you will have another son." Did she deliberately lie to the dying Rachel as a consolation or merely misunderstand the gravity of her situation? Or perhaps this is another example of the horrifying objectification of women. We shall not know for sure.

Rachel's death also testifies about the ironic ways in which barrenness and blessing interact, as well as illustrate the continued surprising success of the last born. Rachel's desire for offspring brings her demise, but she also bears yet another son, who is to be the ancestor of the Saulide dynasty. While she calls the son Benoni ("son of travail"), her husband Jacob calls him Benjamin ("son of my right hand")—that is, either *favored son* or *southerner*, as the right hand and the south were identical when facing east. The irony is, of course, that her own suffering has brought blessing to others.

And, of course, whenever legitimacy of inheritance is the subject of the myth, political power lies underneath the story as well. The Rachel tribes, Joseph (Ephraim and Manasseh, the largest northern tribes) and Benjamin (the smallest southern tribe, but the staunch ally of Judah) turn out to have special status. The Davidic dynasty comes from Judah, but the Saulide dynasty is from Benjamin. In the J epic, both Joseph and Benjamin are looked after and saved by Judah, the ancestor of the Judean kingship (Genesis 37:26, 44:16–33).

So Rachel eventually gets what she so dearly wanted, and we return to the themes with which we began. The story of Sarah in distress is a dramatic way to illustrate her barrenness, which is afterward changed into a blessing of fertility. That blessing comes from God, and it also comes from the trickster patriarch relying on God. Not only is Sarah barren, but while she is in disguise in the foreign households, so are they. The same with Rebecca. In each of the three episodes, Abraham or Isaac, the trickster, leaves enriched for his trickiness. There is a blessing for each of the foreign kings in whose employ the patriarch was found. These are stories that assume Israel had no political power and, in fact, warn foreign powers that their well-being depends on Israel's well-being. No wonder they have resonated to Jews throughout the ages. But their origin is unlikely to be in the sixth century BCE. They look like they started far earlier than that.

In fact, in spite of the biblical perspective focusing on the man and a man's understanding of enrichment, each cycle—let us take the Abraham cycle, the Jacob cycle, and later the Samson and Samuel cycle—begins with a barren woman who, in her plight, asks for a divine oracle and is promised children. The response of YHWH can come in different ways. In Genesis 18, divine messengers come to tell Abraham, who serves them a meal, and is given the promise of children. In Judges 13, Manoah, Samson's father, is visited by a divine messenger, who forecasts Samson's immediate birth. When Manoah attempts to serve a meal, as Abraham does, the angel refuses and disappears into heaven in flames. Similarly, in the call story of the judge Gideon, the angel appears but Gideon is skeptical. Gideon attempts to feed the stranger, but the angel refuses to speak his name and ascends to heaven as in the case of Manoah. It looks like the angel messenger is participating in a covenantal meal.

In Genesis 12 Sarah's fertility leads to further promises of well-being, wealth, land, and many offspring. Each of the patriarchal stories end with the primary blessings of fertility, increase of flocks, and land. These are certainly the prime concerns of the early Israelites as they settle the land before the monarchy. And throughout the period of the judges we see that the young and inexperienced—the least likely—is the one whom God chooses. This theme continues well into the life of the monarchy with the election and repudiation of Saul as king, the election of David, the promise that his dynasty is chosen forever, and finally, the election of Solomon. Each cycle begins in death and barrenness and features a person not obvious to be the savior of Israel. In the end, the story ends in blessing, land, and offspring.

Moses and Jacob

Genesis 12 anticipates the Exodus. But then Jacob is, in a way, a prototype for Moses, as has also been noted by several scholars.[27] What they all have in common is the theme of the trickster. Abraham's trickiness is transferred to Moses. Of course, Moses's story evinces a great many other motifs as well, but he certainly attempts to deceive Pharaoh by asking him to allow the Israelites to leave Egypt temporarily to celebrate a festival to the Lord. The Israelites are always the underdogs and tricksters; they are always the vulnerable ones; they are always the ones who need to exercise their devious minds to prevent the superior powers from completely enslaving them.

In all those trickster stories, whether the opponent be Egypt or Abimelech or the Philistines, with a "willingness" to make women available as wives the trickster is able to derive untold benefits. One important aspect of the trickster theme is that he can take enormous risks—in fact, he can risk everything, even his wife's honor or his special child promised by God—because he knows that God is with him. He knows that God is with him because he represents the Israelites themselves, and they want their myths to tell them that.[28]

Myth and Legend

Michael Fishbane, who studied the fertility motifs in detail, says that they are traditional but meant to move the reader forward into the narrative. The fertility element he sees as a continuation of the curse of Genesis, hence as a vision of the whole: "The contrastive pair *barrenness/fertility*, in its variety of expressions, lies at the heart of the personal anxieties of Rebekkah and Rachel, and the interpersonal tensions between Rachel and Leah. The fact that all the major women in Genesis, and many outside it, are initially barren and struggle for their matriarchal inheritance is undoubtedly a hint at the continuity of the curse of Eden" (pp. 60–61).[29] He also stresses that behind this theme lies a deep anxiety over biological and cultural continuity and lack of power. I can agree, provided we understand that these are mythical characters and not only historical individuals. And there is one more provision: the stories of the patriarchs are meant to mediate difficulties in the succession or the national life of Israel during First Temple times.

One day we may find evidence that the patriarchs existed. But it is safe to conclude that the stories of the patriarchs are framed more by experience of the later editors who lived in the times of the monarchy. So the anxiety and worry over blessing/curse, barrenness/fertility must be understood not just as belonging to Leah and Rachel but even more as a communal and social concern, not a personal one. One suspects that these are universal issues in biblical culture, going all the way back to the beginning of Israelite history. They are absolutely crucial to tribal peoples. The continuing Israelite issue is when is it appropriate to intermarry with the others and when is it too dangerous.

The difference in style between the stories is enough to suggest that they are not a single-authored work, but one that has been edited into a unity.

The patriarchs and matriarchs are actually presented in a very undetailed way. That is, we get no direct statements of their internal states, only objective correlatives to them. The characters in the Pentateuch are not, as a general rule, drawn in enough detail to get more than a general sense of what their internal experience may have been. The narrator is much more interested in outcomes than in characterization along the way. And everything else is schematized. Everything outside the center spotlight of the story loses its peculiarity and fades into the background. God, in the first four books of Moses, on the other hand, is always active and speaks directly to the patriarchs, whether in person or in dreams, and personally directs the history of the patriarchal families and the children of Israel. God is, in a way, the only really well-drawn character in the drama. This is a mythical world for the Israelites; it is explicitly different from their own experience. And it is very different from the narrative in the former prophets. But it is clear that these stories are themselves the most salient ethnic markers of the people Israel. The stories tell the hearers who they are. And they work as identity and ethnicity markers in tribal society, in city society, in exile, and in return. The stories of the Pentateuch are the primary identity markers of the Israelite people in First Temple times. The Bible becomes the same as Israelite and later Jewish history as it continues.

In the former prophets—Joshua, Judges, 1 and 2 Samuel, 1 and 2 Kings— by contrast, we find that the relationship between God and humans is distant and unsure, in many ways closer to our experience: "The word of the LORD was rare in those days; visions were not widespread" (1 Samuel 3:1). To be sure, the word for *rare* means "expensive" or "dear" in Hebrew. But the meaning of the phrase is clear enough: God is not directly present in these stories, as he is in the stories of the patriarchs. He speaks to Samuel briefly, but, on the whole, can be said to be the author of history but not a conversation partner with the personages of the period. YHWH, or more likely his angel, may rarely appear in these stories, but, by comparison with the stories in the patriarchs, these books show humanity on its own, seeking God's help but not always finding it. Occasionally, as we have seen in the comparison between the snake in Genesis 3 and Micaiah ben Imlah, God can deliberately mislead those whose ruin he seeks: "go forth and do so" (1 Kings 22:21–22).

This is a much more morally complicated world than the child's world that confronts Adam and Eve. In this world, God can actually mislead his prophets. It is a world in which Israelites sometimes act like their neighbors who do not have a covenant and hence engage in raping and murdering. It is a world in which even small but terrible events can bring about a terrible and wasteful internicene tribal civil war. It is a world in which the stories of the patriarchs need to be read and understood by the aristocracy and ordinary persons so as to figure out how to act in the world and have confidence in God. And that is why oral and written traditions together helped bring them into existence—tales of terror that instruct the literate and nonliterate classes in times of trouble. The process of mythologization, which yields a divine message, is indeed a complex one. And it also enforces ethnic identity, as has been clear throughout.

Solomon, the Younger Child

Strangely enough, this generates a number of different stories about how the younger child inherits in place of the older child: Abel over Cain, Isaac over Ishmael, Jacob over Esau, Joseph over his brothers, Perez over his brother Zerah, Ephraim over his brother Manasseh, Saul (and the Benjamites) over the other candidates for nagid, David over everyone else for king of a united Israel, and now, as we know, Solomon over his older brother Adonijah to succeed David. It is the royal succession of Solomon that thrusts the other stories to prominence. The JE epic, slowly told and retold by narrators and scribes, eventually imposes this upon the text in order to give David's rise to power and Solomon's succession divine sanction.

In a real way, the stories in the former prophets, the conquest, the stories of the judges, and the court narrative presented the Israelites (both Judeans and their northern neighbors) with contradictions and horrors that had to be explained. This was done through oral traditions out of which myths arose. Thus, the story of Absalom's vengeance murder of his brother Amnon, for example, could be understood and reunderstood through stories about Cain and Abel. The horrible story of the concubine of the Levite, which launched a terrible, internecine tribal war, could be reflected upon through the story of Abraham's rescue of Lot in Sodom and Gomorrah. The latter was an etiology, explaining the ruins on the southern shore of the Dead Sea. But it became a story that explained why Israelites should treat their tribal brothers with more respect or risk destruction. The stories of Jephthah's daughter and the binding of Isaac are both etiologies for religious rituals, a northern rite of women's lament and the placement of the sacrificial cult at the Temple in the south.

In a way, it is a much more complicated world even than that faced by the Deuteronomic writer, because it is a world laced with unexpected losses and gains. The Deuteronomistic Historian, too, thought that the world could be governed under the orderly law of God. But, in the end, King Josiah was killed unexpectedly in a meaningless skirmish with Egypt, ending the Deuteronomic reform.

Still, it stimulated new interpretations by the DH to the former prophets and eventually produced the historical books as a corpus. The characters in the former prophets do not automatically see their way through moral ambiguity. David's mismanagement of his family causes huge dynastic difficulties, but in the end it brings Solomon to the throne. It is a world we understand. One can hope that events will work out in a moral way. But that is almost never clear to the characters in the drama. The Deuteronomistic Historian (really the school of scribes who act in that capacity) can contend that God's justice is evident in the end. That is an interpretation of events. Rarely do those who arrogantly assert their rectitude triumph in these stories. Underneath these grander themes are the more personal ones: survival of the family, fertility, increase, and wealth, despite the lack of power. And, in the case of Solomon, it is quite possible that cautionary tales about intermarriage remained particularly relevant.

CONCLUSION

Synoptic Sinning

Ancestor Stories Create an Ethnic Identity

Though we have hardly run out of terrible stories, we have seen enough to move to some conclusions. First, we should note that biblical writers have no compunction about reporting terrible stories about their ancestors. This is quite at odds with any theory that the Pentateuch was written in the sixth century BCE, especially so if the theory presupposes that the narrator is trying to generate an ethnic identity for the first time.[1] One clear result of reading the stories of the patriarchs is to see how the stories about ancient family relationships mediated stress points and built an ethnic identity based around common ancestry, real or imagined. We were only able to find a relative chronology. Most of the stories we saw appear to be written after the united kingdom (1000 BCE–922 BCE) but before the Deuteronomistic Historians (after 621 BCE but extending into the exile).

Furthermore, we have seen that in the stories themselves there is an enormous range of motivations for different, often distinct editors over many centuries of time. They are much less self-conscious, detailed, and full of embarrassing particulars and much less influenced by Aramaic and Greek than they would have been were they written in Second Temple times. In the Second Temple period the style of Hebrew, as well, would have been different, unless we can demonstrate that the stories are purposely archaized.[2]

Indeed, we have seen that various stories from the time of the patriarchs are unlikely to have been written down at first at all. There are lots of reasons to believe that they existed orally and that the oral form existed together with a written source for a while before it reached the form we have. We have seen that implicit in the stories is a relative chronology. We have been able to sketch the relative chronology logically by the way in which the stories have developed; we have seen how the Deuteronomistic Historians were able to write a more explicitly parenetic moral reason for the same events that the mythical materials originally organized. That is to say, the DH replaces or adds to the mythical analysis of the historical events in Israelite tradition with a moral analysis of historical events that are expressed sermonically in Deuteronomic style. Thus it seems likely that the Pentateuchal materials precede the DH, and the DH begins to work after the Deuteronomist is published in 621 BCE. There is no reason to suppose that the Deuteronomist is of any different time period than his stylistic contemporary, Jeremiah (621 BCE–586 BCE). We were able to look at the relative stages in the development of the DT stories. If we now compare these stories and the relative chronology we have been able to ascertain for them with known, fixed dates from archaeology and the chronology of events in the ancient Near East, we will be able to give the stories a more exact, absolute date. But before that, let's look at the themes privileged by the patriarchal myths.

Terrible Stories for Us, Myths for Them

This book has also argued that the stories of the patriarchs come from different periods: some can be dated closely, others cannot, some seem to respond to issues in the First Temple period, occasionally one seems even older than that, as we shall explore in this chapter. Most seem to have had an oral history as well as a written history. But wherever and whenever they come from, they serve as the mythical substratum to Israelites living in the time of the First Temple period. They reflect the issues and span the seeming contradictions in life during First Temple times, as evidenced by the historical writings in the former prophets in the Bible. The stories were, in turn, sometimes reinterpreted after the Deuteronomic Reform (621 BCE) and then, even later, by the Deuteronomistic Historian. The DH often added a more strictly moralistic and historical interpretation of events as an explanation for the terrible outcomes.

But the DH, coming much later than the JE epic, knew more actual history of the Davidic monarchy and the states of Judah and Israel. Obviously, that gave the DH a clear advantage in understanding historical outcomes as God's pleasure and displeasure. Nevertheless, DH had to stay within that series of parameters. For example, DH certainly thought that bad outcomes were due to sinning and could turn to the destruction of the north by the Assyrians. The earlier writers had no such information. They used the story of the golden calf at Sinai to make their point. The earlier writers, conversely, certainly knew that David and Bathsheba sinned. But since Bathsheba became the queen mother during Solomon's time, the criticism had to be muted. Even the DH had to mitigate his criticism of that particular issue. Because of the nature of the editing, we can often see both explanations in the biblical corpus.

We first isolated the earliest mythic and folkloric layer of the Bible in the three stories describing a matriarch in distress: Sarai, Sarah, and Rebecca are each described as put in danger by the behavior of their husbands. The earliest form we could discern was the presumed oral prototype to all three of the stories: Genesis 12, 20, and 26.

This triplet also showed us that not every story in the Bible is still readily understandable to us today. Apparently, the ancient trickster motif and the warning against intermarriage were more important at one very ancient level of tradition than anything else we might today consider morally significant. It explained as possible and prototypical the rape of Tamar by Amnon and, even more obviously, the rape of the concubine of the Levite. But, as time went on, other, more moral interpretations grew in popularity, as different documents or voices were added to Israel's national epic. In the case of this puzzling story, three more rationalized stories grew up as the three different versions of the stories evolved.

The earliest datable layer in the traditions we have studied has mythical characteristics. An obvious characteristic of the layer of mythological writing in the Bible is that God, or one of his surrogates, communicates directly with the biblical characters. The stories illustrate the Hebrew equivalent of deus ex machina, where God intervenes directly in the affairs of humanity and settles issues with either a boon or a punishment. He can choose Abraham to carry out his plan for humanity or strike the inhabitants of Sodom blind so that Abraham and the family of Lot can escape. We might ourselves choose a god who is less interested in fire and brimstone, but everyone fantasizes about a god who speaks to us individually.

They were different from us, I hope. Sometimes they wanted a divinity who could even the score. Other times they wanted and needed advice about the legitimacy of offspring or marriage or relationship in general. The Hebrew Bible's mythical layer has some easily identifiable characteristics. First, in the mythical layers of Genesis and Exodus, and especially in the strand of tradition that we have been calling J, God speaks to the main characters, intervenes in the situation, and puts every situation to right. Regardless of what may lay behind these stories in history, this presentation of reality is a fictional, mythological world that did not fit most people's experience then as today, but the stories functioned to adjudicate difficult historical questions for them.

It is possible to see how the mythic layer functioned by pairing stories in Genesis and Exodus with legends and historical events in the former prophets. One example of this pairing would be the rape of the concubine and the attempted homosexual rape of Lot, together with the three stories of the matriarch in peril, which have parallel events or structure. In the mythical level of these stories, God intervenes and saves the matriarchs, or Lot, while in the more realistic and difficult stories the concubine of the Levite and Tamar actually suffer the abuse. By means of this deliberate parallelism, the rape of the concubine could be explained as evil not just as a single terrible event but because the people of Benjamin were acting like Sodomites or, by extension, like the Philistines or Egyptians. The story of Lot and the Sodomites, in turn, explained the ruins of cities long vanished around the Dead Sea. They were destroyed by God because they were terrible sinners. It does not matter which story began to be told first. It was the period of oral transmission that brought them together in that interesting way, followed by a clever DH editor who made the connection even more obvious and brought out the point that these savageries demanded the rise of kingship for the people Israel to govern itself. But the mythical connection of the Benjamites with the Sodomites applies to a very early layer of tradition, much earlier than the DH, which explained the ruins on the east side of the Dead Sea.

This is to be distinguished from the foreground of the legendary-historical narrative in Judges or 1 and 2 Samuel, as a counterexample. Think again of the story of the concubine of the Levite, where the word of YHWH is dear, not widespread. His will must be divined from analyzing events or consulting the proper oracle, being careful to interpret them correctly, even returning to the oracle a second time and asking for clarification. This is a non-mythical perspective. Although the stories concern people at a completely different level of technology and cultural attainment, the whole narrative seems more like experience as we know it than the Pentateuch does in one crucial way, with its continuous divine interventions.

This does not turn the narrative in Judges into historical fact, without applying the hermeneutics of suspicion. But it makes clear that there is a difference between the two types of narrative presentment and the latter possibly has a historical kernel.

Golden Calves Lead the Flock to Understanding

The story of the golden calves of Jeroboam really makes this link clear. Many of the pairs of stories that we studied contain no hints as to which story may precede historically, but the two stories about the gold calves of Jeroboam seem to precede the story of the golden calf in Exodus. Each story contains the phrase "These are your gods, who brought you out of Egypt." Since there are two calves in the Jeroboam story, but only one at Sinai, it seems more likely that the Jeroboam story precedes the story in Exodus. The story in Exodus, however, represents a satire of the actual religious practice of the northern kingdom, which was worship of the god of Israel but involved an icon of a calf. The story in Exodus, then, would function as a a polemical myth, condemning and explaining the secession of the northern tribes. Once one of the later layers of editing by DH knew that the northern kingdom was destroyed by the Assyrians, a more effective polemic was available, which shows up in 2 Kings: they sinned and God eventually destroyed them. This explanation was not available to the JE epic—meaning that it had to be created before the destruction of the northern kingdom in 721 BCE.

The same kind of analysis informs the story of the concubine of the Levite. The narrative has a realistic feel, quite specific details of a type always missing from the patriarchal and Exodus narrative. This hardly guarantees that any or every detail in that story in Judges is historical. But historians must make judgments about believability of texts based on the texts of the time.[3] The gift of the virgins of Jabesh-gilead to Benjamin (Judges 20) may easily be a legend of the type one sees in the rape of the Sabine women, partly based on fact and partly on storytelling. That does not necessarily disqualify it from having a historical kernel either. I do not believe this particular problem is resolvable at this time.

Nor does it mean that every pair of stories that we studied should be understood to have developed in the same way. It is not always the case that the story in the former prophets is historical while the one in the patriarchs is mythical. Since they both evolve orally in the same scribal schools, either side or neither may be considered to be source of some traditions. They may both be fictional. But the events in the former prophets are the only ones that can be supported with archaeology at this moment in time. It does very often turn out that the stories in the Pentateuch are somehow commentaries, either constructive or subversive, on issues that show up in the former prophets, issues taken as real by the narrative.

One alternative to the typical case is the pair including the sacrifice of Isaac and the sacrifice of Jephthah's daughter, which evolved together through oral development. But both stories are mythological in nature, explaining two different ritual practices. The binding of Isaac, in its current location, is an etiology for the sacrificial cult in Jerusalem. The sacrifice of Jephthah's daughter is an etiology that explains an otherwise lost ritual of weeping for Jephthah's daughter. Neither are historical as events, but they are historical in the sense that they reflect authentic First Temple era mythology supporting rituals at the Jerusalem Temple and in the northern hills. We can also tell that they developed together as a pair, especially because the story of Jephthah's daughter could be taken up into the propaganda attack against the northern kingdom and also connected to the sinful practices of the Moabites. We cannot demonstrate that Mesha actually sacrificed his son; indeed, it looks like the Bible has recorded a piece of self-serving political propaganda. But the many polemics against human sacrifice in the prophets and law codes and the loss of Moab as a possession in the period suggest that this time period gives us a credible context for the discussion of human sacrifice in First Temple times. Indeed, it looks as though the story of Mesha's sacrifice functions as propaganda to cover the embarrassing loss of the land of Moab to Mesha.

The binding of Isaac is appropriate to the text of the Mesha inscription (approximately 840 BCE) because it contains a polemic against the kind of human sacrifice that Mesha attempts, according to the Bible's estimation, and it promises the Israelites exactly what the Moabites get by performing the sacrifice: "'By myself I have sworn, says the LORD.... And your offspring shall possess the gate of their enemies, [18] and by your offspring shall all the nations of the earth gain blessing for themselves, because you have obeyed my voice'" (Genesis 22:16–18). According to the Bible, the Moabites perform the sacrifice and protect their gates, while the Israelites do not and get the same blessing. It is certainly no proof that Mesha actually sacrificed the crown prince, only that the issue is appropriate to the time of that polemic in the Bible. The story of the binding of Isaac comes up as political propaganda as a response to Mesha's successful bid for independence against the Israelites.

Troubles in the Royal Family

We have discussed two chapters in the history of the Davidic family. They are hardly the kind of stories that dynasties want to record about themselves. Rather, in these chapters, one needs to read both synoptic stories to understand the complexities of the situation. The difficult story of David and Bathsheba, which really continues until David decides for Solomon as his heir, is due to the very subtle machinations of Nathan and Bathsheba. This story is more or less paralleled and explicated in the story of Adam and Eve, the human comedy of sexuality, and in the story of Rebecca and Isaac, the power a mother can wield over the destiny of her son. Both reflect upon issues that are clearly central to the succession of Solomon to the throne, which turns out, not surprisingly, to be the climax of the JE epic. Neither the story of Adam and Eve nor the story of Judah and Tamar can be understood separately from the story of David and Bathsheba. The stories in Genesis speak to the succession narrative. In a way, Adam and Eve can be thought of as a commentary or even a satire on the story of David and Bathsheba and the ways of men with women. It is part of a longer theme throughout the JE epic in which the younger supplants the older, as Jacob (Israel) supplants Esau (Edom), for example, and the Israelites supplant their older relatives living in the land of Israel/Canaan. Nothing would serve the Solomonic throne and the house of David better than stories like that, even if Edom did not actually settle its area near Seir until sometime later in the monarchy.

Some of the material edited by the DH seems to reflect actual circumstances: who would make up the story of David and Bathsheba or Amnon and Tamar out of whole cloth? Frankly it makes no sense to make up stories like the concubine of the Levite or the woes of the Davidic dynasty; they speak so badly for the succession. On the other hand, its role in arguing for kingship is undeniable. That is part of the DH's master plan. Probably DH had access to original documents from a royal source, and certainly he knew a great many oral traditions that would otherwise have been lost. We have seen how there must have been multiple different redactions of many different traditions, and the Deuteronomistic Historians are no exception. Probably there was more than one editorial stage in the production of this huge portion of the historical period. Perhaps the editing continued, one gloss at a time, over a long period. Perhaps there were distinct editings, as many as three variants.

In the same way, the story of Rebecca's helping Jacob take the birthright from Esau is a commentary on the rise of Solomon to power. The way that Rebecca helps Jacob take the birthright seems very close to the story of Bathsheba and Solomon, where it offers a justification for the kingdom going to Solomon and, at the same time, a critique of David and Bathsheba.

The DH supplements and, in a way, supplants the JE epic by adding less mythical and moralistic comments of its own, which reflects the dominant understanding of historical motivation in its day. Furthermore, the DH revamps part of the history, Joshua through 2 Kings, by ranking the actions and the personages based on how closely they come to the superior morals promulgated by the book of Deuteronomy under King Josiah. It reedits the JE epic and gives it a logical conclusion in Josiah's rise to power.

Rather than just forget the stories of horror and disgust that we have looked at, the DH finds a moral lesson in them, that the LORD rewards and punishes according to the offense. This theme was present in the earlier material, but it was never so obvious, and it was often left unexpressed. Before Deuteronomy, the biblical writers appear to have sensed the difficulties in the stories and to have told stories of the patriarchs that somehow encompassed the contradictions between them and provided ancient paradigms that better resolved the issues than their contemporary circumstances. These stories, in the re-presentation of the DH, were fashioned into a late monarchy and exilic courtly history, after the society grappled with the seeming contradictions in them through mythical means, like Cain and Abel, Dina and Shechem, and others, that broach the problems of the succession. Instead, it is much easier to see how they begin to bend the mythic reconsiderations of these terrible themes in the primeval history into a drama of human action and divine reward. The reasons to make up stories about the primeval history seem clear enough; the reasons to make up scandalous stories about the succession or the Court History in exilic times are virtually nonexistent.

A Relative Chronology

All of these paired stories in the Pentateuch, therefore, should precede chronologically the more strictly moralistic DH. Most all the mythological writing must have been in current shape before the DH, because the historian added more realistic-sounding prophecies when further historical events were known. We can see this with regard both to David and to Josiah. Otherwise, it is hard to understand why glosses and later paragraphs in prophecies are always restrictions on the good news of the first paragraph. They appear to be altered when the earlier prophecies seem to be in danger of becoming false.

In any event, archaeology rarely gives us much information about individuals, but it can give us ways to turn relative chronologies into exact ones. Actually, other archaeological finds give us more important clues as to dating. This would be a good moment to fill in the rest of the significant archaeological information, telling us of a First Temple period occupation by the Israelites, and to show that some biblical literature actually does go back to the earliest periods of settlement. The inscriptional and archaeological evidence gives us an entirely new and independent voice that helps demonstrate that the stories are appropriate to the time period.

Archaeology Provides a Step-by-Step Absolute Chronology: The Stela of Merneptah

The princes are prostrated, saying "Peace!"
None raises his head among the Nine Bows.
Tjehenu is desolate, Hatti pacified.
Canaan is plundered with every hardship.
Ashkelon is taken, Gezer captured, [and] Yano'am reduced to nothing.
Israel is laid waste, his seed is no more.
Hurru has become a widow for Egypt.
All lands are pacified together.

(The Hymn of the Stela of Merneptah; my emphasis)

Line 6 describes a great Egyptian victory against a tribal people called Israel. This is a rare and quite wonderful find—over a century ago—which gives us a chance to begin to fashion an absolute chronology: In approximately 1206 BCE, Pharaoh Merneptah (1212–1202 BCE), who was the most powerful man in the Western world at the time, erected a public monument at his funerary temple in Thebes to commemorate his victories against a variety of enemies who had massed in the delta to defeat Egypt. After Merneptah defeats his enemies, he goes on a further excursion to punish any who may have supported this alliance. In the course of punishing his enemies, he mentions his defeat of Israel. When it was rediscovered by Sir Flinders Petrie in 1896, the reaction of nineteenth-century Europe went far beyond any reaction to Merneptah's ancient victory.

It may have been lost, but it was not inconsequential. Even in the ancient world, it was a major victory, because the stela was a significant construction: it was a large black basalt stela some seven and a half feet tall. We have even found a second, fragmentary copy of it at the Cour de la Cachette at Karnak, together with illustrations that may depict the events of the stela.

Merneptah evidently had several victory hymns written and incorporated in this text. In the one important for Israel, the beginning points out the conventional enemies of Egypt, "the Seven Bows." In this hymn, however, Merneptah gets far more specific. He brags that he has destroyed a whole group of countries, cities, and a people called *Israel*. Since the place names are organized geographically, it looks as if this people called *Israel* was living in the hill country of Judah.

The word *Israel* is preceded by a determinative, a writing convention in Egyptian hieroglyphics that gives the reader of the stela an idea of what kind of thing the next word represents: Tjehenu (Libya), Canaan, Hurru, and Hatti are preceded by the determinative that means "foreign land," which is accurate. Ashkelon, Gezer and Yanoam are likewise preceded by the same determinative that here represents "city-state," which is accurate. And Israel was preceded by a different determinative that means "migratory people." There is no reason to doubt its accuracy. That makes Israel a migratory people, living in the Judean hills, at the end of the thirteenth century BCE. The date of the stela suggests that the snapshot of Israel we get from the Merneptah inscription is from approximately 1230 BCE, which is consistent with the most obvious consensus date in the biblical account.

Though the stone for the stela was cannibalized from an earlier inscription of Amenhotep III (1390–1352 BCE), Merneptah's scribes used the back of the basalt slab, as well as carving a particularly beautiful semicircular relief at the top. On that ornamental relief is an illustration that depicts

Merneptah as receiving the characteristic Egyptian sword of command and rule from the major god of Thebes, Amun-Re. Even putting aside the conventional exaggeration characteristic of most every Egyptian document, the victory was significant enough to mention on a stela, so there is every reason to think that Merneptah handed the tribes of Israel a defeat otherwise unmentioned in the biblical record. This suggests that the Bible is historical in the way that other documents from the time period are historical: winners exaggerate while losers control the damage with silence or tendentiousness.

Because the Merneptah stela is the earliest mention of the name *Israel* anywhere outside of the Bible, it effectively not only marks Merneptah's victory but also represents the first witness of the people Israel in history. In other words, it currently divides history from legend and myth in biblical studies. Note that if we define the distinction between history and legend on the basis of a mention of Israel in a nonbiblical source, the border is movable and depends entirely on nonbiblical sources. If something else is found, the border can move earlier.

Not everything in the Bible after Merneptah's stela is history, but we know that everything before the stela, the entire patriarchal period and the Exodus, must remain a legend or a myth until such time as we can find convincing external, archaeological evidence (or some independent data) that it happened.

Some centuries of what follow the Israel inscription are also legend. For example, the conquest model under Joshua is barely evidenced in the archaeological sources. As an alternative, one might hypothesize as more believable the slow infiltration model of the book of Judges, which was described and advanced by the German scholars writing in the early- to mid-twentieth century, Albrecht Alt and Martin Noth.[4] A slow infiltration model suggests that the nomads or transhumant pastoralists (herders who go from summer to winter pasturage but do not wander aimlessly) eventually became agrarian as they settled in the Judean high country. This has some possibility of being true, but there is little way of demonstrating it archaeologically so scholars have abandoned it. One wonders if that is wise. But there are many shades and hues to this theory.

Another model, the so-called Mendenhall model that was so popular in the last half of the twentieth century, posits that the Israelites are a group of refugees or rebels from Canaanite cities, people who left or revolted against the oppressive government in the city.[5] This served as an ideological argument for the existence of socialistic or communist theories. They were projected back on the period of settlement on the basis of almost no actual data. There is little evidence of a rebellion against the Canaanite cities resulting in the creation of a twelve-tribe Israelite confederacy. Even thinking that there was a single fixed agreement among the tribes of YHWH seems far more detailed than can be affirmed by archaeological or literary evidence, although it is clear that the biblical description of covenant is one of the most important themes of the Bible.

An extreme form of skepticism is evidenced in the work of Robert Coote and Keith Whitelam.[6] On principle, they do not rely on any biblical evidence but take the archaeology and various other theories to suggest that the Israelites were originally city dwellers who had to leave the coastal plain and sought to exploit and deforest the highlands. This is, in a way, a form of the Mendenhall hypothesis, and it too has little archaeology to support it. Furthermore, they are very grudging in their acceptance of archaeological evidence that does not fit their model and very generous to modern ideological theories that can be bent to their interests.

As for the Merneptah inscription itself, recently, people politically committed to the Palestinian cause have suggested that the inscription is either a fraud or does not mention Israel at all. The extreme minimalists need to disqualify this archaeological evidence because it states that there was an Israel in the thirteenth century BCE and that the people of Israel were likely living in the highlands of Judah and recognizable to the Egyptians—all this long before the start of the Second Temple period, which began in the sixth century BCE, or the First Temple period, which began in the tenth century BCE.

The arguments that it is not really Israel but some misreading for another nation are clearly generated by the minimalists' need to discredit any early evidence. And they have been shown to be misjudgments. So, unless a new argument or new data are found, it is safe to assume that the Merneptah inscription is a very lucky early reference to Israel, and it is in a completely credible context with an apolitical provenance. That the group called Israel by the Egyptians existed in the hill country of Judea at the end of the thirteenth century BCE is itself evidence for some kind of political and ethnic unity.

That is quite a bit to conclude, but it does not include the biblical Exodus or any of the other dominant metatheories for the arrival of a group of people from Egypt or for the democratic, socialist, or even Palestinian Canaanite background of the Israelites. It does say they were there, and the archaeology of the area tells us that new homes are being built. They develop into a characteristic four-room house, and the people use characteristic collared-rim jars. We also know that from time immemorial the peoples of the Middle Eastern cities were forced to give up city life when economic conditions worsened. The first and most probable hypothesis is actually that among these people is the Israel mentioned by the Egyptians. Possibly all these processes were going on simultaneously. Israel could have been made up of a variety of different people: people leaving the city, people coming from Egypt, anyone settling the highlands, and people coming from the Amorite districts to the east and north of Israel. In this case, the stories of the patriarchs and the stories of the Exodus could represent movements of tribal peoples, eventually unified into a single group by another story, the story of Abraham, but originally happening at approximately the same time as the groups that came from the area around Egypt and the Canaanite cities.

This, in fact, was the Albright synthesis, or the part of it that still remains possible but unproven. What the early history of the Israelites in Canaan appears to show and to show extremely well, both in the archaeology and the Bible stories, is the passage of a people from a pastoralists to agriculturalists and then later from a tribal form of government to a kingship. It does chronicle the nature of the threats facing the tribes of Israel, their technological innovations, as well as the social, religious, and political institutions that evolved, as well as the history of the leadership in transitioning from tribal culture to a central government. I think the evidence coheres, though it certainly does not give us more than a bare minimum of what we want to know.

History and Archaeology Thereafter

No, we cannot assume that the Bible after Merneptah's inscription is suddenly a wholly reliable historical source. No one would even consider such an assumption unless the book were the Bible, where supernatural claims to truth are so easily assumed among nonhistorians. It turns out, as we know, that the Bible is a tendentious historical source, shading events with the same kind of biases that are characteristic of other historical sources. That is why we should not give up the standard historical hermeneutics of suspicion in reading it. That is why, by the same token, it is a historical source; we cannot make the Bible say anything we want it to say.

Furthermore, we know that the story has been conventionally told and retold, and when that happens a number of folkloric themes and exaggerations find their way into it. So we also know there is a long period of oral development in the stories as well. And most of the stories of the patriarchs, no matter where they may have originated, have been tuned to events in the monarchy so that they wind up functioning as myths. That is to say, the latest editor has had the biggest effect on the story, though the editor is not the only voice in the Pentateuch.

While the stela dates from the New Kingdom period for Egypt, and hence more than a millennium after the great pyramids of Giza were constructed, it is right at the very beginning of Israel's occupation of the land of Israel. Before this date, we are dealing with entirely legendary or mythical stories in the Bible. After this event we get a peculiar combination of legend and historical detail for hundreds of years. But this is one of the few places in which we can see that the single term *Israel* is used to describe the entire people.

It would be great to have some more information about Israel from this stela. Several scholars think that we do. At the Cour de la Cachette, the inscription is surrounded by illustrations. Recently, Frank Yurco started a very well-publicized debate by claiming, in the pages of the popular archaeological journal *Biblical Archaeological Review*, that the reliefs found on the inner eastern face of the court illustrate Pharaoh Merneptah's victory over Israel.[7] In the scene the Israelites (if they are such) are wearing the skirts and headbands characteristic of Canaanites. In response, Anson Rainey not only challenged this conclusion but suggested that another one of the panels at the Cour de la Cachette describes the Israelites.[8] In this depiction the Israelites would be wearing skirts and turbans characteristic of nomadic peoples in Canaan and Sinai whom the Egyptians called *Shasu.*

But neither of these popular articles needs actually to be correct about their descriptions of the Israelites; they both depend on an ingenious hypothesis, that the illustrations in the Temple depict the victories of Merneptah. What it does illustrate is the power of any archaeological discovery that can be connected with the Bible to grab the American people's imagination.

As we have seen in detail, everything in Israel's history before the Merneptah inscription is certainly legend. That means all of the stories of the patriarchs Abraham, Isaac, Jacob and his children, Joseph, Moses, and Joshua should be treated as legendary, until and unless some outside evidence is found to substantiate them. Many function as myths.

Over the last century it has come to seem reasonable to assume that the story of Joshua's quick conquest of the land is at odds with most of the archaeological record to date. The stories we have in the book of Judges suggest a slow process of infiltration of Israelites and at the same time a mixing of cultures and peoples, with the biblical record taking a firm stand against it. Even that contains a moral idealization that the Israelites triumphed when they prayed to the Lord. But we now know that a great many of the legends preceding the settlement in Israelite lore functioned simply and completely as myth for the Israelite people living in First Temple times, whatever their status as legend or history may have been.

Archaeology and Extreme Biblical Minimalism

The controversial Israeli archaeologist Israel Finkelstein has cautioned against reading the Bible as the explanation for the archaeological remains in the land of Israel. Fair enough. One should not dig at any site with the sole expectation that one is going to find exactly what the Bible says about it. The data have to be understood independently, in their own right. That is a hard task, given that archaeologists have also usually studied the Bible thoroughly. But once the archaeology has given us what it can, are we methodologically justified in applying that to what we know about the Bible? A historian would have to say "yes," enthusiastically.[9] One should not write off a class of evidence merely because it is difficult to interpret or because it does not support a preexistent ideological commitment. That is why scholarship is always a group enterprise and a multigenerational one. No source of information can be ignored; exactly how the conflicting evidence might be evaluated is, as it has always been, within the purview of each historian. Good method should tell us when not to consider biblical evidence and when biblical evidence must be considered.

The Israelite conquest of Jerusalem is even more controversial. We know that Jerusalem existed as a Canaanite city (the Bible calls its inhabitants Jebusites; we have no nonbiblical attestation of that term) before David conquered it and made it his private possession. For this reason, Jerusalem is often called the city of David. There is not yet any confirmed archaeology in Jerusalem itself that is datable to the time of David and Solomon. On the other hand, there is no particular reason to believe that any evidence would survive. David's palace and Solomon's Temple have been built over a dozen times. Besides, contemporary politics make most archaeological research on the Haram Ash-sharif or the Temple Mount impossible. The continuing argument and violence over every incident ensures that it remains one of the most contested patches of land on the globe.

This sad contemporary fact, however, is not necessarily connected to biblical minimalism; it is just good sense. Finkelstein sees plenty of evidence of new habitation in the Judean hills during the late Bronze and early Iron Ages. Chances are that among these peoples is the Egyptians' Israel. Whether these people are Israelites, non-Israelites, proto-Israelites, or pre-Israelites is of secondary importance. They leave a distinctive mark on the land, with an evolving style that culminates in the four-room house. Why they develop a four-room house in this context is difficult to say, just as it is hard to say why they show a preference for collared-rim pottery. (The pottery styles, in fact, develop uniformly from the thirteenth century BCE through the sixth century BCE and argue for a continuity of habitation of the people Israel.) Likely both are due, at their root, to the particular environment, the hill country, in which they lived, rather than to any particular religious or ethnic issue.

These are considered, conservative, and minimal conclusions, from a person often described as a biblical minimalist. He does not call himself an extreme minimalist, even though he is critical of some more maximalist positions taken about Jerusalem and the united monarchy in previous generations of scholars. He allows that we have both archaeological and literary evidence by the ninth century BCE. Biblical minimalism is therefore a relative position. His comments are meant to critique the easy assent of previous archaeologists to the biblical narrative, indeed even to try to prove the Bible right. But they also point up the importance of his own research in rural areas, rather than in the cities. To downplay what is available in cities is also to emphasize his own work in the Judean hills, which is fair.

The Limits of Finkelstein's Biblical Minimalism

Finkelstein does go on to describe what he calls "biblical minimalism" (we have been calling it extreme biblical minimalism), with which he disagrees:

Biblical history totally lacks an historical basis and its character as a largely fictional composition or wholly imaginative history is motivated by theology of the time of its compilation in the Persian or Hellenistic periods, centuries after the alleged events took place. At best, it contains only vague and quite unreliable information about early Israel. Yet, the continuing power of the biblical narrative is testimony to

the literary skill of the authors as they produced a compelling propa-
gandistic work to a highly receptive public.[10]

He is right about the ability of extreme minimalists to make the text a
basis for their own myths. It is the position of a small group of individuals,
made up mostly of scholars who do not specialize in the time period and are
not archaeologists but have strong political ideologies about the contemporary political situation in Israel/Palestine. Finkelstein's own work in the Judean highlands, while it is critical of reconstructions of the united kingdom
of Israel under David and Solomon, does suggest that the settlements in the
Judean hills are significant Israelite finds. These are, coincidentally, where
most of his own work has been centered.

Exactly what that means is partly a matter of the definition of what an
Israelite is and when one becomes an Israelite. If none of the continuities
actually bespeak ethnic identity to us, it is not necessarily the end of the issue. One wonders whether nineteenth-century definitions of ethnicity and
nationalism should apply to the tenth century BCE. We might look at the
development of script or language or other material that is not strictly archaeological but involves archaeological expertise. The fact is that we have
rightly been concentrating on processual archaeology, watching the development of various technologies, and that may not be the right way to find an
ethnic identity.

The Testimony of Hebrew 1: Early and Late Hebrew

Hebrew has its own testimony to give in the issue of dating and the phenomenon of ethnicity. While many scholars have assumed in an unwarranted
way that Hebrew is uniform throughout the biblical period, differences in
Hebrew have made the documentary hypothesis plausible. Certainly, the
hypothesis depends heavily on a difference in vocabulary between each of
the sources, starting with the varying words for God but also including dif-
fering words for many other things. However, recognition that changes in
Hebrew syntax can be dated has been slower to be accepted. For one thing,
Hebrew, like all other languages, could have developed a specific style, where
an archaic literary dialect became standard and thus later writing contained
archaizing tendencies. This was certainly true in English translations of the
Bible, which were salted with archaic forms like *thou* until quite recently.

Scholars like Avi Hurvitz and his students have shown that, despite all these difficulties, one can actually isolate the characteristics of different historical periods in biblical Hebrew.[11] They began by studying postexilic Hebrew, called Late Biblical Hebrew (LBH), to avoid the charge that they were studying archaizing texts instead of archaic ones. They compared the Hebrew found in the datable documents like the postexilic literary prophets and Chronicles and found many clearly understandable grammatical, syntactical, and lexical similarities. Then they compared these characteristics with earlier texts, dubbed Early Biblical Hebrew (EBH), in which they found distinct differences. It turns out, for example, that the P document is composite and parts of it can be shown to evince the characteristics of EBH, while other parts evince the characteristics of LBH. The same is true of Genesis, which has some late characteristics and a large variety of early ones. If one factors in that there will be some archaizing in the text and also some updating of geographical names, it does look like significant parts of the Pentateuch are preexilic. Of course, as in all means of dating, to be really convincing they must also cohere with other, independent means of dating. Luckily there are many more linguistic features that cohere in an early date for Genesis and the Hebrew of the Pentateuch in non-P places.

The Testimony of Hebrew 2: Vernacular Alphabets and Languages as Ethnic Identifiers

Seth Sanders has pointed out how the development of the Hebrew language is itself an ethnic marker.[12] Those who use the vernacular language in alphabetic form, instead of a cuneiform language, a royal and official language used in statecraft, are developing and expressing their ethnic identity. It would follow that those who have developed Hebrew as a medium for imaginative expression are also ethnically Hebrew or Israelite. The vernacular languages of the area are quite plentifully attested in inscriptions by the end of the ninth century BCE. In other words, the Northwest Semitic language scripts—Hebrew, Moabite, Ammonite, Edomite, and especially Aramaic—can be assumed to emerge at approximately the same time in the ninth and eighth centuries BCE. Sanders credits that particular kind of use of the vernacular, especially royal inscriptions, with growing ethnic identities.

But over three decades ago F. M. Cross identified at least four inscriptions and one seal from four different sites in thirteenth-century BCE Palestine.

They are all alphabetic and written in Proto-Canaanite or Proto-Sinaitic.[13] Another inscription was recently found in early Hebrew at Qeiyafah (likely the biblical Sha'arayim), again written in the Proto-Sinaitic script of the late eleventh or early tenth century BCE, which is being translated by Yossi Garfinkel and Haggai Misgav.[14] The archaeology suggests a major city with a large defensive wall. If Hebrew writing is known here, at the border with Philistia, then one expects at least as much from Jerusalem shortly thereafter, which was about to enter the period of David and Solomon. So vernacular forms of writing are already developing in the thirteenth through tenth century BCE period, and it does take a certain amount of time for these closely associated Northwest Semitic speaking groups to articulate their differences, which may have started even earlier than the thirteenth century BCE, and express them in a Northwest Semitic alphabet.

Sanders himself stays close to what can be demonstrated through inscriptions, thus he emphasizes the ninth and eighth centuries BCE for when the scripts begin emerging and stelae are set up. Assuming that there is an oral phase to the Hebrew vernacular language that precedes the use of the vernacular alphabet in inscriptions, it seems rational to think the Hebrew language was developing from the thirteenth century BCE, which is just as the Bible leads us to believe, as we shall shortly see in more detail. The institutionalization of scribes in the hands of the governments of the time and an imaginative literature makes probable that Hebrew existed as early as the settlement and the united monarchy. Along with the name Israel, the language and the stories in oral form were ethnic identifiers. But the written stage, starting at the end of the ninth century BCE, certainly galvanized nationality even further.

Furthermore, we find a variety of vernacular succession stories of personal success by the ninth century BCE, fascinating stories of the kind that could have served as a pattern for David's rise to power and the succession narrative to Solomon. For example, we find the story of Kilamuwa, an Aramaic king of Yaudy at Anatolian Zinjirli. We also know about the so-called Apology of Esarhaddon, another exciting story of how a lesser son of Sennacherib manages to succeed to the eighth-century throne of the Assyrian Empire and become a major figure in the ancient Near East.

The story of David, however, is a unique story in that it records how a tribal chief becomes a king with the rudiments of a state. We certainly have then a credible cultural context for the recording of the rise of David. But the biblical writing may have come some time after the actual events; we have seen from internal literary characteristics that it was certainly edited and reedited, redacted and reredacted throughout the Davidic dynastic period and even thereafter.

All we can know for sure is that some of the hill people were identifiable as Israel to the Egyptians at the end of the thirteenth century BCE, and so it is reasonable to assume that they must have been identifiable to themselves as Israel in some way. Vernacular language is one obvious ethnic identifier. Common architecture and pottery styles may also turn out to be others. Later on, settlers from the area begin to be identifiable as Israelites living in the First Temple period (950–587 BCE), the Iron Age, when they develop other ethnic identifiers like avoidance of pork. It seems clear that some of the inhabitants of the four-room houses who used collared-rim jars were Israelites. What did being Israelite mean in that period? The archaeology does not help us much. But the Bible gives us a rare view of the extreme past through its poetry. It appears to allow us to fill in some blanks.

Archaeological and Scriptural Point of View Together:
The Song of Deborah

Obviously, we can make certain conclusions by looking forward and seeing that a group of people living in the area grew into Israelites in the first millennium BCE. It is one thing to know that there was a people named Israel who inhabited the Judean highlands at the end of the thirteenth century BCE, according to Egyptian records, and to know that eventually a great many of the people in this area identified with a God named YHWH and wrote in Hebrew. It is quite another thing to say for sure when or how these people became Israelites. It does not look like archaeology alone can answer this question, though we can always hope that evidence one way or the other will show up, like more understandable inscriptions. Once the archaeological evidence is surveyed neutrally, we can ask whether we learn anything from texts that fall naturally as part of this historical context and not later ones.

There are some scriptural passages, all poetic set pieces, that seem to come from the earliest level of Hebrew, even from the level of the settlement: Exodus 15 (the Song at the Sea), Psalm 78, Deuteronomy 33, possibly the Blessing of Moses, and Judges 5 (the Song of Deborah). All the songs appear to have archaic spellings and language forms. It is always possible they are later texts that have been deliberately created with archaizing characteristics.

So we should analyze each individually to attempt a secure judgment. The most important of these scriptural passages to understand the earliest period of settlement is the Song of Deborah in Judges 5, with its prose setting in Judges 4, which is admittedly from the DH.[15] Indeed, the differences between the DH prose narrative of the events and the song's narrative makes clear that they were written at different times.

The song retells the story of the defeat of the Canaanite Sisera by Israelite tribal militias under the control of Deborah and Barak. Sisera's death itself is accomplished by another woman, Jael, who was renowned for great valor in this early time. All this is mentioned in the song, though it is only recounted in the prose narrative of Judges 4. One expects, of course, that the song is subject to the same kind of exaggerations and heroization that would happen to any tradition that was carried on orally for so many generations, and this is certainly what one finds. That limits its use as a historical source. But it does not disqualify it completely.

What makes the Song of Deborah so intriguing is, first of all, the puzzling Hebrew. It does not contain a few archaisms in an otherwise understandable context. It is archaic in virtually all its aspects. To me, it seems to be a window into the formation of what we call the Hebrew language. Second, it describes a political reality that fits the time of the judges, even to the embarrassment of the prose narrative. Finally, the listing of the tribes is appropriate to an early period of Israelite settlement and not to the editorial level of the narrative. Let us take each of these issues up in a bit more detail.

The Twelve Tribes as Myth

According to the story in Genesis, Jacob had twelve children through two wives and two concubines. The Leah tribes are Reuben, Simeon, Levi, Judah, Issachar, Zebulun, and the daughter Dinah. From Jacob's second wife, Rachel, Benjamin and Joseph are descended but Joseph, in turn, had two sons, who gave rise to the tribes of Ephraim and Manasseh. Gad and Asher come from Jacob's concubine Zilpah while Dan and Naphtali descend through Jacob's concubine Bilhah.

This is an ideal, mythic order. Clearly, the stories in the five books of Moses are powerful ethnic identifiers, just as we have seen. This tribal model is an intentional order of power relations consciously taken from the past, and it provides a mythic model of society and government as well as family descent. The patriarch Jacob-Israel presents us with the pattern, his offspring each standing for a tribe. And he himself is depicted as living in the northern part of the land of Israel and visiting the cultic centers of the north. We have already seen the relationship between the story of Jacob's strife with the angel and the cultic center of Bethel. Abraham, on the other hand, lives near and visits the cultic centers of the tribe of Judah. So, in a very real way, the story of Abraham—if not the historical Abraham himself—represents the founder of the cultic centers of the south, while in the narrative Jacob becomes the founder of the cultic centers of the north. That is an ethnic identifier, even if it is not a demonstration that there really was an Abraham or a Jacob.

But we find something less than ideal when we look at the Song of Deborah itself. The Song of Deborah represents a state of affairs before the united monarchy, because it is definitely not the order of the developed monarchy under Solomon, who sets up administrative districts that cut across tribal holdings. The song must come from a time when a social order was using the stories to explain and rationalize the political order: the geographical distribution of the tribes of Israel and their holdings. So it is likely that the early statements of the mature tribal system come from the period before kingship or when kingship was just arising.

Let us look at the evidence in more detail. The later listings of the tribes show a great deal of evidence of a later editor's hand. We find the tribes listed in their entirety three times in the five books of Moses: Genesis 49:1–27, Numbers 1:5–15, and Deuteronomy 33:1–29. Each of them places a great deal of emphasis on the number twelve, as it always comes up with exactly twelve tribes, so that is part of the intentional social order of the society, imposed on the data by a later editor. We can be sure the order is imposed because, in fact, no two lists of tribes themselves are identical. In Numbers 1:5–15 Levi is missing (perhaps because it has no tribal holdings, but, rather, the tribe lives as religious functionary among the other tribes). In this list Joseph is divided up into Ephraim and Manasseh to keep the count at twelve.

The Actual Tribal System in the Song of Deborah

In the Song of Deborah, we appear to penetrate Israelite history before any ideal order of twelve tribes existed as no such twelve-tribe confederacy is articulated. Levi, Simeon, Judah, and other southern groupings like Caleb are not mentioned at all. It is a time not of unity but of disunity and banditry when travel on the main roads was dangerous (Judges 5:6). Indeed, according to one understanding of Judges 5:6 followed by a number of translators, it is the Israelite tribes themselves who are the source of the banditry, making clear that some of the tribes were supporting themselves by raiding the caravan routes. It seems unlikely that this would be the invention of a poet singing after the establishment of the monarchy. Again, the uncomfortable detail argues for the antiquity of the song over the prose explanation.[16]

It is a song that depicts Israel as a militant hill people, consistent with the Merneptah stela, and clearly the people of YHWH as well, a statement that is frequently repeated in the early part of the poem. So Israel is organized as a brotherhood tribal structure through its articulation of a covenant with YHWH, though it is not the idealized twelve-tribe confederacy of the JE level of tradition. Obviously, stories of Jacob and his children reinforce the tribal structure and are likely already to exist in some form.

Although as many as ten tribes are mentioned in the song and Zebulun is mentioned twice, it is hard to establish exactly which tribal militias joined the battle and which did not. This is far more likely to represent the actual situation before monarchy arose, when it took a charismatic judge to energize the tribal militias. Only the specific tribes affected by the crisis respond to the call of Barak and Deborah, though Deborah is able to spur some to action by playing on her female gender to shame the tribes into participating.

The identity of the tribes is an argument for the song's antiquity. The tribe of Manasseh is missing, too, but appears to be represented by Machir, who is listed in later texts as a descendant of Manasseh and, arguably, the westernmost moiety or clan in the tribe, while the other part of the tribe was dwelling east of the Jordan, perhaps. This could mean that the tribe of Manasseh had not yet actually organized itself and that its major parts were still known at the time by its most significant part. Or, it could be, for example, that parts of the tribe claimed territory east of the Jordan, as the text says, and so do not participate in the battle. Gad, likewise, appears to be represented by Gilead, its westernmost branch.

There have been, of course, an enormous number of theories trying to explain all of these characteristics, but almost all have suggested that the Song of Deborah represents the earliest stages in the development of the twelve-tribe tradition and may actually, given its compact nature and specific genre, have survived from hoary antiquity before the monarchy.[17]

Form Criticism of the Song

It is exactly this kind of writing that is likely to survive from the distant past. We know from the form critics that such identifiable genres, or *Gattungen*, that have specific functions in a society (their situations in life, or *Sitz im Leben*) and arise in specific situations are more likely to survive intact. We might call them *literary form*s in English. Looking at the probable birth of this song in oral literature is therefore called form criticism in English.[18] What form criticism seeks to do is to find the social setting that produces these literary forms and allows them to be transmitted intact for a long time.

The Song of Deborah is an example of one such *genre* or *Gattung* or *form*. The song is itself a well-understood form. It is not the only poem we can isolate from the early texts. The editors sometimes claim to be quoting from a yet more ancient text, the book of Jashar, a compendium of ancient Israelite poetry, quoted in Joshua 10:12b–13a (Joshua's command to the sun and moon), 2 Samuel 1:19–27 (David's lament for Saul and Jonathan), and probably 1 Kings 8:12–13, a couplet embedded in Solomon's prayer at the dedication of the Temple, which survives in fuller form in the Septuagint.[19]

The Song of Deborah is first of all the story of an ancient victory, and it is framed as a victory song, which has a very stable existence as a form in many societies. In its way, it is the oral equivalent of a stela. It is also a song that taunts the enemy. In our own society, taunt songs like "Mary, Mary quite contrary," have survived in oral/written form for centuries, in this case from the time of Mary, Queen of Scots. There is no telling how old the oral children's taunt "*N*a-na, *na*-na . . . *naaa*-na" is. Indeed, unless you use the exact oral rhythm, which is not apparent in its written form, you cannot know what the taunt is. In the Bible itself, we appear to have accounts of origins that have survived for centuries in oral form:

Are you not like the Ethiopians to me,[20]
O people of Israel? says the LORD.
Did I not bring Israel up from the land of Egypt,
and the Philistines from Caphtor and the Arameans from Kir?

(Amos 9:7)[21]

These historical kernels are appropriate and likely survived for considerable time in oral form. So while we cannot tell how exactly Israelites thought
about themselves and their ethnic identity in the thirteenth to twelfth centuries BCE, we do have a vernacular literary form that began from approximately the middle of the period of the Judges.

The literary issue about identifying the Israelites as the inhabitants of
the high country exists in that we have a biblical record of other groups living in the highlands in this period: "The Amalekites dwell in the land of the
Negeb; the Hittites, the Jebusites, and the Amorites dwell in the hill country;
and the Canaanites dwell by the sea, and along the Jordan" (Numbers 13:29).
To accept this record that the Israelites had non-Israelite neighbors in the
highlands, one has to accept the biblical record. Many radical scholars do
not. But the Jebusites, for example, who are associated with the city of Jerusalem, and are often claimed to be the ancestors of today's Palestinians, are
not mentioned any other place than in the Bible. Carrying ancient myths
into the present uncritically leads to many difficulties for any ideologue.

It is not logical to accept that there may be other people living in the highlands without also accepting that the Israelites were there. So the best that
may be said about the earliest period of the Israelites in the land is that there
are different groups in the area and the Israelites could differentiate themselves from them, even if we cannot yet do so from our archaeological data.
Only ideological positions prevent this easy conclusion from being universal. We also know that the Egyptians do differentiate the Israelites from the
other people in the area. So while we do not know which ethnic identifiers
made these distinctions possible, we know that distinctions were being made.

The kinds of archaeology that have been practiced for the last two generations are unlikely to discover Israelites. Processual archaeology's purpose is
to find laws that underlie various settlements, not unique aspects. It is possible to sidestep the methodological problem by calling the people who lived
in these settlements pre-Israelites or proto-Israelites, but the issue, it seems
to me, is a slightly different problem from knowing exactly when Israelites
developed. We know that they were there; they knew how to identify themselves from others. We just do not know exactly how they did it. Perhaps it
was because they worshipped another god, as the texts and the archaeology
repeatedly tell us. The best solution would be to review the various ethnic
identifiers that exist later in the culture and to posit that some of them probably existed in the earliest period.

Starting with the Song of Deborah, the enemies of the Israelites are not pictured as other tribal people, but as city dwellers. For example, Sisera's mother peers out of a city window, not a tent flap, and not an upland hut. Sisera visits Jael in a tent. This is not archaeological proof that other tribes, even opposing tribes, did not exist in the hill country, but it is suggestive that the Israelites considered themselves residents and rulers of the high ground and considered the cities their enemies.

Our Lack of Knowledge about David and Solomon

We move forward. Not only do we have but sparse knowledge about the archaeology in the time of the settlement, the same situation obtains with the kingdom of David and Solomon, as Israel is urbanizing. Even our literary evidence about David is complex and difficult. We think, for example, of the famous conflict between David and Goliath, whose story climaxes in 1 Samuel 17:49–50: "And David put his hand in his bag and took out a stone, and slung it, and struck the Philistine on his forehead; the stone sank into his forehead, and he fell on his face to the ground. So David prevailed over the Philistine with a sling and with a stone, and struck the Philistine, and killed him; there was no sword in the hand of David." This story, as famous as it is, is disputable. The Bible contains other traditions that are just as clear about who killed Goliath, and it is not David: "And there was again war with the Philistines at Gob; and Elhanan the son of Jaareoregim, the Bethlehemite, slew Goliath the Gittite, the shaft of whose spear was like a weaver's beam (2 Samuel 21:19). In 2 Samuel 23:24 we find an Elhanan ben Dodo, who is probably the original killer of Goliath before the court scribes rewrote the story. Notice that his father's name, Dodo, is quite similar in Hebrew to "David," which may be the bridge uniting the two stories. And finally, in postexilic 1 Chronicles 20:5, we find an attempt to resolve the contradiction by synthesizing it into a single tradition: "And there was again war with the Philistines; and Elhanan the son of Jair slew Lahmi the brother of Goliath the Gittite, the shaft of whose spear was like a weaver's beam." We may suspect that in the centuries after the events, the house of David's "public relations department" was very active in the formulation of the dynamic and imaginative story of David's killing of the giant. But we must conclude that the story is disputable in the form in which it is given to us.[22]

But if so we must have an immense respect for the scribes in Judean employ because they certainly made a believable and very intriguing story of how David killed Goliath. Is it complete fiction? Was Elhanan the ruddy youth who killed the giant and who deserves to be remembered in the famous taunt song "Saul has killed his thousands, but Elhanan his tens of thousands?" Or, perhaps, is Elhanan another word for David? Neither way instills any confidence in the stories in Samuel or brings us easily to a historical (rather than a legendary) David, who must be almost completely beyond our reach by current historical methods, even before we add in the uncertain archaeology. It does suggest, however, that stories added to tradition along the way tended to be those that glorified the heroes and did not disparage them.

We see, instead, good reason to make up the story of how David slew Goliath (to add to the glory of David) or to narrate how Solomon received the special gift of wisdom from YHWH (to add to the glory of Solomon) and thus ruled so very wisely over an extended kingdom. But there is no justification for the terrible stories of rape and murder in the Court History unless something like that happened and stimulated a parallel mythical discussion of its significance in the patriarchal period. It is the later Deuteronomistic Historian who finds a moral meaning in them by subjecting them to the principle that every sin will generate its own punishment, every righteous action its own reward.

The Archaeology of Jerusalem and the United Kingdom of David and Solomon

Until recently, there was virtually nothing of archaeological interest in Jerusalem that could be traced to the eleventh or tenth century BCE, which is the time of Saul, David, and Solomon. But David and Solomon were supposed to have ruled the whole land, not just Jerusalem, and there was evidence attributed to them at other archaeological sites. In the 1950s Yigael Yadin, the son of professor Eliezer Sukenik, archaeologist of the Hebrew University, who established the antiquity of the Dead Sea Scrolls, was excavating at Hazor, the largest *tel* (artificial mound, denoting an ancient habitation) in Israel. He identified an Iron Age construction at Hazor as a large city gate. It was of special construction, having three chambers on each side of the gateway, a "six-chambered gate." Yadin remembered that a similar gate had been discovered at another ancient *tel*, Megiddo. He immediately thought of the biblical verse describing Solomon's fortifications at Megiddo, Gezer, and Hazor: "King Solomon conscripted to build the house of the LORD and his own house, the Millo and the wall of Jerusalem, Hazor, Megiddo, Gezer" (1 Kings 9:15). With brilliant insight, he went back to the excavation reports of R. A. S. Macalister, who excavated Hazor in the early twentieth century. There, he found the exact same six-chambered foundation excavations, incorrectly labeled as a "Maccabean Castle" but obviously another example of the six-chambered gate. Yadin then presented his evidence, together with 1 Kings 9:15, that all three cities had been rebuilt by Solomon in his own reign and thus finished before 930 BCE. Thus he had found an example of architecture from the united monarchy.

And this theory had a great deal to recommend it. At the time, one of its strong points was considered to be that it unified the archaeological evidence with biblical texts. But actually, upon further reflection, it shows the circular logic that relying on biblical text produces for archaeologists. Archaeologists would rely on the text of the Bible in framing their hypotheses, while thereafter historians would reunify the context with the text, which made a perfect circle.

In fact, it is hardly clear that the gates date from the same time period or were made by the same builder. And it is not at all clear that the constructions were Solomonic. It does seem clear that they are an Israelite building form from the First Temple period, probably within a century of David in any case. But since there is nothing in Jerusalem that could be with surety dated to the time period of David and Solomon, the direct evidence for the period of Solomon and David has moved from the category of "demonstrated" to the category of "possible."

At the same time, Eilat Mazar began digging in Jerusalem, in the area called the city of David, or the oldest part of the city, on the slope below the Dung Gate and outside the contemporary city walls. The city walls that so grandly surround the city of Jerusalem today date not from biblical antiquity but from Suleiman in the sixteenth century CE. Some of the original "city of David" lies inside Suleiman's walls.

But the ancient city extended outside the contemporary walls on this southern side. Mazar has studied and continued to uncover there a large city wall at the "stepped structure," which she claims is from the time of David and Solomon. Part of this structure was already known before her excavations, but she is finding promising new evidences of its antiquity because of the abutting structures, which include a very thick wall. She has made a very good case for her identification. Time will tell whether she is correct, but so far there is no undoubted archaeological evidence there was even a period of David and Solomon from Jerusalem or elsewhere. But there is evidence of a continuous band of settlement in the hills from earlier to about this period. It also seems as if the hilltop settlements described by Finkelstein were abandoned during this period, and it is as good a theory as anything else to say that they were denuded by the flight to cities that accompanies a strong and reliable government, such as the ones the Israelite kings produced. It appears likely those rulers existed—even the united monarchy rulers, of course—but we have not yet found anything that can be ascribed to them. But the current lack of evidence does not yet amount to evidence of lack. And now, of course, we have discovered Hebrew inscriptions (in proto-Sinaitic script) from the eleventh and tenth centuries BCE at the ancient city of Sha'arayim.

Pharaoh Shishak's Campaign

There is one more important piece of evidence about the presence of the Israelites in the tenth century BCE. That is the campaign of Pharaoh Shishak (of biblical fame), whose actual name in Egyptian sources is Pharaoh Shishonq. What makes this pharaoh worthy of mention is that the Bible has him invading the land of Israel early in the reign of King Rehoboam, Solomon's successor. In a completely independent source, he also wrote about it on a victory relief at Karnak. The biblical report covers the campaign in this fashion: "In the fifth year of King Rehoboam, King Shishak of Egypt came up against Jerusalem; he took away the treasures of the house of the Lord and the treasures of the king's house; he took everything. He also took away all the shields of gold that Solomon had made" (1 Kings 14:25–26). Not a happy visit for the Judeans. But it appears to have been a campaign for booty, not conquest. This was the fifth year of Rehoboam or probably 926 BCE, according to the consensus chronology of the Judahite and Israelite kings. Furthermore, and this is the most important part, Libyan Pharaoh Shishonq I, founder of the twenty-second dynasty, did invade Israel in the tenth century BCE according to his own claims. We know this because he recorded his military victories on the outer wall of the great Hypostyle Hall of the Temple of Amun at Karnak. This has led to virtual assurance that this is the same pharaoh mentioned by 1 Kings. That is significant because it is the very first event explicitly mentioned in both the Bible and an outside source.

Prior to the invasion, the text of 1 Kings 11:40 tells us that Jeroboam, fugitive from Solomon, sought and received refuge in Shishak's Egypt before he returned to captain the secession of the northern tribes. The text of 1 Kings exactly fits the Egyptian chronology, which is virtually impossible if the Bible were being written at the beginning of the Second Temple period in the sixth century BCE or even later at the beginning of the Hellenistic period in the fourth century BCE. The Egyptian inscription would certainly have been lost even to the most astute historian of the sixth century BCE, and yet the two sources agree chronologically exactly.

That is as far as our archaeological evidence takes us for now. Unfortunately, there is no mention of the land of Judah in his relief; no mention of Jerusalem either. What is worse, no clear geographical order is discernable in the groupings of the conquered cities and areas in the Shishonq stela. One can, by piecing together the 154 towns mentioned, come up with a plausible invasion route, even several plausible ones, but no one route is explicit in the text. A few cities from Judah and Samaria are mentioned as destroyed. Jerusalem would not have appeared here because it capitulated and paid a gigantic tribute and was not "destroyed." A town called "Fort Abiram" does appear in the contemporary dialect of Egyptian. This can well be a reference to the name Abraham, given the orthographic rules of the day, and so suggests both the existence of Judahite settlements and the Hebrew language. Yet one might expect some more forceful mention of having forced Rehoboam to submit to Pharaoh Shishonq's power. On the other hand, the relief is fragmentary, and, since there is no discernible order in the list, it is always possible that an important reference to Beth David or Jerusalem or Ephraim was on the missing part of the relief and has been lost. Certainly, we may be underinterpreting this evidence as well: Fort Abiram could be the Egyptian word for Be'er Sheba, Fort Abira[ha]m.

Biblical scholars have for a long time used this event to demonstrate, if not the truthfulness of the historical work in the Bible, the Bible's rough historicity from this time forward—in the sense that all documents are historical, with tendentiousness and perspective. Extreme biblical minimalists, conversely, strongly stress how little we know about this campaign. But this is an argument from silence. The synchronic appearance in both places, as universally admitted, coming from completely independent sources, puts the historicity of the chronology of the Bible's account beyond dispute, however one may want to argue for or against any specific outcomes.

All that evidence has not yet yielded the name of David or Solomon per se. But it does make the existence of a united monarchy virtually certain. We would have to make up an alternative story for how Rehoboam got on the throne that did not include David or Solomon, and this seems vastly improbable. The fact that we have no archaeological evidence does not mean that the events did not happen. So while we know the stories about David and Solomon are certainly the products of long literary traditions—oral and written—that exaggerated the extent of their power, it is quite a different thing from saying that neither king existed at all or that the united monarchy is nothing but fiction. Unfortunately, many people envision the biblical accounts of the united monarchy as great moments of national splendor, where history is written against huge palatial movie sets (like the film *David and Bathsheba* starring Gary Cooper and Susan Haywood), when they are more likely to have taken place in much more restricted circumstances.

But archaeology can sometimes add a more exact and absolute chronology because inscriptions can help connect relative chronologies with explicit events. The story of the golden calf at Sinai, for example, must have been written after Jeroboam's revolt but likely before the DH, from whom we have a quite different polemic about Jeroboam. For the same reason, the story of the sacrifice of Isaac is appropriate to the time period of the Mesha stone, even though human sacrifice is not mentioned in Mesha's own description of his campaign against Israel. It was clearly part of the polemic of the Israelites against their Canaanite neighbors. Also Pharaoh Shishonq's campaign in the fifth year of King Rehoboam is a quite obvious parallel between the Bible's historicity and Egyptian history. There is no reason, a priori, why traditions should not go back to the united monarchy, and there is reason to believe that the Bible contains and transmits traditions that go back that far. But, with material that old, one should expect that the transmission is not historically accurate in the way we demand today but rather obeys rules of folkloric transmission before it gets to us.

Israelite Inscriptions

There is a great deal about Israel to be learned from Israelite inscriptions. We have reviewed the major places where Israel is mentioned before the end of the ninth century. We need to add to that the large number of inscriptions in Hebrew by Judeans and Israelites living in the land. Archaeologically, the presence of these inscriptions virtually certifies a Hebrew-speaking population in First Temple times: the Gezer calendar (possibly Canaanite), the Samaria ostracon, the "Barley Letter" from Samaria, the various ostraca from Kuntillet 'Ajrud including the abecedaries (alphabet lists), the illustration dedicated "to YHWH and his Asherah," the enormous stone bowl with blessing inscription, a looted inscription from Khirbet el-Qom, the Uriah epitaph, which was recovered from Khirbet el-Qom, saved from the private antiquities market by the fortunate intervention of William Dever, the Siloam tunnel inscription of King Hezekiah's water tunnel,[23] the Silwan inscription, the Yavneh Yam ostracon, the Lachish ostracon and letter, and the Arad ostracon. Lastly, an actual biblical quotation from the Pentateuch was found on tiny silver scrolls in 1980 by Gabriel Barkay during the excavation of a tomb at Ketef Hinnom.

This evidence not only bespeaks a single ethnic identity but also the development of a script and a language that is specifically Hebrew. The materials are unlikely to be frauds. This clarifies that there is an ethnic identity speaking Hebrew remarkably early. And we think that they must also be telling stories of the patriarchs and later reading them as well.

Besides this evidence, there are innumerable other examples of ethnicity in the (signet) seals and *bullae* (a *bulla* is the clay impression from a signet seal, the seal itself was impressed in soft clay and then hardened) found in the Judean hills. To be sure, bullae are relatively easy to fake or forge. Probably most of the ones found in the antiquity stores in Jerusalem are fakes. But many have been found in legitimate digs and so have unassailable provenance.

Luckily, it is characteristic of names in the ancient Near East that many contain the name of a god, what we call a *theophoric* name. A great many of the legitimate seals and bullae contain names that are theophoric, and, of those, a great many are names that carry the name of Israel's God, YHWH—like 'Ahaziah or Yehoab. The former is an example of a name with the theophoric element -*iah* at the end, signifying the divine name YHWH; the latter is an example of the theophoric element *Yeho*- at the beginning, which also signifies the divine name YHWH. So both people had some kind of relationship to the God YHWH. Since these seals and bullae are stratigraphically datable to and throughout the First Temple period, we know that there were people who identified in some way with the divine name YHWH from early times through the end of the First Temple period.[24] That certainly does not make them Jews in today's sense, or even guarantee that they were strictly monotheistic Yahwists or even decent Yahwists, but it is an argument demonstrating that devotion to a divinity called YHWH became an ethnic identity marker for people living in the Judean hills even as early as the end of the second millennium and in the cities thereafter.

One additional argument, which comes from later in the archaeological record, but still in the First Temple period, concerns the large number of very well-attested inscriptions from non-Israelite sources, which talk about Israel and Judah and their kings. We have just spoken about the Merneptah inscription. Previously, we have looked at the crucial importance of the Moabite stone as an actual historical document with a quite different perspective on events mentioned in the Bible.

These are only the beginning of a number of important inscriptions found in the capitals of foreign lands and attesting to the existence of a "house of David" or a "Judah" during First Temple times (950 BCE–587 BCE): the black obelisk of Shalmaneser III (King Ahab is mentioned, and, on a panel, probably unlucky King Jehu [2 Kings 9–10] of Israel is depicted making obeisance and paying his tribute), the Taylor prism, the annals of Sennacherib, and the Rassam cylinder (all of which describe the Assyrian invasion of Judah in 2 Kings 18:13–19:8, equivalent to 2 Chronicles 32:1–22 and Isaiah 36:1–37:8).[25]

By the time of the exile then, we can be sure, from evidence gathered in ancient world capitals and on their borders, that there were two political and ethnic entities of the Israelite people: Israel, Ephraim, or the Omride dynasty (*beth Omri*) in the north and the Davidic dynasty (*beth David*) or Judah in the south. They were active in world politics, and they also contained a series of legends about their forefathers that match the issues of the First Temple period as related by the Bible.

Most recently (1993–1994), the Tel Dan ("house/dynasty of David") inscription has given us a very persuasive reference to the existence of the Israelites—Judah, Ephraim, and even hints of the united Israelite kingdom of David and Solomon. This Aramaic, severely broken inscription, erected by an unidentified Aramean king, mentions "house of David" as the name of its defeated enemy. It should be dated within 150 years of David's life. It seems almost incontrovertible evidence of the existence of the Davidic dynasty and hence of David himself.

The Tel Dan inscription has been rather difficult for extreme biblical minimalists to accept. They have claimed that the inscription is a fake and even that Israelis "salted" the archaeological site. This kind of accusation, without any evidence whatsoever, is prima facie evidence that the extreme minimalists have accepted an ideological position and are no longer following ordinary rules of academic discourse.

In fact, there is no reason why any inscriptional evidence should survive in this war-torn area of the world, but many have. My list itself is not exhaustive, only representative of what has been archaeologically studied. Many references about Judah and the Israelites have survived from the great powers and enemies of Israel in antiquity. These references, no matter how tendentious and inaccurate, help us establish that there was an ancient Israel and that it played a role in world politics. The text of the Bible uses a Hebrew that is appropriate to the First Temple period. Spelling and forms of expression differ in the Second Temple period. So, if the issue is whether there was an ethnic identity of Israelites in the First Temple period, the inscriptions, the archaeology, and the stories they told, which eventually became biblical text, make clear that they were a people with a common culture and understanding.

The Main Issues of the Biblical Stories

The central issue of the Bible—JE, D, and P—is certainly the *covenant*. There are versions of the covenant that are mentioned in the great songs of the Bible, but also quite explicitly and frequently in JE, D, and P. For example, in Genesis 15 we find YHWH's covenant with Abram: "On that day the LORD made a covenant with Abram, saying, 'To your descendants I give this land, from the river of Egypt to the great river, the river Euphrates, the land of the Kenites, the Kenizzites, the Kadmonites, the Hittites, the Perizzites, the Rephaim, the Amorites, the Canaanites, the Girgashites and the Jebusites'" (Genesis 15:18–21).

He promises that the descendants of Abram will inherit a swath of land not from the Nile (the river of Egypt does not mean the Nile) but from the Wadi el-Arish in Gaza to the Euphrates River—not in Iraq but in the north in Syria. This is what Solomon claimed, and he arguably was the largest power in that area at that time. It was certain that Solomon lived at a lucky moment when the great powers were in decline and several local Levantine kingdoms developed mini-empires.[26] One might expect that there is some exaggeration of what Solomon could have controlled politically or militarily.

Solomon's empire could not have been a modern state. Perhaps it means that he had control of the trade roads. Nor does it mean that any Canaanites living there were or will be dispossessed. One must not ever confuse modern governments with ancient ones or make modern conclusions from ancient evidence. That is unscholarly and unworthy of university discussion.

But what is important here is the nature of the agreement between Abraham and YHWH. It is a kind of treaty, but not so much the kind established by great nations as we see patterned in Deuteronomy or in the P source. This covenant is more like the kind of agreement that two tribal chiefs might make, with YHWH actually being pictured as a smoking fire pan going between the pieces of the cut-up animals. Of course, Deuteronomy especially will picture the covenant as an Assyrian vassal treaty or, more exactly, the anti-Assyrian vassal treaty. The people who look at the covenant in this fashion are the king's bureaucracy, his scribal schools and the scribal schools of the priesthood, who, after the kingship has been disestablished, make their strongest appearance in the P material.

So too the prophets also made their contribution to the idea of the covenant. They use other models for an agreement enforced by an oath. Hosea pictures the covenant between Israel and YHWH to be a marriage. We know that men swore oaths as part of marriage contracts going back to the second millennium BCE in Aramaic and other Semitic languages. Hosea sees the relationship between YHWH and his people as a marriage, a bad one that needs to be renewed. And, when it is renewed, YHWH will again be the loving husband he has already promised to be: "And I will betroth you to me forever; I will betroth you to me in righteousness and in justice, in steadfast love and in mercy. I will betroth you to me in faithfulness; and you shall know the LORD" (Hosea 2:19–20).

The point is that all the different voices in the society add to the covenant imagery by picturing it in the most comfortable way to their own social positions. JE finds the covenant most closely resembling an agreement among tribal chiefs. The D source, as we have seen, takes an Assyrian vassal treaty as its model. The P source finds the covenant renewal ceremony that was celebrated first in Josiah's Passover and transfers it to the renewal of government under Ezra and Nehemiah. At that point, covenant changes in the imperial Persian period, when treaties between nations are no longer necessary. Covenant then becomes more and more to be identified with circumcision, the quintessential P marker of belonging. All this makes quite implausible to me the idea that the Bible's interest in covenant could have emanated from the Persian or Greek periods. What goes through all these stories of covenant is that they not only specify a contractual relationship between God and the people Israel but also specify the level of government each description of the covenant entails.

Our main subject has been the fearful and loathing stories of the Pentateuch, the rise of kingship, and the Court History. These are much more difficult stories to understand; but they are incomprehensible as stories from the Second Temple period, with its imperial rule. It has been my contention that the stories in the Pentateuch have served as the mythical expression of the problems brought up by events and stories that are to be found in the former prophets. Whether they report history or folklore, the way the stories grow together into doublets or synoptic stories certainly shows us central nodal points in the mythology of Israel.

These are universal themes, even if the method of expressing them is local. They occur in a single historical context and cannot just be transferred to the modern period and used as a paradigm for national policy. They should not just be adopted as myth today. Or let me be more exacting about this. All over the world people do adopt ancient myths and accept them as ways of creating their own understandings of nationalism. To study that process is certainly fair game in the university. But to accept the arguments of one group or another is not an occupation that ought to be supported by university life. It is a matter of professional disinterest. The point of the university is to be the one place where these matters can be put aside.

Even more ridiculous would be to accept biblical myth as history and build an opposing polemical myth upon it. Each attempt to use these stories as a blueprint for contemporary policy shows the total lack of a historian's disinterest and the need to return the university to being the one place where these issues can be discussed dispassionately and disinterestedly. For sure, literary criticism allows us to interpret a novel from any perspective we want. And history is certainly available for similar kinds of analysis. There are, however, some important limitations to historical analysis that literary criticism does not share. One is not free to ignore commonly accepted data. For example, John Van Seters, who concluded that the strands of Hebrew tradition were late, did not ignore the results of archaeology that contradicted his position. But to call anything fraudulent that counters one's own theory of Palestinian priority, as some recent scholars have done, ignoring anything that does not agree with them, is simply unprofessional behavior. No theory of the universality of tendentiousness can justify such self-conscious use of one's university membership for propagandizing. One thing is sure: the word of the Lord is still very dear to those who must try to live within history. Sometimes it takes millennia to appreciate this simple fact; it certainly takes a lifetime to understand it. There are no shortcuts to historical understanding.

NOTES

Introduction

1. We will discuss the historicity of this inscription on the stele of Merneptah in the last chapter.

2. I will be using the name *Canaan* to discuss the land inhabited by the tribes of Israel. Whether and when it should be called *the land of Israel* will depend on arguments yet to be made. We will use other terms like *Philistia* and *Palestine* when they are appropriate.

3. See Sean Gaston, *Derrida and Disinterest* (New York: Continuum, 2005), pp. 1–18.

4. George Aichele et al., *The Postmodern Bible* (New Haven: Yale University Press, 1995); see the index entry "historical criticism" on p. 389.

5. See William G. Dever, *Who Were the Early Israelites and Where Did They Come From?* (Grand Rapids, MI: Eerdmans, 2003).

6. Of course, the process is not well understood. Israel may well have developed out of Canaanite religion and into the form we have it now. See, e.g., Mark S. Smith, *The Origins of Biblical Monotheism: Israel's Polytheistic Background and the Ugaritic Texts* (New York: Oxford University Press, 2001).

7. See Norman Gottwald, *The Tribes of Yahweh* (Maryknoll, NY: Orbis, 1979); Guy Swanson, *The Birth of the Gods: The Origin of Primitive Beliefs* (Ann Arbor: University of Michigan Press, 1970); "Monotheism, Materialism, and Collective Purpose:

An Analysis of Underhill's Correlations," *American Journal of Sociology* 80, no. 4 (January 1975): 862–69; "Comment on Underhill's Reply," *American Journal of Sociology* 82, no. 2 (September 1976): 421–23; "Sovereign Groups, Subsistence Activities, and the Presence of a High God in Primitive Societies," in *The Religious Dimension: New Directions of Quantitative Research* (New York: Academic, 1978), pp. 299–310; John Simpson, "Subsistence Systems and High Gods," prepared for the CSSR Annual Meeting, Vancouver, 1983.

8. See D. J. McCarthy, *Old Testament Covenant: A Survey of Current Opinions* (Richmond: Westminster/John Knox, 1972); K. Baltzer, *Das Bundesformulaer* (Neukirchen, 1964); R. E. Clements, *Prophecy and Covenant* (London: SPCK, 1965).

9. Alan F. Segal, *Life After Death* (New York: Random House, 2004), pp. 1–12. Some of the material is quoted from my previous work and is used with permission.

1. The Matriarch in Peril

1. Robert Alter, *The Art of Biblical Narrative* (New York: Basic Books, 2011), pp. 55–78. Alter uses Walter Arend's *Die typischen Szenen bei Homer* (1933) as a basis for his work.

2. This is the favorite language of S. David Sperling, *The Original Torah: The Political Intent of the Bible's Writers* (New York: New York University Press, 1998), pp. 27–40, whose work has also been an important confirmation of my own interest in studying parallelism.

3. See Gary A. Rendsburg, "Investiture Address," the Blanche and Irving Laurie Chair in Jewish History, Rutgers University, October 2004. Rendsburg anticipates many of the methods employed here and has kindly shared his publications with me.

4. Meir Sternberg, *The Poetics of Biblical Narrative: Ideological Literature and the Drama of Reading* (Bloomington: Indiana University Press, 1987).

5. Sarai is saved in the end through divine intervention. If one accepts the interpretation of Judy Klitsner, the gift of Isaac's birth to Sarai in her old age represents a reward for her exemplary conduct in this frightening circumstance. But I remain unconvinced because nothing like that is said in the text. Judy Klitsner, *Subversive Sequels in the Bible: How Biblical Stories Mine and Undermine Each Other* (Philadelphia: Jewish Publication Society, 2009), pp. 129–30. Rather, the importance of Sarai's salvation by God is precisely that it is divine intervention in a circumstance in which very few people can expect to be saved. We shall see this in more detail later in chapter 5.

6. Mark Zvi Brettler, *How to Read the Jewish Bible* (New York: Oxford University Press, 2007), 57–58. Originally published as *How to Read the Bible* (Philadelphia: Jewish Publication Society, 2005). See also Mark Zvi Brettler, *The Creation of History in Ancient Israel* (New York: Routledge, 1995).

7. The final editor of the stories, P, officially understands the names as referring to the same persons by saying that YHWH changes their names (Genesis 17:5). But the difference in names may just as well have originally reflected local differences in the stories.

8. We shall also see that it will help if we remove the stories from the time of the patriarchs in the second millennium BCE and put them in the time period of the settlement and the monarchy in the first millennium BCE. We shall have to wait to the end of this chapter to see how. And then we shall have to wait a few chapters to see exactly why we have to do this.

9. Ilana Pardes, *Countertraditions in the Bible: A Feminist Approach* (Cambridge: Harvard University Press, 1992), p. 4. Pardes very astutely states that her goal is "to explore the tense dialogue between the dominant patriarchal discourses of the Bible and counter female voices which attempt to put forth other truths."

10. Tzvetan Todorov, *The Poetics of Prose* (Ithaca: Cornell University Press, 1977), pp. 53–65.

11. J and E will turn out to be rather longer and more complex narrators than just this story. There will also turn out to be a lot of argumentation about whether each of these strands of tradition is a united narrative or only a series of related stories.

12. The Hebrew name for the book, *tanakh*, would take us in a different direction. The Hebrew name comes from a bit later in time than *ta biblia* because it is a rabbinic concept while the Greek translation gives us an older, underlying conception of what the Bible is. We will see that the underlying principle behind the collection of the books in the Bible is covenant. Everything in the book has something to do with covenant. The Latin word for covenant is *testamentum*, inherent in our use of the terms *Old Testament* and *New Testament*. So our English words for the sections of the Bible emerge from an English translation of a Latin translation of a Greek translation of a Hebrew word, *brith*, which means covenant.

13. For example, Abraham Ibn Ezra (1092–1167) suspected that the text of the Bible was composed of different sources written at different times. Most famously, he cautions silence in interpreting the now famous crux in Genesis 12:6: "The Canaanite was then in the land." The verse states that when Abraham entered the land, Canaanites were already there. This has indeed proved historical because there already had been "Canaanite" cities for millennia. But what is more interesting is that Ibn Ezra

notes that the word *then* implies that this is quite different from the narrator's own time. He comments: "It is possible that Canaan seized the land from someone else. And if this is not so, it has a great secret and the person who understands will keep quiet."

14. The earliest written documents in the Bible are thus likely to be songs or poems that survived because they were repeated generation after generation—set pieces like Exodus 15 (the Song at the Sea) and Judges 5 (the Song of Deborah). In part, archaeology has figured in the argument, as we have not yet been able to find sure evidence of a Davidic or Solomonic Jerusalem. We will take up these problems in the last chapter.

15. The one scholar whose work has been devoted to showing the late date of the sources of the Pentateuch is John van Seters, most recently in his *The Biblical Saga of King David* (Winona Lake, IN: Eisenbrauns, 2009). Though the work has been going on for decades and is very interesting, there are some reasons to be skeptical. Later scholars dating the material late often have ideological reasons for doing so. For a much more sophisticated and interesting summary of new developments in the documentary hypothesis, see David Carr, "Changing Positions in Pentateuchal Studies," in Magne Saebo, ed., *The Hebrew Bible/Old Testament: The History of Its Interpretation*, volume 3: *Modern Interpretation of the Hebrew Bible/Old Testament: The Nineteenth and Twentieth Centuries*, part 2, *The Twentieth Century: From Modernism to Postmodernism* (Göttingen: Vandenhoeck and Ruprecht, 2010).

16. See William F. Albright, "The Patriarchal Background of Israel's Faith," *Yahweh and the Gods of Canaan* (Garden City, NY: Doubleday, 1968); see also John Bright, *A History of Israel*, 3d ed. (Philadelphia: Westminster, 1981), pp. 67–102.

17. See Ephraim A. Speiser, *Genesis*, Anchor Bible 1 (Garden City, NY: Doubleday, 1964).

18. As scholars like to say, it was contained in the West Amorite onomasticon or the list of names in common use.

19. Speiser, *Genesis*, p. xi. See also "The Wife-Sister Motif in the Patriarchal Narratives," in A. Altmann, ed., *Biblical and Other Studies* (Cambridge: Harvard University Press, 1963), pp. 15–28.

20. G. Ernest Wright, *Biblical Archaeology* (Philadelphia: Westminster, 1962), p. 40; See also James Kugel, *How to Read the Bible: A Guide to Scripture, Then and Now* (New York: Free Press, 2007), p. 101.

21. R. David Freedman and Samuel Greengus, "The Patriarchs' Wives as Sisters—Is the Anchor Bible Wrong?" *Biblical Archaeological Review* 1 (1975): 91–94, 151–52.

22. See also Rendsburg, "Investiture Address."

23. David Daube, in *Studies in Biblical Law* (New York: Ktav, 1969), pp. 78–82, has argued that even as late as the exilic period the matter of marriage to a half sister was still an unsettled question. In this same category also is the law against marrying two sisters, as Jacob did with Leah and Rachel (see Leviticus 18:18).

24. Carolyn J. Sharp, *Wrestling the Word: The Hebrew Scriptures and the Christian Believer* (Philadelphia: Westminster John Knox, 2010), pp. 51–54.

25. Susan Niditch, *A Prelude to Biblical Folklore: Underdogs and Tricksters* (Urbana: University of Illinois Press, 1987).

26. Robert Pelton, *The Trickster in West Africa* (Berkeley: University of California Press, 1980), pp. 6–7; Daniel Brinton, *The Myths of the New World* (New York: Leypoldt and Holt, 1968), pp. 161–62.

27. Mac Linscott Ricketts, "The North American Indian Trickster," *History of Religions* 5, no. 2 (Winter 1966): 336.

28. Mac Linscott Ricketts, "The Structure and Religious Significance of the Trickster-Transformer-Culture Hero in the Mythology of the North American Indians," Ph.D. diss., University of Chicago (1964), p. 589.

29. Paul Radin, *The Trickster* (New York: Philosophical Library, 1956), pp. 133, 136–37.

30. Pelton, *The Trickster in West Africa*, p. 14.

31. See David M. Carr, *Writing on the Tablet of the Heart: Origins of Scripture and Literature* (New York: Oxford University Press, 2005); Karel van der Toorn, *Scribal Culture and the Making of the Hebrew Bible* (Cambridge: Harvard University Press, 2007). Van der Toorn's hypothesis that there was no royal scribal school, only a temple one, is not relevant to this discussion. It is also not convincing to me in its major hypothesis, though a great deal may be learned from reading his work.

32. Carr, *Writing on the Tablet of the Heart*, 17–46.

33. Peter Machinist, "The Question of Distinctiveness in Ancient Israel: An Essay," in *Ah, Assyria . . . : Studies in Assyrian History and Ancient Near Eastern Historiography Presented to Hayim Tadmor* (Jerusalem: Magnes, 1991), p. 211.

34. Erich Auerbach, *Mimesis: Representations of Reality in Western Literature*, trans. Willard Trask (Princeton: Princeton University Press, 2004 [1953]).

2. The Golden Calf

1. Amihai Mazar, "Cult Site from the Time of the Judges in the Mountains of Samaria," *Eretz Israel* 16 (Jerusalem, 1982) [in Hebrew]. The site was dated to the period archaeologists call Iron Age, IA—about 1200 BC—a time when, the Bible tells us,

the Israelite tribes started their permanent settlement of the Land of Israel. This was a one-period site. It had been used for only a short time and was then abandoned. The bronze figurine of the young bull was probably used in the days of the Judges in the land assigned to the tribe of Manasseh. See also Mazar's article "Bronze Bull Found in Israelite 'High Place' from the Time of the Judges," *Biblical Archaeology Review* 9, no. 5 (September/October 1983): 34–40.

2. *The BAS Biblical World in Pictures*. Biblical Archaeology Society, 2003; P. Kyle McCarter Jr., *Ancient Inscriptions: Voices from the Biblical World* (Washington, DC: Biblical Archaeology Society, 1996).

3. Or "fashioned it with a graving tool": meaning of Heb uncertain.

4. Gk Vg compare Tg: Heb: "Today ordain yourselves."

5. Gk Heb Mss: MT "before you"; Compare 2 Samuel 7:26, 29.

6. Israel Knohl, *The Divine Symphony: The Bible's Many Voices* (Philadelphia: Jewish Publication Society, 2003), p. 80. See also chapter 7 of this book.

7. Gk Syr: Heb: "us."

8. Gk Vg: Heb: "he."

9. Or "shall go up in flames."

10. Compare Gk: Heb: "To these they say sacrifices of people."

11. Gk Syr: Heb: "calves."

12. Cn: Heb: "exult."

13. Cn: Heb: "to a king who will contend."

14. Cn: Heb: "counsel."

15. Moses Aberbach and Leivy Smolar, "Aaron, Jeroboam, and the Golden Calves," *Journal of Biblical Literature* 86, no. 2 (June 1967): 129–40; "Jeroboam's Rise to Power," *Journal of Biblical Literature* 88, no. 1 (March 1969): 69–72.

3. A Historical Tragedy

1. It used to be believed that the Succession Narrative (SN), the Court History (CH), and even David's Rise to Power (DRP) were written fairly close to the events. The reasons for this were simply that the story seems historical, as the narrator has considerable inside knowledge. However, major theories of these writings since the 1960s have diverged greatly. It could be written close to the time (Julius Wellhausen) or long after the time (D. M. Gunn) or in the days in between. In this work we will take an intermediate position. Some of the material will be seen to be fairly close to the events, others will be added, and still others will be late, even as late as the exilic

period. This makes necessary approximately three different recensions of the story. I am fairly dubious that any single theory, based on the logic or predisposition of an individual scholar, completely describes both the historicity and literary skill of the redactors.

2. Robert Wright, *The Evolution of God* (New York: Little, Brown, 2009).

4. The Concubine of the Levite

1. Phyllis Trible, *Texts of Terror: Literary-Feminist Readings of Biblical Narratives* (Philadelphia: Fortress, 1984), p. 65.

2. Gk OL: Heb "prostituted herself against."

3. The Bible leaves no room for a husband to forgive his wife in case of her adultery, but one might speculate that it could happen if the husband were willing to "forego" his honor in the situation. Such understandings are common in tribal societies even today.

4. Gk: Heb: "she brought him."

5. Cf. verse 7 and the Greek: Heb "they."

6. A great deal of speculation, both ancient and modern, has gone into the issue of what happened to the third angel. The favorite theory is that as soon as its mission was done the angel disappeared. The first angel's mission was to announce the birth of Isaac, and so only two angels are to be found later with Lot in Sodom.

7. Why the repetition of the name LORD? Is it to indicate that YHWH can appear as a kind of angel himself, but a very special one who also participates in the LORD? Later Christian interpreters see in this verse justification for a preexistent Christ who is the second LORD in the sentence. Later Jewish commentators counter by saying that one should not get the idea that there are "two powers" from this passage.

8. Avi Hurvitz, "Can Biblical Texts Be Dated Linguistically? Chronological Perspectives in the Historical Study of Biblical Hebrew," in A. Lemaire and M. Sæbø, eds., *Congress Volume: Oslo 1998* (Leiden: Brill, 2000) and *A Linguistic Study of the Relationship Between the Priestly Source and the Book of Ezekiel: A New Approach to an Old Problem* (Paris: Gabalda, 1982).

9. See Walter Rast and R. Thomas Schaub, "Have Sodom and Gomorrah Been Found?" *Biblical Archaeology Review* 6, no. 5 (September/October 1980): 27–36.

10. So Marc Brettler, for example, in his interesting article "The Book of Judges: Literature as Politics," *Journal of Biblical Literature* 108, no. 3 (1989): 395–418; see especially p. 417.

11. So Susan Niditch, with appropriate diffidence about the challenge in deciding on a prior relationship. See Susan Niditch, *A Prelude to Biblical Folklore: Underdogs and Tricksters* (Urbana: University of Illinois Press, 1987).

12. Compare Gk and Heb: "And all who saw it said, 'Such a thing has not happened or been seen.'"

13. See Baruch Halpern, *The First Historians: The Hebrew Bible and History* (University Park, MD: Pennsylvania State University, 2004).

14. To call this system an amphictyony is to impose a Greek model on the society. Clearly, however, no matter how idealized the picture, a twelve-tribe structure was one description of government before the monarchy; see Baruch Halpern, *The Emergence of Israel in Canaan* (Chico, CA: Scholars, 1983) and *The Constitution of the Monarchy in Israel* (Chico, CA: Scholars, 1981).

15. Brettler, "The Book of Judges."

16. The great Bible interpreter Martin Noth, for example, sees this as an independent northern tradition. But that is hard to understand in a book with such obvious southern sympathies. See Martin Noth, *The Deuteronomistic History* (Sheffield: University of Sheffield, Department of Biblical Studies, 1981) and *The Old Testament World*, trans. Victor I. Gruhn (Philadelphia: Fortress, 1966).

17. Moshe Weinfeld, *Deuteronomy and the Deuteronomic School* (Oxford: Oxford University Press, 1972), p. 355.

5. The Horror of Human Sacrifice

1. Erich Auerbach followed by hundreds of literary analyses; see Erich Auerbach, *Mimesis: Representations of Reality in Western Literature*, trans. Willard Trask (Princeton: Princeton University Press, 2004 [1953]).

2. Note the use of terminology: "blood of innocents."

3. See Baruch Margalit, "Why King Mesha of Moab Sacrificed His Only Son," *Biblical Archaeology Review* 12, no. 6 (November/December 1986): 62–63. Margalit is convinced from this passage; I am not wholly convinced, based on the difficulty with the word *offspring*. But note the correspondence of language with Mesha and the binding of Isaac. We shall see that there is a great deal of supporting evidence in favor of the existence of human sacrifice in Canaan and Phoenicia; we are not looking at merely a biblical polemic.

4. Edmund Leach's essay, "The Legitimacy of Solomon," originally a journal article and reprinted in his book of essays *Genesis as Myth*, is quoted from *The Essential Edmund Leach* (New Haven: Yale University Press, 2001), 2:48.

5. Lévi-Strauss's structuralism always posited a polar and dualistic pair. I do not necessarily agree; but here we have a case in which Lévi-Strauss's theory works without much resizing.

6. Claude Lévi-Strauss, *Structural Anthropology*, trans. Claire Jacobson and Brooke Grundfest Schoepf (New York: Basic Books, 1963).

7. See Paul G. Mosca, "Child Sacrifice in Canaanite and Israelite Religion: Study in Mulk and Mek," Harvard University, Ph.D. diss. (1975); John Day, *Molech: A God of Human Sacrifice in the Old Testament*, University of Cambridge Oriental Publications 41 (New York: Cambridge University Press, 1989); Joseph A. Greene and Lawrence E. Stager, "An *Odyssey* Debate: Were Living Children Sacrificed to the Gods? Yes," *Archaeology Odyssey* 3, no. 6 (November/December 2000): 28–31; Francesca Stavrakopoulou, *King Manasseh and Child Sacrifice: Biblical Distortions of Historical Realities* (New York: Walter de Gruyter, 2004). The entire argument is well summarized by Frank Moore Cross, "A Phoenician Inscription from Idalion: Some Old and New Texts Relating to Child Sacrifice," in Michael D. Coogan, J. Cheryl Exum, and Lawrence E. Stager, eds., *Scripture and Other Artifacts: Essays on the Bible and Archaeology in Honor of Philip J. King*, pp. 93–107 (Louisville: Westminster/John Knox, 1994); and George C. Heider, *The Cult of Molek: A Reassessment* (Sheffield: JSOT, 1985).

8. Cross, "A Phoenician Inscription," p. 97.

9. See Nicole Ruane, "Social Status and the Sacrifice of the First Born," unpublished paper; and Catherine Bell, *Ritual Theory, Ritual Practice* (New York: Oxford University Press, 1992) and *Ritual: Perspectives and Dimensions* (New York: Oxford University Press, 1997).

10. The next sections are deeply indebted to P. Kyle McCarter Jr., *Ancient Inscriptions: Voices from the Biblical World* (Washington, DC: Biblical Archaeology Society, 1996), pp. 90–92.

11. André Lemaire, "'House of David': Restored in Moabite Inscription," *Biblical Archaeology Review* 20, no. 3 (May/June 1994): 31–37.

12. Ibid.

13. See William G. Dever, *Who Were the Early Israelites and Where Did They Come From?* (Grand Rapids, MI: Eerdmans, 2003), pp. 32–34.

14. The translation of W. F. Albright in the "Palestinian Inscriptions" section of James B. Pritchard, ed., *Ancient Near Eastern Texts Relating to the Old Testament* (Princeton: Princeton University Press, 1950), p. 320.

15. Charles Clermont-Ganneau, "La Stèle de Mésa," *Revue Critique* (September 11, 1875): 166–74, quote p. 173; and "La Stèle de Mésa, examen critique du texte," *Journal Asiatique* 9 (8th series, 1887), p. 107.

16. Mark Lidzbarski, "Eine Nachprüfung der Mesainschrift," in *Ephemeris für semitische Epigraphik I* (Giessen: J. Ricker, 1900), pp. 1–10.

17. René Dussaud, *Les monuments palestiniens et judaïques: Moab, Judée, Philistie, Samarie, Galilée* (Paris: E. Leroux, 1912), p. 5; compare also D. Sidersky, *La stèle de Mésha, index bibliographique* (Paris, 1920), p. 11; A. H. Van Zyl, *The Moabites* (Leiden: Brill, 1960), addendum 1.

18. Lemaire, "'House of David,'" 36.

19. See André Lemaire, "'House of David' Restored in Moabite Inscriptions," *Biblical Archaeology Review* 20, no. 3 (May/June 1994): 31.

20. See, for example, Lawrence J. Mykytiuk, *Identifying Biblical Persons in Northwest Semitic Inscriptions of 1200–539* B.C.E., Society of Biblical Literature Academia Biblica 12 (Atlanta: Society of Biblical Literature; Leiden: Brill, 2004), pp. xix, 327.

21. See Ada Yardeni's section entitled "They Would Change the Dates of Clearly Stratified Inscriptions—Impossible!" in the article "Defusing Pseudo-scholarship: The Siloam Inscription Ain't Hasmonean," *Biblical Archaeology Review* 23, no. 2 (March/April 1997): 47.

22. See Dever, *Who Were the Early Israelites?* especially pp. 239–41.

6. Ways of a Man with a Woman

1. The ambiguities of Bathsheba's character are well explored by Alice Bach, *Women, Seduction, and Betrayal in Biblical Narrative* (Cambridge: Cambridge University Press, 1997), pp. 128–65.

2. Meir Sternberg, *The Poetics of Biblical Narrative: Ideological Literature and the Drama of Reading* (Bloomington: Indiana University Press, 1987).

3. Tikva Frymer-Kensky, *Reading the Women of the Bible* (New York: Schocken, 2002), 143–56.

4. Jon D. Levenson and Baruch Halpern, "The Political Import of David's Marriages," *Journal of Biblical Literature* 99, no. 4 (December 1980): 507–18.

5. See Sternberg, *Poetics of Biblical Narrative*, pp. 186–229. Sternberg stresses the ambiguity, suggesting many different possibilities for the knowledge of each character at every moment. I think that the ambiguity is present but not so total. What follows is my take on what each character knows.

6. So also ibid., p. 221.

7. Pace Sternberg, who thinks that both the messenger and even Uriah may be aware of the ruse.

8. I don't mean to suggest that the succession narrative is a separate document composed by one single person. It's just a convenient way to refer to these chapters of text. Bathsheba makes an especially strong entrance in 1 Kings 2, where she goes to David, explains the rebellion of Adonijah, and essentially spares her own and Solomon's life by convincing David to back Solomon's party of Bathsheba, Benaiah, and Nathan. See the next chapter.

9. Gary A. Rendsburg, "Investiture Address," the Blanche and Irving Laurie Chair in Jewish History, Rutgers University, October 2004; Joseph Blenkinsopp, "Theme and Motif in the Succession History (2 Sam. xi 2ff.) and the Yahwist Corpus," *Volume du Congrès: Genève 1965*, SVT 15 (Leiden, 1966), pp. 44–57; and see also the work of R. E. Clements and S. David Sperling.

10. See James B. Pritchard, ed., *Ancient Near Eastern Texts Relating to the Old Testament* (Princeton: Princeton University Press, 1950), 37–41, for the story of Enki and Ninhursag.

11. See Alan F. Segal, *Life after Death* (New York: Random House, 2004), throughout.

12. Alternatively, it may signify the Tigris or the Nile in an anachronistic way.

7. No Peace in the Royal Family

1. David Daube, in *Studies in Biblical Law* (New York: Ktav, 1969), pp. 78–82, has argued that even as late as the exilic period the matter of marriage to a half sister was still an unsettled question. In this same category also is the law against marrying two sisters as Jacob did with Leah and Rachel (see Leviticus 18:18).

2. David Noel Freedman, ed., *The Anchor Bible Dictionary* (New York: Doubleday, 1992), 5:1182.

3. See Dean Andrew Nicholas, *The Trickster Revisited: Deception as a Motif in the Pentateuch*, Studies in Biblical Literature 117 (New York: Peter Lang, 2009), pp. 58–59.

4. Freedman, *The Anchor Bible Dictionary*, 5:1183.

5. See Susan Niditch, *Judges: A Commentary*, The Old Testament Library (Louisville: Westminster John Knox, 2008), pp. 138–72.

6. Freedman, "Samson," *The Anchor Bible Dictionary* 5:950–954.

7. Edmund Leach, *Genesis as Myth and Other Essays* (London: Jonathan Cape, 1969), p. 39. Edmund Leach's "The Legitimacy of Solomon" originally appeared in the *European Journal of Sociology* 7 (1966): 58–101 and has been reprinted in *The Essential Edmund Leach* (New Haven: Yale University Press, 2001), 2:48.

8. James B. Pritchard, ed., *Ancient Near Eastern Texts Relating to the Old Testament* (Princeton: Princeton University Press, 1950), p. 41.

9. In this perception, both S. David Sperling and Gary Rendsburg (*The Redaction of Genesis* [Winona Lake, IN: Eisenbrauns, 1986] and "Investiture Address," the Blanche and Irving Laurie Chair in Jewish History, Rutgers University, October 2004) have preceded me, though I am embarrassed to say that I taught the material for a number of years without the benefit of their perceptions.

10. Gk Syr Vg: Heb "Therefore."

11. Freely adapted from Robert C. Culley, *Studies in the Structure of Hebrew Narrative*, Semeia Supplements (Missoula, MO: Scholars; Philadelphia: Fortress, 1975), p. 108.

12. My formulation, not Culley's.

13. Michael Fishbane, *Biblical Text and Texture: A Literary Reading of Selected Texts* (Oxford: One World, 1998); pp. 26–27 for this table. Fishbane credits U. Cassuto, *A Commentary on the Book of Genesis*, part 1 (Jerusalem: Magnes, 1961), pp. 212, 218, 225, 228.

14. Of course, we know that the argument between the farmer and the shepherd is a millennia-old mythical motif that can be traced back to the disputes between Dumuzi and Enkidu in Sumer. These stories may represent the alternation between these occupations necessary in the ancient Near East.

15. Papyrus Anastasi, 6:54–56, in James B. Pritchard, ed., *Ancient Near Eastern Texts Relating to the Old Testament* (Princeton: Princeton University Press, 1950), p. 259. A possible fifteenth-century BCE reference may be found in a list of Thutmose III. See Freedman, *The Anchor Bible Dictionary*, under "Edom," 2:287–301.

16. That is, "He supplants or He takes by the heel."

17. Or see "of."

18. Or "and of."

19. Meaning of Heb uncertain.

20. See Baruch Halpern, *David's Secret Demons: Messiah, Murderer, Traitor, King* (Grand Rapids, MI: Eerdmans, 2001), p. 470.

21. In fact, Deuteronomy commands Judah not to try to conquer Edom or Ammon.

22. That is, "House of God."

23. See also Genesis 35:22, where Reuben catches his stepmother Bilhah in the field and cohabits with her.

24. John Van Seters, "Jacob's Marriages and Ancient Near East Customs: A Reexamination," *Harvard Theological Review* 62, no. 4 (October 1969): 377–95.

25. Martha A. Morrison, "The Jacob and Laban Narrative in Light of Near Eastern Sources," *Biblical Archaeologist* 46, no. 3 (Summer 1983): 155–64.

26. Freedman, *The Anchor Bible Dictionary*, 4:113.

27. Nicholas, *The Trickster Revisited*, pp. 63–71.

28. Ibid., p. 100, but note that I disagree with Nicholas's dating of these traditions.

29. Fishbane, *Biblical Texts and Texture*.

Conclusion

1. That hypothesis, at first blush, has not much to recommend it; some of its proponents are excellent scholars; others merely like it because it is convenient for their current political opinions. But actually the date at which the Israelites become an ethnic group should have nothing to do with modern politics.

2. There is a mounting pile of ingenious and very scholarly studies of the development of Hebrew as a language and, particularly, the differences between early and late biblical Hebrew and oral and written dialects. On the subject of oral versus written styles and how this helps us understand First Temple Hebrew, see, for example, Frank H. Polak, "The Oral and the Written: Syntax, Stylistics, and the Development of Biblical Prose Narrative," *Journal of the Ancient Near Eastern Society* 26 (1998): 59–105.

3. Disqualifying evidence or alternative positions merely because of ideological assumptions—for example, the modern land belongs to the Palestinians or the Israelis—is always wrong. Anything scholarly will take a look at all positions that are argued in a scholarly way. In my opinion that does not relieve us of the task of applying the hermeneutics of suspicion all the time, not just about opposing positions, and utilizing all the evidence at our disposal. To believe otherwise is simply personal bias masquerading as method.

4. Martin Noth, *The Old Testament World*, trans. Victor I. Gruhn (Philadelphia: Fortress, 1966); Albrecht Alt, "The Settlement of the Israelites in Palestine," *Essays on Old Testament History and Religion*, trans. R. A. Wilson (Oxford: Blackwell, 1966 [1953]).

5. George Mendenhall, *The Tenth Generation: The Origins of the Biblical Tradition* (Baltimore: Johns Hopkins University Press, 1973); Norman Gottwald, *The Tribes of Yahweh: A Sociology for the Religion of Liberated Israel, 1250–1050* BC (Maryknoll, NY: Orbis, 1979).

6. Robert B. Coote and Keith W. Whitelam, *The Emergence of Early Israel in His-torical Perspective* (Sheffield: Almond, 1987). See also Thomas L. Thompson, *The Bible in History: How Writers Create a Past* (London: Jonathan Cape, 1999). Whitelam and Thompson clearly know biblical studies quite well. Whether their interest in late dat-ing is a result of their scholarship—as is that of Van Seters (see note 15 in chapter 1)—or a result of a preexistent bias—like Palestinian apologist Nadia Abu El-Haj—is not entirely clear. Whitelam shares the same assumptions as Abu El-Haj in her book *Facts on the Ground: Archaeological Practice and Territorial Self-fashioning in Is-raeli Society* (Chicago: University of Chicago Press, 2001). She relies on the results of Whitelam and the Copenhagen school in a completely uncritical manner (she has no basis for making scholarly decisions in this field and adduces no other reason than that they agree with her predispositions). Thus her discussion of biblical history is entirely ideological and has no basis in method. Not so in her dissertation, which seems a valid if not particularly original discussion about how archaeology has insin-uated itself into Israeli politics. Had she stuck entirely to the issue of how Israelis use archaeology as foundation myths for their society, she would have been on a lot more solid ground. As it is, there is not much of scholarly interest in her book, though her dissertation, on which it is based, remains an interesting piece of evidence of how someone capable of scholarship can be lured into tragic and disastrous enterprises that have little to do with scholarship.

7. Frank J. Yurco, "3,200-Year-Old Picture of Israelites Found in Egypt," *Biblical Archaeology Review* 16, no. 5 (September/October 1990): 20–38.

8. Anson F. Rainey, "Rainey's Challenge," *Biblical Archaeology Review* 17, no. 6 (November/December 1991): 56–60, 93.

9. Pace Philip R. Davies.

10. Israel Finkelstein and Amihai Mazar, *The Quest for the Historical Israel: De-bating Archaeology and the History of Early Israel*, ed. Brian B. Schmidt (Leiden: Brill, 2007), p. 5.

11. Avi Hurvitz, "The Relevance of Biblical Hebrew Linguistics for the Historical Study of Ancient Israel," in Ron Margolin, ed., *Proceedings of the Twelfth World Con-gress of Jewish Studies: Division A, The Bible and Its World* (Jerusalem: World Union of Jewish Studies, 1999), pp. 21–33, "Can Biblical Texts Be Dated Linguistically? Chronological Perspectives in the Historical Study of Biblical Hebrew," in A. Lemaire and M. Sæbø, eds., *Congress Volume: Oslo 1998* (Leiden: Brill, 2000), pp. 143–60, "Early and Late in Biblical Language—the Characteristics of Late Biblical Hebrew," "The Archaeological-Historical Debate on the Antiquity of the Hebrew Bible in the Light of Linguistic Research of the Hebrew Language" [Hebrew], in I. L. Levine and A. Mazar, eds., *The Controversy Over the Historicity of the Bible* (Jerusalem: Yad Ben-

Zvi/Dinur Center, 2001), pp. 34–46; M. F. Rooker, *Biblical Hebrew in Transition: The Language of the Book of Ezekiel* (Sheffield: JSOT, 1990).

12. Seth L. Sanders, *The Invention of Hebrew* (Urbana: University of Illinois Press, 2009), p. 85.

13. These include Lachish bowl no. 1, the Lachish ewer, the Goetze seal (Soreq Valley), the Beth Shemesh sherd, the Hazor Dipinto, and perhaps the Tell el-Hesi sherd. F. M. Cross Jr., "The Origin and Early Evolution of the Alphabet," *Eretz-Israel* 8 (Jerusalem: Israel Exploration Society, 1967): 8*–24*. See Richard S. Hess, "Literacy in Iron Age Israel," in V. Philips Long, David W. Baker, and Gordon J. Wenham, eds., *Windows Into Old Testament History: Evidence, Argument, and the Crisis of "Biblical Israel"* (Grand Rapids, MI: Eerdmans, 2002), pp. 82–102, quote p. 85.

14. Hershel Shanks, "Prize Find: Oldest Hebrew Inscription Discovered in Israelite Fort on Philistine Border," *Biblical Archaeology Review* 36, no. 2 (March/April 2010): 51–54.

15. See Robert Alter's work.

16. The meaning of the text is perhaps best construed as the Israelites' lack of heroes to assert their ability to control and raid the highways against the major powers. See, e.g., Baruch Halpern, *The Emergence of Israel in Canaan*, Society of Biblical Literature Monograph Series 29 (Chico, CA: Scholars, 1983), pp. 212–13; and Susan Niditch, *A Prelude to Biblical Folklore: Underdogs and Tricksters* (Urbana: University of Illinois Press, 1987), pp. 67, 71, 78.

17. For an excellent summary and plausible reconstruction of the period of the Judges, see Halpern, *The Emergence of Israel in Canaan*, especially section 3, "The Making of Historical Israel," pp. 109–86.

18. And *Gattungsgeschichte* in German, *histoire de genres* in French.

19. David Noel Freedman, ed., *The Anchor Bible Dictionary* (New York: Doubleday, 1992).

20. Or *Nubians*; Heb *Cushites*.

21. Ronald S. Hendel, "Finding Historical Memories in the Patriarchal Narratives," *Biblical Archaeology Review* 21, no. 4 (July/August 1995): 52–55, 58–59, 70–71.

22. See Finkelstein on the importance of David's armor for dating. But he dates the whole section on that basis. See Israel Finkelstein and Neil Asher Silberman, *The Bible Unearthed: Archaeology's New Vision of Ancient Israel and the Origin of Its Sacred Texts* (New York: Free Press, 2001); Finkelstein and Mazar, *The Quest for the Historical Israel*. How prescient is Robert Alter, who knows from his sensitive, close reading that, even if certain details of the story of David are embellished, the story itself must have a historiographic subject. See Robert Alter, *The Art of Biblical Narrative* (New York: Basic Books, 2011), pp. 40–42.

23. The attempt by Rogerson and Davies to redate this inscription to the Hellenistic period and to brand it as an early fraud is wholly unsuccessful. See *Biblical Archaeology Review* 23, no. 2 (March/April 1997), composed almost entirely of the article "Defusing Pseudo-scholarship: The Siloam Inscription Ain't Hasmonean," with excellent commentary by Hackett, Cross, McCarter, Yardeni, Lemaire, Eshel, and Hurvitz, all criticizing some aspect of the identification made by Rogerson and Davies. Only extreme minimalism requires that this inscription, which dates to the time of Hezekiah's water tunnel, be a fake.

24. See the very interesting study of Jeffrey H. Tigay, *You Shall Have No Other Gods: Israelite Religion in the Light of Hebrew Inscriptions* (Atlanta: Scholars, 1989).

25. Baruch Halpern has helpfully summarized the synchronisms between the Assyrian kings and their Israelite and Judahite counterparts: Adad-Narari III and Joash (of Samaria); Tiglath-pileser III and Ahaz (of Judah) and Menahem, Pekah, and Hosea (of Israel); Sargon II (721–705 BCE) mentions the kingdom of Judah, and Sennacherib (704–681 BCE) mentions Hezekiah and known rulers of other states. Esarhaddon (680–669 BCE) and Ashurbanipal (668–631 BCE) refer to Hezekiah's successor, Manasseh. The biblical chronology of kings is remarkably accurate. Baruch Halpern, "Eyewitness Testimony," *Biblical Archaeology Review* 29, no. 5 (September/October 2003): 50–57.

26. Kenneth A. Kitchen, "The Controlling Role of External Evidence in Assessing the Historical Status of the Israelite United Monarchy," *Windows Into Old Testament History*, pp. 111–30.

INDEX

Aaron, *see* Golden calf of Aaron
Abel, *see* Cain and Abel
Aberbach, Moses, 75–78
Abihu (son of Aaron), 76–77
Abijah (son of Jeroboam I), 76
Abimelech (son of Gideon), 135, 156, 160, 188
Abimelech of Gerar (Philistine king), 27–30
Abishag the Shunamite, 199, 206–7
Abraham (Abram), 3; anachronisms and, 48; argument with God about sparing Lot, 106, 117; covenants and, 16–17; cultic centers of south and, 243; descendants of, 125; different names of, 27, 44, 261*n*7; in Egypt, 25–27; as father of Israelites, 24–25; God's testing of, 50–51, 123; Sarah and, 24–29, 48, 49, 51, 183; wife-sister motif and, 1, 25–29, 49, 186; *see also* Sacrifice of Isaac
Absalom (son of David), 172
Absalom and Amnon, 2, 193–94, 198, 199, 220
Abu El-Haj, Nadia, 272*n*6
Achish (mercenary), 210
Adam and Eve, 7, 165–79; David and Bathsheba compared to, 165–66, 168,

171–72, 174–75, 178–79, 228; gender of author of, 171; structure of, 198
Adapa (wise man), 178
Adonijah (older brother of Solomon), 2, 159–60, 165, 172, 199–202, 206–7, 269*n*8
Adonizedek (king of Jerusalem), 91
Adoram, stoning of, 65
Adultery: in David and Bathsheba, 2, 154–57, 161–62; forgiveness for, 102, 265*n*3
Ahab, 144, 147, 175–76
Ahaz (king of Judah), 136, 191
Ahithophel, 207
Ai, capture of, 91
Akkadian language, 54
Albright, W. F., 43–44
Albright synthesis, 43–45, 234; downfall of, 46–47
Allegories, 23–24
Alt, Albrecht, 51, 232, 271*n*4
Altar and sacrifice, 187
Alter, Robert, 23
Amaziah, Amos and, 71–73
Amenhotep III, 231
American democracy, 12
Ammon (nation), 108
Ammonites, 130

Amnon (son of David, half brother of Tamar), 2; *see also* Absalom and Amnon; Tamar and Amnon

Amon (king), 85, 89

Amorites, 44–45, 48

Amos: Amaziah and, 71–73; on covenant, 19; Hosea and, 70–71, 79

Amphictyony, 266n14

Amun-Re (god), 232

Anachronisms, 48

Anath (goddess), 41

Angels: birth of Isaac announced by, 105, 265n6; in Lot in Sodom, 105, 119, 265n6; worship of, 67; YHWH as name of, 67, 124–25

Animals: in creation story, 167; cut-up oxen, 104, 113; parable about poor man and lamb, 157; in place of human sacrifice, 125–27, 132, 146, 150

Apocalypse and day of judgment, 61

Aqedah story, *see* Sacrifice of Isaac

Archaeology, 9, 41, 43–44, 230–37, 272n6; history and, 234–36; of Jerusalem, 248–50

Archetype, conceptual, 13

Asa (king), 84

Asher (child of Jacob and Zilpah), 242

Asherah (goddess), 41

Ashkelon site, 58–59, 74

Ashurbanipal (Assyrian emperor), 87

Assyrians: empire collapse of, 87; northern kingdom conquered and destroyed by, 69–71, 73–74, 80–81, 98–99; vassal treaty, 89–90, 256

Athena (goddess), 95

Auerbach, Erich, 56

Azariah (king), 84

Baal (god): bull as symbol for, 59; worship of, 66–67

Baal-berith, temple of, 187

Bab edh-Dhra (city), 109

Babylonian exile (587 BCE–532 BCE), 86–87

Bacchus (god), 132

Bamah (high place), 68, 76

Barkay, Gabriel, 253

Barrenness and fertility, 134–35, 211–12, 216–18

Bathsheba (wife of David), 153; *see also* David and Bathsheba

Bathshua (Bath Shua), 163

Benaiah (son of Jehoiada), 160–61

Benjamin (son of Rachel), 215–16

Benjamites, 113–17, 118, 225

Bethel: angel worship at, 67; calf shrine at, 66, 71–72, 76; Jacob's dream at, 205–6

Beth-El (Beth-Aven), 74

Beth-shemesh (town), 188, 189, 191

Bible: as anthology, 11–12, 261n12; English translations of, 238; as historical document, 122, 234; as prescriptive document, 41, 192; rhetorical devices in, 51; as theological document, 149; *see also* Stories

Biblical Archaeological Review, 235

Biblical history, 264n1; beginning of, 3–4; morality and, 1–2; Shechem (city) in, 186–88; understanding of, 59; *see also* History

Biblical minimalism, 236–38, 251; *see also* Minimalists

Biblical Text and Texture: A Literary Reading of Selected Texts (Fishbane), 197–98

Bilhah (concubine of Jacob), 242, 270n23

Binding of Isaac, 50; *see also* Sacrifice of Isaac

Blessing: curses and, 211, 212, 218; from Isaac, 203–4

Blindness: of men in Sodom, 107, 118; of Samson, 189, 190

Bloom, Harold, 171

Book of life, 61

Boqer (herdsman or meat supplier), 72

Brettler, Marc, 120

Brith (covenant), 14, 261n12

Broschi, Ofer, 58

Bull: as symbol for Baal, 59; as symbol for God, 79

Bullae, seals and, 253

Cain and Abel, 194–99, 220

Calf figurines, 58–59, 74, 263n1; *see also* Golden calf

Calf shrines, 66, 68, 71–72, 76, 121

Canaan, 259n2; conquest of, 90–91; history of, 3–4

Canaanites: golden calves worshiped by, 59; intermarriage of Israelites and, 163, 184–85, 192; Israelites compared to, 17–18, 33, 40–41, 149, 209; phase, 43; sacrifice by, 127–29, 135, 136, 266*n*3

Cannibalism, 132

CH, *see* Court History

Chemosh (god), 136, 143, 145

Cherubim, 79

Christ as second LORD, 265*n*7

Circumcision, 135, 183

City of David (Jerusalem), 236, 249

Civil war: Israelites and Benjamites in, 114–17; oracles in, 114–15, 119

Clermont-Ganneau, Charles, 140–41, 146

Code of Hammurabi, 15

Composite authorship, theory of, 36

Conceptual archetype, 13

Concubine of the Levite (Judges 19), 100–5; consequences of, 113–14; cut-up corpse in, 104, 113; death of, 102, 104; Gibeah in, 103, 110, 121; hospitality in, 102–3; kingship and, 112–13; Lot in Sodom compared to, 56, 105, 107, 110, 117–22, 178, 182, 220, 224–25; matriarch in peril compared to, 110–12; rape in, 103–5, 113–14, 117, 224–25; tribal war and, 104, 112; as victim, 152

Conquest model of Israel, 232

Contract, 14

Coote, Robert, 233

Corpse, cut-up, 104, 113

Corvée tax and building projects of Solomon, 63, 64

Counteridentity, 55, 128–30, 185, 193

Cour de la Cachette at Karnak, 231, 235

Court History (CH; 1 Samuel–2 Kings), 56, 93, 264*n*1

Covenant, 14–20, 255–57, 261*n*12; in Deuteronomy, 18–19, 179; Josiah and, 15, 16, 17, 19, 86, 89; as marriage, 19–20, 256; moral discernment and, 179; myths as, 14–15; Old Testament and, 14–15, 261*n*12; patriarchal stories and, 15, 16; punctual aspect of, 17; Ten Commandments as, 18

Covenant renewal, 89–90; of Ezra, 15, 16, 17; in First Temple period, 15; at Passover, 15, 86, 89

Creation story, 166–68, 170; *see also* Adam and Eve

Critical history, 9

Cross, F. M., 239

Culley, Robert C., 196

Cultic centers of north and south, 243

Curses: Assyrian vassal treaty and, 90; blessing and, 211, 212, 218

Dabar (sexual abuse), 117

Dan (child of Jacob and Bilhah), 242

Dan (city), 66, 68, 71, 121

Danites, 120

David, King: evaluation of, 84, 120; Goliath and, 94–95, 247–48; kingdom of, 38; life narrative of, 161; prophecies regarding, 95–98; story of, 240–41; *see also* City of David; House of David; United Kingdom

David and Bathsheba (2 Samuel 11): Abishag the Shunamite in, 199, 206–7; Adam and Eve compared to, 165–66, 168, 171–72, 174–75, 178–79, 228; adultery in, 2, 154–57, 161–62; ambiguities in, 154, 159–60, 162, 268*n*6; Joab in, 155–56, 158–62, 202, 207; Judah and Tamar compared to, 163–65, 228; LORD in, 157–58; objectification of women in, 153, 160, 161–62; punishment in, 181–82; Solomon as son of, 153, 159–61, 165, 181–82, 200–202; summary of, 153–57; Uriah in, 2, 154–56, 180, 268*n*7

David and Bathsheba (film), 252

Davidic dynasty: end of, 3, 13, 97; history of, 82, 97, 216; rebellion against, 62–65

David's Rise to Power (DRP), 264*n*1

Dead Sea, ruins around, 109–10, 112, 220, 225

Dead Sea Scrolls, 42–43, 248

Deborah, 129; *see also* Song of Deborah

Delilah, 188–89

Descartes, René, 5

Descendants: root metaphor of family descent, 17; sexuality, endogamy and, 134–37; *see also specific individuals*

Desert wanderings, 3, 77

Deus ex machina, 224

Deuteronomic Reform (621 BCE), 151, 223

Deuteronomistic Historian (DH), 37, 39; editing characteristics of, 93–94,

Deuteronomistic (*continued*)
208–9, 223–24, 229; on golden calf,
68–70, 80–81, 98; Joshua, book of,
and, 90–91; strong hand of, 120–22;
voice of, 84, 87–93, 95, 221
Deuteronomy: as Assyrian vassal treaty,
89–90; covenant in, 18–19, 179; finding book of, 83–85; identifying voice
of, 83; Josiah and, 83–86, 94; Moses
and, 85, 86; prophecies in, 94, 95–98
Dever, William, 253
Devotional deities, 41
DH, *see* Deuteronomistic Historian
Dhiban (ancient Dibon), 139, 142
Die Maerchen (fairy tales), 51
Dinah (daughter of Leah), 212
Dinah story (Genesis 34), 135, 183–86,
191, 193
Dionysus (wine god), 132
Disinterest, 4–6; biases compared to, 4,
6, 8; myths and, 7, 10; types of analy-
sis and, 7–8, 10
Divine intervention: JE epic and, 95; in
Lot in Sodom, 119; Sarah and, 260*n*5
Documentary hypothesis, 33–38; history
of, 41–42; of Pentateuch, 33, 35–38,
40–43, 83; phases in development
of, 43
Doublet, 23–24, 25, 27
DRP, *see* David's Rise to Power
D source, 36, 37, 39, 42; *see also* Deuter-
onomistic Historian
Dumuzi, *see* Enkidu and Dumuzi,
story of
Dynastic principle, 159, 201–3

Early Biblical Hebrew (EBH), 239
Early Bronze Age, 109
EBH, *see* Early Biblical Hebrew
Edom (nation), 108, 109, 203–5
Eglon (obese Moabite king), 114
Egypt: Abraham and Sarah in, 25–27;
Joseph's journey to, 3, 36; Solomon
and, 207–8
Egyptian bondage, 17, 19
Ehud (judge), 114
El (fertility god), 59, 66
Elhanan ben Dodo, 247–48
Eliezer of Damascus, 48
Elisha (prophet), 141

Elohim (God): as term for, 37, 38, 78;
worship of, 66
E narrator, 31, 261*n*11
Endogamy, 134–37
Enki and Ninhursag (myth), 167
Enkidu (wild man), 178
Enkidu and Dumuzi, story of, 195,
270*n*14
Enticement, 175–76
Ephraim: Manasseh and, 64, 220; as
name for Israel, 63; Shechem (city) as
capital of tribal holdings of, 187; tribe
of, 100, 242
Epic literature, 7
Er (child of Judah and Shua), 163
Esarhaddon, Apology of, 240
Esau, 202–4, 220, 228
E source, 36–40, 42; Exodus and, 60, 79;
sacrifice of Isaac from, 124, 126
Esther, 77
Ethics, 16; ethical settlement of modern
Middle East, 150; eudaimonism in,
93–94
Ethnic identity, 109, 210, 220, 222–23,
271*n*1; Hebrew language and, 239–41
Etiologies: family as, 108; Lot in Sodom
as, 108–10; ruins around Dead Sea
as, 109–10, 112; of Temple cult, 127,
220
Euphrates River, 17
Eve, 166, 195; *see also* Adam and Eve
The Evolution of God (Wright, R.), 99
Exodus, 3; E source and, 60, 79; identity
and, 20; prototypes of, 27, 33
Exodus 15 (The Song at the Sea), 241,
262*n*14
Exodus 32, *see* Golden calf of Aaron
Extreme maximalists, 9
Extreme minimalists, 9, 148–50, 236–38
Ezra, 15, 16, 17

Fairy tales, 51
Families: as etiology, 108; offspring and,
130, 134; relationships, 95; *see also*
Descendants; Royal family
Farmer and pastoralist, 195, 199, 270*n*14
Feifa (city), 109
Fertility, 139; barrenness and, 134–35,
211–12, 216–18; marriage and, 188,
189, 192

Fiction, 11
Finkelstein, Israel, 236–38, 250
First Temple period (950 BCE–587 BCE):
covenant renewal in, 15; historical
origin of stories in, 143; Israelites
during, 13, 20; maximalists on, 9;
minimalists on, 9, 65, 148–49; myths
and, 10, 13, 20–21; postcolonial stud-
ies of, 6
Fishbane, Michael, 197–98, 218
Flood story, 7, 36
Folkloric approach, 51–53; see also
Mythology; Wife-sister motif
Foreign women, 130, 135, 188
Form criticism, 245–47
Former prophets, stories of (Joshua,
Judges, 1 and 2 Samuel, 1 and 2
Kings), 57, 62, 219
Fort Abiram, 251
Franco-Prussian War (1870–1871),
140
Fratricide, 194, 196, 199
Friedman, Richard, 113
Fundamentalism, 7, 9
Future Messiah, concept of, 98

Gad (child of Jacob and Zilpah), 242
Garden of Eden, 165–77
Garfinkel, Yossi, 240
Genealogy, proper, 192
Genesis: different narrators in, 31–34,
261n11; marriage in, 1–2; wife-sister
motif in, 1, 25–31; see also Creation
story; Wife-sister motif
Genesis 1–11, as myth, 7, 8–9, 12–13, 43,
148
Genesis 3, 197–98
Genesis 4:3–16, 197–98
Genesis 12, see J narrator; Matriarch in
peril
Genesis 19, see Lot in Sodom
Genesis 20, see E narrator; Matriarch
in peril
Genesis 22, see Sacrifice of Isaac
Genesis 26, see J narrator; Matriarch in
peril
Genesis 34, see Dinah story
Genesis 38, see Judah and Tamar
Genre criticism phase, 43
Genres (Gatungen), 245

German Bible Scholars, 51
Ghettos burning in United States, 75
Gibeah (Israelite settlement): in concubine of the Levite, 103, 110, 121;
Solomon's dream at, 207–9
Gibeon, treaty with, 91
Gideon, 129, 217
Gilgamesh epic, 44, 178
Gloss (statement added later), 106, 130,
209
God: Abraham's argument with, about
sparing Lot, 106, 117; Abraham tested
by, 50–51, 123; bull as symbol for, 79;
covenant between people of Israel
and, 14–20; as name, 37, 38; plural
form for, 78; punishment by, for
golden calf worship, 61–62; punishment by, for sins of father, 158; see
also Divine intervention; Elohim;
YHWH
Goddess worship, 148
Golden calf of Aaron (Exodus 32),
60–61; golden calves of Jeroboam
I compared to, 56, 75–81; as myth,
80–81
Golden calves, 58–62, 113, 226; Canaanite worship of, 59; destruction of, 60,
76; DH on, 68–70, 80–81, 98; Hosea
on, 67–71, 74; Israelite worship of,
59–60, 67; kissing, 73–74; prophecies
against, 70–74
Golden calves of Jeroboam I (1 Kings
12:28–30): golden calf of Aaron
compared to, 56, 75–81; historicity
of, 79–81
Goliath and David, 94–95, 247–48
Gomorrah, 108
Good and evil, 168–70, 175, 177
Graf, Karl Heinrich, 42
Greek myths, 10, 189; family relationships in, 95; human sacrifice in, 151;
mourning rituals and, 132
Greek period, 9
Gresham's law, 132
Grimm brothers, 51
Gunkel, 51

Hammurabi, (Babylonian king), 15
Hannah, 134, 211, 212
Hannebala (sexual abuse), 117

Happy ending: in Lot in Sodom, 107, 108–10; in matriarch in peril, 110–11, 118–19

Haram Ash-sharif (Temple Mount), 236

Hazor: destruction of, 91; excavation of, 248–49

Hebrew, as term, 39

Hebrew language, 39, 45, 54; authority of, 72; development of, 271*n*2; early and late, 238–39; ethnic identity and, 239–41; vernacular, 239–41

Henotheism, 15

Hera (wife of Zeus), 95

Hermeneutics of suspicion, 6–7, 146, 149, 226, 234, 271*n*3

Hermes (god), 6

Hero, birth of, 23

Hezekiah (king), 84

Hirah (friend of Judah), 163

Hiram (king of Tyre), 163

History: archaeology and, 234–36; of Canaan, 3–4; critical, 9; of Davidic dynasty, 82, 97, 216; of documentary hypothesis, 41–42; fiction compared to, 11; four books of Moses and, 82, 219; historical criticism, 6, 259*n*4; of Israel, 3–4, 33, 46; of Israelites, 55–56, 96, 241; myth and, 10–11, 14, 82, 178, 257; study of, 4

Hitler, Adolf, 77

Homeland and offspring, 17–19

Homer, 23, 24

Homosexual rape, 103, 104, 106, 107, 135

Hosea: Amos and, 70–71, 79; on covenant as marriage, 19, 256; on golden calf, 67–71, 74

Hospitality, 102–3, 105

House: four-room, 233, 237, 241; multiple meanings of, 97, 98

House of David, 254; Mesha stone and, 146–47, 150; as southern kingdom, 63

House of Omri (name for Israel), 63

Hozze (seer), 72

Huldah (prophetess), 88–89

Human sacrifice, 123–51; animals in place of, 125–27, 132, 146, 150; *see also* Sacrifice of Isaac; Sacrifice of Jephthah's daughter; Sacrifice of Mesha; Tophet

Hurrians, 45, 46–47, 48

Hurvitz, Avi, 239

Hypertypical story, 24

Ibn Ezra, Abraham, 261*n*13

Identity, 20; *see also* Counteridentity; Ethnic identity

Idolatry, 73–74, 120; *see also* Golden calves

Iliad (Homer), 23, 24

Illud tempus (that time), 81

Imagination, stories and, 10

Immortality, loss of, 169, 179

Incest: in Judah and Tamar, 164–65, 207; laws, 28–29, 135; Lot and, 108; of Reuben and Bilhah, 270*n*23

Inheritance, legitimacy of, 216

Innocence, 168–69

Iphigenia, sacrifice of, 131

Iron Age, IA, 263*n*1

Isaac, 1, 3; birth of, 105, 260*n*5, 265*n*6; blessing from, 203–4; covenants and, 16; Ishmael and, 220; Rebecca and, 25, 29–30; *see also* Binding of Isaac; Sacrifice of Isaac

Ishmael, 220

Israel: conquest model of, 232; covenant between God and people of, 14–20; end of exile of, 39; history of, 3–4, 33, 46; Jacob as name for, 67, 202–4; land of, 3, 259*n*2, 264*n*1; Mendenhall model of, 232–33; Moab's relationship with, 108–9, 137–38, 144–46; other names for, 63; in Six Day War, 75; slow infiltration model of, 232, 235; Syria's relationship with, 213–15; as word in stela of Merneptah, 231–34

Israelite inscriptions, 109, 252–55, 274*n*23; *see also* Mesha stone; Stele; Tel Dan inscription

Israelites: Abraham as father of, 24–25; ancestors of, 16; Canaanites compared to, 17–18, 33, 40–41, 149, 209; civil war between Benjamites and, 114–17; conquest and settlement by, 90–91; during First Temple period, 13, 20; golden calf worshiped by, 59–60, 67; history of, 55–56, 96, 241; intermarriage of Canaanites and, 163, 184–85, 192; as term, 39

Issachar (son of Leah), 212

Jabesh-gilead, virgins of, 116, 118, 226
Jacob, 3; covenants and, 16; cultic
    centers of north and, 243; descen-
    dants of, 191, 242–43; in Dinah story,
    184–85, 193; dream at Bethel, 205–6;
    Esau and, 202–4, 220, 228; Laban
    and, 213–15; Leah, Rachel and, 1–2,
    212–13, 263n23; Moses and, 217–18;
    as name, 44; as name for Israel, 67,
    202–4; Rebecca and, 202–5, 229; as
    tricksters, 202, 205, 217–18
Jael (woman), 242
Jamil, Sheikh, 140
Jebus (Jerusalem), 103, 121
JE epic, 36–37, 40, 45, 93, 220; divine
    intervention and, 95; ending of, 113;
    Joseph and Benjamin in, 216; Rje as
    redactor of, 36, 79
Jehoram, 144, 146
Jehoshaphat (king), 84, 176–77
Jehu (king of Israel), 66–67
Jephthah's daughter, see Sacrifice of
    Jephthah's daughter
Jeremiah, 126, 223
Jericho, 91
Jeroboam I (922–901 BCE), 64–65; see
    also Golden calves of Jeroboam I
Jeroboam II (786–746 BCE), 73
Jerusalem: archaeology of, 248–50; as
    capital of Southern kingdom, 66;
    conquest of, 97, 236–37; see also City
    of David; Jebus
Jerusalem Temple: sacrifices at, 66; wor-
    ship at, 84
Jews: covenant and, 20; saving of, 77; as
    term, 39
Jezebel, 177, 183
J narrator, 31, 261n11
Joab (servant of David): in Absalom
    and Amnon, 194, 199; in David and
    Bathsheba, 155–56, 158–62, 202, 207;
    perspective of, 158–61
Jordan, crossing of, 90–91
Joseph, 216; birth of, 213; bones of, 187;
    descendants of, 242; journey to
    Egypt, 3, 36
Joshua, book of: DH and, 90–91; as
    historical book, 84; see also Former
    prophets, stories of
Josiah (king of southern kingdom): birth
    of, 69; covenanting of, 15, 16, 17, 19,
    86, 89; Deuteronomy and, 83–86, 94;
    Passover celebration of, 15, 17, 19, 86,
    89; priests slaughtered by, 76; proph-
    ecies about, 87–89; reform stages
    of, 86–87; reign of, 84–85, 120, 209;
    tragedy of, 87–89
Jotham (king), 84
Journal of Biblical Literature, 75–78
J source, 36–40, 42
Judah, rulers of, 3
Judah and Tamar (Genesis 38): David
    and Bathsheba compared to, 163–65,
    228; incest in, 164–65, 207; summary
    of, 162–65
Judean, 39
Judges: epilogue or appendix of, 100,
    120; as historical book, 84; names
    of, 129; period of, 3; stories from,
    2, 91–93; see also Former prophets,
    stories of
Judges 5; see Song of Deborah
Judges 11; see Sacrifice of Jephthah's
    daughter
Judges 19; see Concubine of the Levite
Judgeship, theory of, 96
Juntillet Ajrud (archaeological site), 41

Karavaca, Ya'qub, 140
Khanazir (city), 109
Kilamuwa, story of, 240
Kingdom of Israel, 63
Kingdom of Judah, 63
1 and 2 Kings: editing of, 93; as histori-
    cal books, 84, 87; see also Former
    prophets, stories of
1 Kings 12:28–30, see Golden calves of
    Jeroboam I
2 Kings 3, see Sacrifice of Mesha
Kingship, 84, 274n25; concubine of the
    Levite and, 112–13; of Saul, 96, 97,
    113; tribal systems compared to, 115,
    117, 119–20
Klein, F. A., 139
Kosher laws, 105

Laban, Jacob and, 213–15
Languages, 53–54; Northwest Semitic,
    54, 141, 239–40; vernacular, 239–41,
    273n13; see also Hebrew language;
    Northwest Semitic language
Late Biblical Hebrew (LBH), 239

Laws, divine origin of, 15, 18, 19
LBH, *see* Late Biblical Hebrew
Leach, Edmund, 133, 135, 139, 165, 192–93
Leading words, 197–99
Leah: barrenness of, 134, 211; Jacob, Rachel and, 1–2, 212–13, 263n23; tribes of, 242
Legend, 3, 218–20, 225
"The Legitimacy of Solomon" (Leach), 192–93
Lemaire, Andre, 146–47
Levi (son of Jacob), 184–85, 193
Levirate marriage, 164
Lévi-Strauss, Claude, 94, 133–34, 165, 267n5
Levites, 76; *see also* Concubine of the Levite
Lidzbarski, Mark, 146–47
Literary approaches, 50–51
LORD: in David and Bathsheba, 157–58; as name, 37, 38, 265n7
Lot: Abraham's argument with God about sparing, 106, 117; incest and, 108; mixed-breed origin of Ammonites and Moabites and, 130; wife turned into pillar of salt, 108, 109
Lot in Sodom (Genesis 19), 56, 105–10; angels in, 105, 119, 265n6; concubine of the Levite compared to, 56, 105, 107, 110, 117–22, 178, 182, 220, 224–25; divine intervention in, 119; as etiology, 108–10; happy ending in, 107, 108–10; hospitality in, 105; rape in, 106–8, 113, 117, 224–25

Macalister, R. A. S., 249
Machinist, Peter, 55
Madrassahs (schools), 54
Maenads, story of, 132
Manasseh (king): Ephraim and, 64, 220; reign of, 85, 89; tribe of, 145, 242, 244, 264n1
Mandrakes, Rachel and, 213, 215–17
Manoah (father of Samson), 217; wife of, 212
Mari (ancient city), 44–45
Marriage, 1–2; covenant as, 19–20, 256; endogamous, 134, 135; fertility and, 188, 189, 192; between half siblings, 28–29, 48–50, 181, 263n23, 269n1;

institution of, 168; intermarriage, 163, 184–86, 188–92, 214–15, 224; Levirate, 164; after rape, 183
"Mary, Mary quite contrary" (taunt song), 245
Masculinity, honor, shame and, 50–51
Matriarch in peril (Genesis 12, 20 and 26), 25–35, 41–42, 44, 186, 224; concubine of the Levite compared to, 110–12; happy ending in, 110–11, 118–19; marriage between half-siblings in, 28–29, 182–83; morality and, 39; *see also* Wife-sister motif
Maximalists, 8–10
Mazar, Amihai, 58
Mazar, Eilat, 249–50
Megiddo, 44, 249
Mendenhall model of Israel, 232–33
Merneptah, Pharaoh, 231; stela of, 3, 9, 144, 230–36, 254
Mesha (king of Moab): as *boqer*, 72; proclamation of, 143–44; *see also* Sacrifice of Mesha
Mesha stone, 139–51, 252; analysis of, 141–43; authenticity of, 148–51, 254; colonial intrigue regarding, 140–41; house of David and, 146–47, 150; reconstruction of, 144–47
Micaiah ben Imlah, 175–76
Mimesis (Auerbach), 56
Minimalists, 8–10, 112; extreme, 9, 148–50, 236–38; on First Temple period, 9, 65, 148–49
Misgav, Haggai, 240
Moab: Israel's relationship with, 108–9, 137–38, 144–46; prophecy against, 142–43
Moabites, 130
Moabite stone, *see* Mesha stone
Monotheism, 15, 16, 37, 178
Moral discernment, 177, 178–79
Morality: biblical history and, 1–2; matriarch in peril and, 39; myths and, 81, 94–95, 98–99; wife-sister motif and, 26–27, 29–30, 40, 52
Mordechai, 77
Morrison, Martha A., 213
Mortality, wisdom and, 169–70
Moses: Deuteronomy and, 85, 86; golden calf and, 60–61, 80; Jacob and, 217–18; as law giver, 15, 18,

19; Ten Commandments and, 18, 59–60

Moses, five books of, 9, 14, 242–43; *see also* Pentateuch

Moses, four books of (tetrateuch), 82, 219

Mother, role of, 205

Mt. Moriah (Temple Mount), 124, 126

Mourning rituals, 74, 132

Mythology, 14, 33, 95

Myths, 12–13; covenant as, 14–15; disinterest and, 7, 10; durable aspect of, 17; First Temple period and, 10, 13, 20–21; functions of, 13, 165; Genesis 1–11 as, 7, 8–9, 12, 13, 43, 148; golden calf of Aaron as, 80–81; Greek, 10, 95, 132, 151; history and, 10–11, 14, 82, 178, 257; legend and, 218–20, 225; morality and, 81, 94–95, 98–99; patriarchal stories as, 55–57, 218; polemical, 77, 81, 108, 226, 257; prototypes, 20–21; rituals and, 13, 14–15, 17; sacrifice of Isaac as, 125–27; sacrifice of Jephthah's daughter as, 130–31; Second Temple period and, 20; stories compared to, 223–26; twelve tribes as, 242–43; values and, 191–93; *see also* Covenant; *specific myths*

Nabi (profession), 72

Nadab (son of Aaron), 76

Nadab (son of Jeroboam I), 76

Nagid (king), 97

Nakedness, 169–70

Naphtali (child of Jacob and Bilhah), 242

Narrators: in Genesis, 31–34, 261*n*7, 261*n*11; opinion of, 100–1

Nathan, 64; prophecies by, 95–98, 157–58, 200

National origins, story of, 19

Neccho, Pharaoh, 88

Neo-Babylonian Empire, 88

New covenant, 14

New Testament, 14, 261*n*12

Niditch, Susan, 51–52

Nihilists, 8

Nineveh, 87

Noah's flood, 7

Northern kingdom: Assyrians conquering and destruction of, 69–71, 73–74,

80–81, 98–99; as Kingdom of Israel, 63; rule of, 64–66

Northwest Semitic language, 54, 141, 239–40

Noth, Martin, 51, 266*n*16, 271*n*4

Numeira (city), 109

Nuzi tablets, 44–45, 213

Oath taking, 14–15

Odyssey (Homer), 24

Offspring: family and, 130, 134; homeland and, 17–19; use of word, 128, 266*n*3

Og (king of Bashan), 142

Old covenant, 14

Old Testament: covenant and, 14–15, 261*n*12; stories in, 1–2, 10

Omri (king), 144

Onan (child of Judah and Shua), 163–64

Oracles in civil war, 114–15, 119

Oral and written phases of stories, 32–36, 38–39, 46, 53–55

Original sin, 172

Pairs of stories (doublets), 23–24

Palestine: modern state of, 8; name of, 190

Palestinians, 149, 233

Pan-Babylonian phase, 43

Parable about poor man and lamb, 157

Paradise, 167

Parallelism, 225, 260*n*2; parallel synoptic, 121–22; *see also* Repetitions of stories; *specific stories*

Passover, 15, 17, 19, 86, 89

Patriarchal TKPeriod (1700–1500 BCE), 126

Patriarchal stories, 10, 13; covenant and, 15, 16; function of, 21; as legend, 3; as myths, 55–57, 218; *see also* Abraham; Isaac; Jacob; Joseph

Pelton, Robert, 51–52

Pentateuch (five books of Moses): date of, 39, 47, 262*n*15; documentary hypothesis of, 33, 35–38, 40–43, 83; stories of, 21, 56–57, 122, 219

Persian period (532–ca. 333 BCE), 86

Petermann, J. H., 139

Petrie, Sir Flinders, 231

Philistines, 188–91

Philo of Alexandria, 24

284

Pillar of salt, 108, 109
Plague, 61–62
P narrator, 261n7
Polemical myth, 77, 81, 108, 226, 257
Pork, 190, 241
Postcolonial studies, 6
Pottery, 237, 241
A Prelude to Biblical Folklore: Under-
  dogs and Tricksters (Niditch), 51–52
Priestly source, 37; see also P source
Priests, slaughter of, 76
Progressive revelation, theory of, 42–43
Proof-texting, 5
Prophecies: regarding David, 95–98;
  in Deuteronomy, 94, 95–98; against
  golden calves, 70–74; about Josiah,
  87–89; of Micaiah ben Imlah, 175–76;
  against Moab, 142–43; by Nathan,
  95–98, 157–58, 200
Prophets, 57; see also Former prophets,
  stories of; specific individuals
Prostitution, 101–2
Prototypes, 23–24; of Exodus, 27, 33;
  mythical, 20–21; to scare sinners, 62
Prototypical story, 24
P source, 36–37, 39, 42
Purim holiday, 77

Rachel: barrenness of, 134, 211, 212;
  Jacob, Leah and, 1–2, 212–13, 263n23;
  mandrakes and, 213, 215–17
Radin, Paul, 52
Rape: in concubine of the Levite, 103–5,
  113–14, 117, 224–25; of Dinah by
  Shechem (son of Hamor), 183–86;
  homosexual, 103, 104, 106, 107, 135;
  in Lot in Sodom, 106–8, 113, 117;
  marriage after, 183; of Sabines, 118,
  226; in Tamar and Amnon, 2, 48–49,
  172, 180–83, 186, 193, 224–25
Rebecca: barrenness of, 134, 212, 216;
  Isaac and, 25, 29–30; Jacob and,
  202–5, 229
Red Sea, crossing of, 61, 90
Rehoboam (son of Solomon, king of
  Judah), 62–63, 65, 210–11
Relative chronology, 3, 222, 230–34
Rendsburg, Gary, 162
Repetitions of stories (doublets), 22–23,
  36; see also Matriarch in peril

Reuben, 2, 270n23
Ricketts, Mac Linscott, 52
Rituals: mourning, 74, 132; myths and,
  13, 14–15, 17
Rje (redactor of JE epic), 36, 79
Root metaphor, 13, 17
Royal family, 180–221, 228–29; see also
  specific individuals

Sabines, rape of, 118, 226
Sacrifices: altar and, 187; by Canaanites,
  127–29, 135, 136, 266n3; to golden
  calves, 75; of Iphigenia, 131; at Jerusalem Temple, 66; see also Human
  sacrifice
Sacrifice of Isaac (Genesis 22): editing
  of, 136; from E source, 124, 126; as
  myth, 125–27; sacrifice of Jephthah's
  daughter compared to, 56, 132–34,
  220, 227; sacrifice of Mesha compared to, 137–39, 150–51, 227–28;
  summary of, 123–25
Sacrifice of Jephthah's daughter (Judges
  11): as myth, 130–31; sacrifice of Isaac
  compared to, 56, 132–34, 220, 227;
  summary of, 129–32, 135
Sacrifice of Mesha (2 Kings 3), 137–39,
  150–51, 227–28
Safi (city), 109
Samaria site, 58, 71, 263n1
Samson, 129; blindness of, 189, 190; foreign women and, 135, 188; Philistines
  and, 188–91
1 and 2 Samuel: editing of, 93; as historical books, 84; see also Former
  prophets, stories of
2 Samuel 11, see David and Bathsheba
Sanders, Seth, 239–40
Sarah (Sarai): Abraham and, 24–29, 48,
  49, 51, 183; barrenness and fertility of,
  134, 211–12, 216–17; different names
  of, 27, 261n7; divine intervention
  and, 260n5; in Egypt, 25–27
Sarna, Nahum, 126
Satan, 174–75
Saul: cut-up oxen and, 104, 113; kingship
  of, 96, 97, 113; Witch of En-Dor and,
  121
Saulide dynasty, 216
Scribal schools, 53–55, 182, 198